VOICES FROM THE INSIDE

Case Studies from a Tennessee Women's Prison

Chinyere Ogbonna
and
Ross Nordin

University Press of America,® Inc.
Lanham · Boulder · New York · Toronto · Plymouth, UK

4501 Forbes Boulevard
Suite 200
Lanham, Maryland 20706
UPA Acquisitions Department (301) 459-3366

Estover Road
Plymouth PL6 7PY
United Kingdom

Printed in the United States of America
British Library Cataloging in Publication Information Available

Library of Congress Control Number: 2009932206
ISBN: 978-0-7618-4806-6 (paperback : alk. paper)
eISBN: 978-0-7618-4807-3

The paper used in this publication meets the minimum requirements of American National Standard for Information Sciences—Permanence of Paper for Printed Library Materials, ANSI Z39.48-1992

Dedication

This book is dedicated to my parents, Chief Daniel and Mrs. Mabel Ogbonna, for their indefatigable support, and to my fabulous children, Nwachi, Chima and Chike McGruder, who allowed me the "concentration time," to work on the book.

Dr. Ogbonna

This book is dedicated to my daughters Rebecca and Emily; my parents, Madge and Jack Nordin and my brother Brent.

Ross Nordin

Contents

Tables

Foreword

In Criminology and Criminal Justice our knowledge-base is inevitably limited by the information available to us as scholars; it is difficult, if not blatantly inappropriate, to either generalize or to speculate beyond the capabilities of the data at hand. Such information itself may be limited for several reasons that are understandable given the financial exigencies of getting the kind of data that we oftentimes "really want"—the kind that is either cost or time-prohibitive (or both), that we have to be patient to get, if we ever get it at all.

And while we all accept that resource constraints are part and parcel to navigating the social scientific process, the consequences of such data limitations are quite clear. For example, we did not "know" about the effects of community-structural characteristics on neighborhood crime rates until scholars from the Chicago School started collecting data on the subject; we did not know about the comparative validity of certain criminological theories until Travis Hirschi started the trend of pitting them against one another in empirical tests 1969; we did not know about the changing nature of peer influences at different developmental stages until we had multiple waves of the National Youth Survey at our disposal; we did not know about life-course transitions until Sampson and Laub ran across a dusty dataset in a Harvard basement; and we did not know about the relative effect of biological characteristics on many forms of antisocial behavior until datasets like the National Longitudinal Study of Adolescent Health became publicly available; and the list goes on.

Other times, our "criminological imagination" is stifled because information is limited simply because we aren't looking in the right places. For example, in the arena of institutional corrections, we did not necessarily consider prisons to be worthy of academic study until Clemmer's *The Prison Community* and, more influentially, Sykes' *Society of Captives* came into the picture and demanded that scholars take notice; we weren't really thinking about the roles of the external environment and social context in how prisons operate until Jacobs' *Stateville* came along and demonstrated that link all too clearly; we weren't really focused on the importance of variations in institutional management styles until DiIulio came out with *Governing Prisons*; and we weren't thinking about the ways that individual and prison-level characteristics interact with one another in important ways until researchers like Kevin Wright and others started collecting multi-level data for use by scholars such as Scott Camp, John Wooldredge, and Michael Reisig.

The same could certainly be said of the treatment and experiences of female inmates within the discipline of criminology and criminal justice—a field that just hasn't been looking in the right places. To be sure, the bulk of the theoretical and empirical literature on prisons and prison inmates has focused almost exclusively on men—a practice implicitly justified by the preponderant gender gap in incarceration rates in the United States. Nevertheless, recent trends in incarceration would seem to render such a justification useless, as over the last couple of decades women have become the fastest growing portion of the American inmate population. Such growth, however, has not been matched by a similar increase in the pace of female inmate-oriented scholarship. The limits of what we know cannot be attributed to data limitations alone, as if such limitations exist in a social vacuum, because just as much information on female offenders has been equally and readily available as it has been for males. The problem is that, as a field, we haven't been looking.

This is where Chinyere Ogbonna and Ross Nordin's book takes us directly. *Voices from the Inside* gives us an intimate look into the lives of women inmates. As Ogbonna and Nordin capture the existence of these women in their own words—their struggles with addiction, their often chaotic and heartbreaking upbringings steeped firmly in economic deprivation, and their struggles to liberate themselves from abusive situations—they add a human element to what is often given the treatment of mere cold hard data by criminologists traditionally. Like other criminological works using a similar methodological approach, the point is to provide a measure of depth and insight that can only be achieved by letting the research subjects speak for themselves, which is exactly what is contained here.

In the end, this book is important because it highlights the importance of taking seriously for study a population of offenders that has been largely neglected by the scholarly community. It is therefore a pleasure to be afforded the opportunity to introduce it.

Travis C. Pratt
Arizona State University
January 2009

Preface

There are striking similarities between current drug policies and the former policies of prohibition era. As the American political climate leans towards "Get Tough" policies on drugs and crime, there has been an attendant increase in the number of tough sentences imposed on individuals charged with drug crimes. These tough policies appear to have garnered consensus within USA's political life and culture. The premise of drug prohibition agenda is that illegal drugs are evil and must be stamped out of our society by any means necessary. This is particularly of importance in inner cities in the USA. A large percentage of the individuals incarcerated for drug offences are from inner cities. At issue is whether due processes are compromised in the current "Get Tough" on crime policies.

Studies show that there is a steady increase in the number of female drug offenders, particularly African American women offenders, yet there is no study as of record that has specifically examined the processes (from the offenders perspective) leading to their arrest and subsequent incarceration. This research examines the literature review with regards to the history of prohibition in the USA with special emphasis on Alcohol and Drug Prohibition, as well as analyzes empirical data pertaining specifically to incarceration of women drug offenders in Tennessee. A subset of the research incorporates results of personal interviews with these incarcerated women drug offenders regarding Criminal Justice processes leading up to and subsequent to their conviction. The experiences of the African American women will be contrasted with the experiences of Caucasian offenders. Included also in the research is information pertaining to the nature and type of their drug offences.

Acknowledgments

I appreciate the help and support of Dr. Linda Nutt, the Director at Tennessee Department of Corrections who was instrumental in getting this research started. I would also like to thank all the other Department of Corrections and Tennessee Prison for Women (TPFW) staff that helped facilitate the interviewing process. Professor Goode, thanks for sharing details about the David Lipscomb Program. Warden Steele, with members of her staff, at TPFW was instrumental in making sure the interviews proceeded smoothly and I especially appreciate the openness of the inmate respondents at TPFW who welcomed my myriad questions regarding their circumstances. Without them this book would not have been possible.

I especially acknowledge the help provided by my former Austin Peay State University student Ms. Linda Quijano, who helped administer the interviews. I would also like to acknowledge my undergraduate criminal justice students at Austin Peay State University, some of whom were subjected to early drafts of this book, for their comments and suggestions. To Ross Nordin it was gratifying working on this project with you.

I extend my gratitude to reviewers of earlier drafts of the book for their insightful comments and suggestions: Alex Sekwat of Tennessee State University and Travis Pratt of Arizona State University, and to the other myriad individuals who cheered me on.

Chinyere Ogbonna

Thanks to all the individuals who helped in the process of making this book a reality. And to Chinyere Ogbonna, it was an insightful pleasure working on this book with you. It is wonderful seeing this book become a reality.

Ross Nordin

Chapter 1

Introduction

> The care of every man's soul belongs to himself. But what if he neglects the care of it? Well what if he neglect the care of his health or his estate, which would more nearly relate to the state. Will the magistrate make a law that he not be poor or sick? Laws provide against injury from others; but not from ourselves. God himself will not save men against their wills. . . . Thomas Jefferson[1]

The crucible of the idea behind the above quote is that government should not make laws concerning individual personal behavior, so long as that behavior does not directly impinge on others. As such, a drug addict should not be punished merely for possessing and using drugs, except and only if that particular drug addict in the course of satisfying his/her addiction impinges on the rights of fellow citizens. How an adult individual chooses to treat himself/herself should not be mandated by governmental laws. The majority of current United States' drug laws are based on the premise of punishing individuals that for whatever reasons expose themselves to drug addiction.

Throughout the course of recorded history there has been some form of restriction or prohibition of narcotic, intoxicating and psychotropic substances. The focus of prohibition is generally to make the prohibited substances unavail-

---

1. Thomas Jefferson in his notes paraphrased the words of John Locke in *A Letter Concerning Toleration.* The letter was originally published in 1689. The full quote from John Locke is as follows: "The Care therefore of every man's Soul belongs unto himself, and is to be left unto himself. But what if he neglect the Care of his Soul? I answer, What if he neglects the Care of his Health, or of his Estate, which things are nearly related to the Government of the Magistrate than the other? Will the magistrate provide by an express Law, That such an one shall not become poor or sick? Laws provide, as much as is possible, that the Goods and Health of Subjects be not injured by the Fraud and Violence of others; they do not guard them from the Negligence or Ill-husbandry of the Possessors themselves." Source: A Letter Concerning Toleration (1969), Edited and Introduced by James H. Tully (Hacklett Publishing Company, 1983), 35.

able to the general population. These substances are usually believed to be detrimental to the physical and moral characters of individuals as well as to general society.

Alcohol prohibition in the United States was the culmination of decades long temperance, or "anti-alcohol" movement. The temperance movement was initiated during the early nineteenth century in America by doctors, ministers and large employers who were concerned about drunken workers and servants.[2] These groups were later joined by women's groups (notably the Women's Christian Temperance Union),[3] and the Anti-Saloon League[4] that were dedicated to the idea of wiping out drunkenness. According to one of the league's publications, "Liquor is responsible for 19 percent of the divorces, 25 percent of the poverty, 25 percent of the insanity, 37 percent of the pauperism, 45 percent of child desertion, and 50 percent of the crime in this country."[5] The League was also interested in trying to put saloon owners out of business, to the extent that they circulated posters that depicted saloon-keepers as evil persons that profited on death and enslavement of others.[6]

The Eighteenth Amendment of the United States Constitution (ratified January 16, 1919) and the subsequent Volstead Act or National Prohibition Act (passed October 28, 1919), made the manufacture, transportation, and sale of alcohol illegal.[7] According to Volstead Act, any beverage that contained greater than 0.5 percent alcohol was prohibited. The Act also vested federal agents with the authority to investigate and prosecute violators. However, neither the Amendment nor the Act was applicable to possession or consumption of alcohol,[8] thus individuals that had made or bought liquor prior to prohibition could legally serve them during the period of prohibition. Initially prohibition was popular, but as the years passed by, it became less popular as it became clear that the stated purposes of Volstead Act were not being realized. The 18th

---

2. Levine, H., Craig Reinarman, 2004. Alcohol Prohibition and Drug Prohibition: Lessons from Alcohol Policy for Drug Policy. http://www.cedro-uva.org/lib/levine.alcohol.html (accessed August 19, 2006).
3. The Women's Christian Temperance Union was formally organized in 1874.
4. The Anti- Saloon League, which was formed in 1895, was one of the most important driving forces behind the eventual enactment of the Volstead Act. The underlying belief of the league was that alcohol was the basis of a host of evils The league was focused not just on prohibition of alcohol but also on making sure that saloons did not thrive, since the saloon was the purveyor of alcohol.
5. Odegard, P.H. , 1928. Pressure Politics: The Story of the Anti-Saloon League. New York: Columbia University Press, 60
6. National Commission on Marihuana and Drug Abuse: History of Alcohol Prohibition. http://www.druglibrary.org/Schaffer/LIBRARY/studies/nc/nc2a.htm (accessed August 17, 2006).
7. Kobler, J. 1993. Ardent Spirits: The Rise and Fall of Prohibition. New York: Da Capo Press,, 14.
8. Kobler, 14.

Amendment was finally repealed by the 21st amendment in 1933, bringing an end to 13 years of federal alcohol prohibition in the United States.

Alcohol prohibition was based on the ideology that alcohol was the root of all the social ills of that era. To the extent that prohibition was undertaken to preclude access to alcohol, and consequently resultant detrimental effects of alcohol, the policy was a failure. Detailed analysis of prohibition reveals that although prohibition was instituted as a panacea to a multitude of social problems such as crimes, poverty, disease, general drunkenness and other social ills, it did not serve that goal.[9] At the beginning of alcohol prohibition it seemed that the policy was actually working and alcohol consumption appeared to have decreased. However, towards the mid-part of the prohibition era, crime increased and consumption of alcohol increased as indicated by various studies.[10] During this time, moon shining and bootlegging began to thrive as a lot of individuals began to produce alcohol illegally.[11] This in effect turned what was once a regulated and legitimate business into an organized criminal enterprise. Without control, the quality of alcohol produced was doubtful and individuals who had no prior experience began to produce alcohol to capitalize on the outstanding profits, made possible by the illegal black market. Unfortunately, this alcohol was more potent in its unregulated form and there were anecdotal evidence of thousands of deaths occurring from poisoning due to improperly denatured alcohol or paralyzing "rotgut" being sold to consumers in the black market. Since alcohol was illegal it was impossible to regulate the production and, as such, illicit consumers of alcohol could never be sure of the contents of what they were purchasing; their illegally obtained alcohol could be a toxically mixed conundrum sold as alcohol within the black market. This same parallel could be applied to the illegal drug market today.

As a policy initiative, Prohibition made it virtually impossible to tax the illegally produced alcohol. It was also almost impossible for the court and prison system to prosecute all violators since so many people were violating the law. The courts and prisons were overloaded with violators of alcohol prohibition and the government had to increase spending in order to enforce the dictates of prohibition law. With so many people producing various forms of liquor at their homes or on their property it became virtually impossible for the authorities to effectively enforce prohibition as a policy.[12] As a policy initiative, Prohibition did not live up to its expectation. According to Hu, "Prohibition destroyed the

---

9. Data from U.S. Bureau of Census indicate that murder rate increased with the start of prohibition and then actually declined for 11 consecutive years after the end of prohibition.

10. Kobler, 14.

11. Moon shiners specifically were involved in illegal alcohol distillation and production, while bootleggers imported and sold alcohol from moon shiners.

12. Hu, T. 1950. The Liquor Tax in the U.S.: 1791–1947, New York City: Columbia University Press, 35–55

manufacturing and distributive agencies through which the demand for liquor had been legally supplied. But the demand remained."[13]

With regards to the effects of prohibition on alcohol consumption, proxy and research data on alcohol consumption relative to occurrence of cirrhosis of the liver would indicate that during prohibition era there was a drop in documented alcohol consumption and cirrhosis of the liver (but it must be noted that cirrhosis of the liver had been declining since 1908 which was prior to prohibition).[14] But generally speaking, published research has shown that there was only a minimal effect of prohibition on alcohol consumption.[15] It should also be noted that there was no drastic jump in cirrhosis of the liver after prohibition was repealed. This makes it difficult to claim that prohibition actually helped reduce the rate of cirrhosis.[16] According to Jeffery Miron, research results indicate that prohibition had only a small statistically insignificant effect on cirrhosis[17] of the liver.[18] Also when data on arrests for drunkenness were analyzed pre and post prohibition, results suggested that prohibition had an appreciable short-term impact and almost zero long-term impact on alcohol consumption and arrests.[19] [20] Thus prohibition did not appear to have had the desired effect with regards to reduction in alcohol consumption; nonetheless, studies indicate that there was a significant increase in crime during the prohibition era. The stated increase was indicated by homicide rate data pre, post and during prohibition. According to Friedman,[21] the period spanning 1920 through 1934 was characterized by high rates of homicide. The high rate of homicides during that period was most likely a consequence of prohibition effect. Jeffrey Miron indicated that the more prohibition was enforced, the less there was the possibility for implicit property rights and legal exceptions (e.g. medical uses) to the prohibition, which increases the size of the black market and therefore violence within the specific

---

13. Hu, 35–55

14. Miron, J., Zweibel, Alcohol Consumption During Prohibition. American Economic Review, 81 (2), 242–247. Warburton, C., "The Economic Results of Prohibition." New York: Columbia University Press.

15. Miron, 242–247.

16. Miron, 242–247.

17. Cirrhosis of the liver can be utilized as an indicator for alcohol consumption, since there is generally a positive relationship between alcohol consumption rates and the rate of cirrhosis.

18. Miron, 242–247.

19. Dills, A., Mireille Jacobson, Jeffrey Miron. 2005. The Effect of Alcohol Prohibition on Alcohol Consumption: Evidence from Drunkenness Arrests. *Economic Letters, vol. 86*, issue 2, 279–284

20. According to Dills et all (2005) It must be noted that alcohol enforcement could have been increased during prohibition thus skewing the results or increasing the perceived rate of arrests.

21. Friedman, M.1991. The War We are Losing. In Searching for Alternatives: Drug Control Policy in the United States. Stanford: Hoover Institution, 53–67

community.[22] There is propensity for violence in the black . ticular substance is illegal but profits that can be generated fr sale of the substance are extremely high. One of the many ways lence can occur is through confrontation between law enforcement a violators.

In United States, drug prohibition developed as an offshoot of constitution alcohol prohibition during the 1920s.[23] But prior to alcohol prohibition, there was the Harrison Act which prima facie did not appear to be a prohibition law. It appeared to be a bill that would regulate the marketing of small quantities of heroin, morphine and other drugs over the counter while necessitating a physician's prescription for larger quantities. As such, registered physicians were merely required to keep records of drugs prescribed or dispensed.[24]

The Bill was "an Act to provide for the registration of, with collectors of internal revenue, and to impose a special tax upon all persons who, produce, import, manufacture, compound, deal in, dispense, sell, distribute, or give away opium or coca leaves, their salts, derivatives, or preparations, and for other purposes."[25]

The (a) portion of the section two part of the Act states, "To the dispensing or distribution of any of the aforesaid drugs to a patient by a physician, dentist, or veterinary surgeon registered under this Act in the course of his professional practice only: Provided, that such physician, dentist, or veterinary surgeon shall keep a record of all such drugs dispensed or distributed, showing the amount dispensed or distributed, the date, and the name and address of the person to whom such drugs are dispensed or distributed; except such as may be dispensed or distributed to a patient upon whom such physician, dentist, or veterinary surgeon shall personally attend; and such record shall be kept for a period of two years from the date of dispensing or distributing such drugs, subject to inspection, as provided in this Act."[26]

The above Act contained a provision for physicians that included the following, "in the course of his professional practice." This clause was interpreted by law enforcement agents to mean that a doctor could not prescribe opiates to an addict. Addiction was not considered a disease, thus an addict could not be considered a patient and as such, opiates could not be prescribed or dispensed to

---

22. Miron,. J. 1999. Violence and the U.S. Prohibitions of Drugs and Alcohol. *American Law and Economics Review 1-2,* 78–114
23. Levine, H., Craig Reinarman, Alcohol and Drug Prohibition: Lessons from Alcohol Policy for Drug Policy. http://www.cedro-uva.org/lib/levine.alcohol.html (accessed September 2006)..
24. Brecher, M. and the Editors of Consumer Reports Magazine. 1972. Consumers Union report on Licit and Illicit Drugs. http://www.druglibrary.org/Schaffer/studies/cu/cu8.html (accessed December 14, 2006).
25. Public Law No. 223, 63rd Congress, approved December 17, 1914.
26. Public Law No. 223

n addict by a physician since it would not be supplied within the context of "in the course of his professional practice."[27] A lot of physicians were arrested or had their careers ruined under this interpretation and some were subsequently convicted and imprisoned.[28] Members of the medical profession soon learned that it was foolhardy to supply opiates to addicts.[29] This interpretation of the Harrison Act was a precursor to the "War on Drugs."

The first U.S. narcotics agents worked for the alcohol prohibition agency. But subsequently in 1930 drug prohibition was separated from alcohol prohibition by Congress.[30] This separation led to creation of a new federal drug prohibition agency, the Federal Bureau of Narcotics.[31] The U.S. government in the 1930s, with help from the Federal Bureau of Narcotics, wrote and gained acceptance for two international anti-drug treaties that were targeted towards suppressing narcotics and "dangerous drugs."[32] The then newly established United Nations (UN) made drug prohibition one of its priorities in 1948, and by 1961 the UN single convention had established the current system of global drug prohibition.[33] During the course of the last 80 years, drug prohibition has been supported by just about every type of government or political party.[34] Global drug prohibition can be alluded to as a sort of continuum whereby there is a range of penalties (which vary from country to country) to deal with violations of drug prohibition. As far as the Western world is concerned,[35] the Netherlands would be on one end of the continuum (where there is a decriminalized as well as regulated form of drug prohibition) and at the other extreme end of the continuum would be countries like United States where long prison sentences are imposed for repeated possession, use and small scale distribution of forbidden drugs.[36] The prohibitory policies of other western countries fall somewhere in between the two, but no western country and very few third world countries have forms of drug prohibition that are as criminalized nor as punitive as that of United States.[37] The vast majority of drug laws in the United States preclude probation

27. Brecher.
28. Brecher.
29. Brecher.
30. Levine, H., Craig Reinarman, 1991 Alcohol and Drug Prohibition: Lessons from Alcohol Policy for Drug Policy. *The Millbank Quarterly, Vol 69. No. 3*, http://www.cedro-uva.org/lib/levine.alcohol.html (accessed September 2006).
31. Levine
32. Levine
33. Levine.
34. Levine.
35. Some countries that are not part of the Western world actually do impose penalties that are more stringent than USA penalties for instance, China, Singapore, Indonesia impose the death penalty for drug trafficking.
36. Levine
37. Levine

or parole or sentencing discretion by judges, leading to an unprecedented number of individuals that are incarcerated for violating drug laws.[38]

According to Levine and Reinarman there are now about 0.5 million individuals in prison for violating drug prohibition laws and the majority of them are poor people of color that are serving time for possession or intent to sell small quantities[39] of illegal drugs.[40] The vast majority of new convictions are drug related, and billions of dollars have been spent on the "War against Drugs." In his book aptly titled, "Some problems of Addiction," Dr. Karl Bowman, indicated that current USA drug policy is a virtual failure.[41] Dr Bowman convincingly makes the case for a change in drug policy. He stated,

> For the past 40 years we have been trying the mainly punitive approach; we have increased penalties, we have hounded the drug addict, and we have brought out the idea that any person who takes drugs is a most dangerous criminal and a menace to society. We have perpetuated the myth that addiction to opiates is the great cause of crimes of violence and of sex crimes. In spite of the statements of the most eminent medical authorities in this country and elsewhere, this type of propaganda still continues, coming to a large extent from the enforcement bureaus of federal and state governments. Our whole dealing with the problem of drug addition for the past 40 years has been a sorry mess.[42]

This viewpoint is especially compelling when data from countries like Netherlands with a more regulatory approach towards its drug problem, is compared with data from the USA with its more punitive approach towards the drug issue. Violent crime rates e.g. homicide in the Netherlands are less per capita than the crime rates in the USA despite the fact that drugs are more tolerated within the Netherlands.[43] Also in a 1958 Joint Committee Report on narcotic drugs, published by American Bar Association and American Medical Association the thrust of the report was that stringent drug law enforcement should not be the main and only response to the drug problem.[44] Many developed countries echo US style rhetoric and logic, without actually imposing heavy sanctions on

---

38. Levine
39. It should be noted that there is also a disparity in sentencing specifically between cocaine possession and crack possession. The current federal guideline for first time offence for possession of crack cocaine is five years in prison with no possibility of parole while possession of five grams of cocaine which is purer pharmacologically is treated as a misdemeanor.
40. Levine
41. Bowman, K., 1958. Some Problems of Addiction. Problems of Addiction and Habituation, ed. Paul H. Hoch and Joseph Zuin. New York: Grune & Stratton, 171.
42. Bowman, 171
43. Table 1.1 of International Comparisons of criminal Justice Statistics 2000, indicate that for the year 2000, the Netherlands had a 1.42 homicide rate versus 5.64 homicide rate per 100,000 people.
44. American Bar Association and American Medical Association Report. 1958, 19-21.

drug offenders.[45] The United States is one of the most strident proponents of incarceration as a policy tool, and is the leader in drug incarceration rates when compared with other industrialized countries, yet there is no conclusive data that this policy as a whole has significantly impacted the availability or supply of drugs.[46] Literature review data indicate that such drug policies or laws do not fall equally across all segments of US society, for instance between 1985 and 1995, there was 200 percent increase in the number of incarcerated females in both state and federal institutions and the majority of these women were incarcerated for non violent drug offences.[47]

> Stringent law enforcement has its place in any system of controlling narcotic drugs. However, it is by no means the complete answer to American problems of drug addiction. In the first place it is doubtful whether drug addicts can be deterred from using drugs by threats of jail or prison sentences. The belief that fear of punishment is a vital factor in deterring an addict from using drugs rests upon a superficial view of the drug addiction process and the nature of drug addiction . . . The very severity of law enforcement tends to increase the price of drugs on the illicit market and the profits to be made therefrom. The lure of profits and the risks of the traffic supply simply challenge the ingenuity of the underworld peddlers to find new channels of distribution and new customers, so that profits can be maintained."[48]

Inherent in the above statement is the idea that perhaps other avenues of dealing with the USA drug problem should be explored, especially considering the fact that the current "Get Tough" policies on illicit drugs have cost billions of dollars, while failing to curtail illicit drug supplies and, at the same time, expanding current USA prison populations. Part of the propaganda against illegal drugs is the idea that addiction and involvement in the drug trade leads to violence and aberrant behavior, but some of the violence should be ascribed to current enforcement processes and the underground nature of illicit drug trade.

According to David Friedman the co-relationship between drugs and violent crime could occur in any one of the following three ways. The first co-relationship assumes that violence can occur as a result of violent crime committed by individuals that use drugs. This relationship assumes that all prohibited drugs lead people to commit violent crime while under the influence. Inherent in the idea is that people would not normally have committed the crime were it not for the fact that they were under the influence. This assumption is made both for

---

45. Bewley-Taylor, D., Mike Trace and Alex Stevens, 2005. Incarceration of drug Offenders: Costs and Impacts. *The Beckley Foundation Drug Policy Programme.* Briefing Paper Seven. June 2005
46. Bewley-Taylor
47. Bewley-Taylor.
48. American Bar Association and American Medical Association Report, 1958, pp 19-21.

drugs for which it is pharmacologically implausible e.g. heroin and marijuana (since they are depressants) and for ones that is entirely plausible such as alcohol. Therefore, the assumption is that drug prohibition will curtail the availability of drugs thus leading to a reduction in violent crime.[49] A sub co-relationship is the contention that drug users commit crimes in order to get the money to pay for their drug habit.[50] If that is the case then prohibition, which drives up prices due to the black market, would lend itself to that contention as opposed to regulation whereby the drugs will be cheaper and hence the implication that drug users will not have to commit crime to fund their drug habits since they can afford the drugs.

The second co-relationship is that violence occurs as a consequence of production and distribution of drugs. This can occur since individuals that are part of the drug industry have their wealth in portable forms (drugs and cash), which makes them susceptible targets. And, since the nature of their business precludes them from calling the police, they then have to utilize private violence to protect themselves.[51] Violence can also occur as a form of dispute resolution since formal legal channels are not viable options for those participating in the drug trade.[52]

Finally violence can occur as a direct consequence of the attempt to enforce drug prohibition and this violence would be in the form of confrontation between drug suspects and law enforcement officers.[53] When the current "War on Drugs" is compared with prohibition, one can see glaringly similar parallels. Both policies involved huge expenditures on enforcement, increased judicial caseloads, increased prison populations (as a direct result of enforcement and prosecutions), increased crime–both directly as a result of enforcement and indirectly due to black-market activity, increased substance related sickness and death from adulterated forms of the prohibited substances; all without specifically reducing consumption or availability of the prohibited substances.

Currently there is increasing opposition to drug prohibition as a general policy initiative. Presently an appreciable number of countries and many regional and local governments are reforming their drug policies while focusing more on harm reduction and adoption of less criminalized forms of drug prohibition.[54] That is the best that they can do without effectively withdrawing from the 1961 convention on drugs. But the possible political fallout that will invariably result if withdrawal were to occur from the single convention of 1961 effectively en-

---

49. Friedman, D. Drugs Violence and Economics. http://www.daviddfriedman.com/Academic/drugs_and_violence.html (accessed September 19, 2006).
50. Friedman.
51. Friedman.
52. Miron, J. 1999. Violence and the U.S. Prohibition of Drugs and Alcohol. *American Law and Economics Review, 1, Fall 1999*, 78–114.
53. Friedman .
54. Levine.

sures that for the time being no nation will make the move to officially withdraw from the United Nations Convention on drugs. At a press conference in December 8, 1995 the then U.S. Surgeon General, Jocelyn Elders, suggested that US government should examine the experience of countries that have decriminalized drugs. She mentioned at the press conference that she understood that crime rate and incidence of drug abuse had actually declined within those countries.[55] The White house dismissed the idea out of hand. It was inconceivable for the White House to envision the possibility of decriminalizing drugs.

Generally speaking the U.S. political atmosphere does not bode well for politicians that are seen as soft on crime. The politically expedient refrain "Tough on Crime" applies equally well to "Tough on Drug" approach. Since this popular refrain seems to impact on the politician that utilizes it, a positive image of a public servant working for citizen's interests is one who is determined to stamp out crime at any cost and protect citizens from drugs as well as crime. From Barry Goldwater to Richard Nixon, this particular refrain appeared to have struck a lucrative chord. Although it did not help elect Barry Goldwater to the presidency in 1964, this refrain was one of the main anthems of Richard Nixon's run for the presidency. During the 1968 presidential primaries, the get tough on crime strategy seemed to have struck a chord in the electorate. So much so that Richard Nixon in a letter to Former President Dwight Eisenhower, wrote that, "I have found great audience response to this [law and order] theme in all parts of the country, including areas like New Hampshire where there is virtually no race problem and relatively little crime."[56] One could reasonably postulate that inherent in this missive was the concept that Richard Nixon recognized that U.S. citizens responded well to this idea of being tough on crime. Another pervasive idea, underscored by the missive was the notion that crime was perpetrated by the "non-Caucasian race." Throughout the decades the message of "tough on crime" has solidified, such that currently the popular refrain amongst politicians of both sides of the political party spectrum (Democrats and Republicans) is that crime must be stamped out at all costs. This has given rise to mandatory sentencing, three strikes out laws, and generally tougher sentences for all spectrums of crimes, including non violent drug crimes.[57] This, despite the fact that research does not give credence to the idea that tougher and longer prison sentences help to significantly reduce crime. Most empirical studies conclude that tougher criminal policies and enhanced incarceration usually result in, at best a small reduction in crime rate while substantially increasing the number

55. Chambliss, W. 2001. Power, Politics and Crime. Boulder: Westview Press, 85
56. Baum, D. 1996. Smoke and Mirrors: The War on drugs and the Politics of Failure. Boston: Little, Brown. Travis Pratt. 2009. Addicted to Incarceration; Corrections Policy and the politics of Misinformation in the United States. Sage Publication Inc., 25
57. Pratt, T. 2009. Addicted to Incarceration: Corrections Policy and the Politics of Misinformation in the United States. Sage Publication Inc., 66–68

of incarcerated prisoners.[58] In fact according to Visher it would require about a 10–20 percent increase in prison population to bring about close to one percent reduction in crime.[59] The general public seems to buy into the popular "Get Tough on Crime" refrain, but that is hardly surprising given the fact that media sources generally lend themselves advertently or inadvertently to propagating the idea that crime is more pervasive than it actually is. In a research study of effect of television news content on citizens' fear of crime, Chirico's, Padgett, and Gertz found that the media played a large role in shaping the extent of people's idea of crime.[60] Thus the more dramatic the news, portraying crimes, the more citizens' perceptions that crime is pervasive.[61] Therefore based on media portrayal, the idea that has remained indelible in citizens' minds is that crime is a huge problem that must be dealt with. In fact most indicia point towards the fact that majority of the public think that crime is on the increase despite the fact that the reverse is true.[62] Within this national atmosphere, the rhetoric of "Tough on Crime" is embraced readily by the public. As such any politician that appears to be "Tough on Crime" would have a ready connection to sentiments of majority of the American public.

The failure and absurdity of putting so many people in prison for drug offences have led police chiefs, prison wardens and even some conservative politicians like former secretary of state George Schultz as well as Milton Friedman to embrace the idea of drug decriminalization.[63] Research also indicates that the majority of drug offenders, whom are currently incarcerated, are in prison for minor non-violent offences.[64] Despite such empirical research, the war on drugs appears to have resulted in enhanced prosecution especially where women from lower socioeconomic background are concerned. That is not to say that women with drug issues are necessarily just women from lower socio economic background, but research shows that there is greater police activity in lower or poorer neighborhood, with subsequent increased arrest there for drug offences. According to Chambliss, the war on drugs in United States has produced a war

58. Pratt, 67.

59. Pratt. 67. Visher, C.A. 1986. The RAND inmate survey: A reanalysis. In Criminal Careers and "Career criminal," ed. A. Blumstein, J. Cohen, J.A. Roth, and C.A. Visher. Washington, DC: National Academy Press.

60. Chiricos, T., S. Eschholz, and M. Gertz. 1997. Crime, News, and Fear of Crime: Toward an Identification of Audience Effects. *Social Problems* 44: 342-57

61. Chiricos

62. According to, Bureau of Justice Statistics, crime 1974-2004, when crime rate is analyzed for the years 1974 through 2004, data shows that crime rate has decreased for all general types of crime. http://bjsdata.ojp.usdoj.gov/dataonline/Search/Crime/State/StatebyState.cfm?NoVariables=Y&CFID=207830&CFTOKEN=35222829 (accessed January 3' 2009).

63. Chambliss, 85–86

64. Maguire, K., and Ann l. Pastore, eds., 1977-1995. Sourcebook of Criminal Justice Statistics, Washington, DC, U.S. Department of Justice, Bureau of Justice Statistics,.

between police and minority youth from the ghetto.[65] There is greater police activity and monitoring of poor neighborhoods. Since residents of poor neighborhoods are constantly under greater scrutiny by police, laws of probability dictate that there would be more likelihood of arresting someone there, in those poor neighborhoods, for breaking the law. That would likewise hold true if the police were to mount a constant vigil at higher end neighborhoods, to try and arrest anyone that engages in any behavior that is against the law. Accordingly young black and Latinos in America's ghettoes are under siege and at war with the police. Thus drug related incarceration rates for minorities and individuals from lower socio-economic backgrounds have increased exponentially. According to Chambliss, with regards to enhanced policing at the ghettoes, women are being targeted even more than men.[66] Therefore, although recent incarceration rates for both men and women have increased dramatically under current get tough on drugs climate, rate of incarceration for women increased at almost twice the incarceration rate for men.[67]

Generally stricter enforcement of punitive drug policies have had an increase on the number of incarcerated women, but the greatest increase in percentage of inmates incarcerated for drug offences are seen in African American women,[68] or generally women of color and women from lower socioeconomic backgrounds. Nationally from 1986 to 1999, the United States has seen an 888% increase in the number of women incarcerated in state facilities for drug related offenses,[69] and African American women comprise a disproportionate percentage of the incarcerated women. This is despite the fact that such women usually have minimal to no direct involvement with organized drug trade, yet they are still harshly prosecuted under auspices of the expansive and stricter drug laws. This does not mean that upper income women do not abuse drugs. The media inundates us with stories of wealthy stars that have drug addictions. But the criminal judicial course for them seems destined for a path that is divergent from that of women from poor socioeconomic background. There is the case of Kate Moss, a super model and entrepreneur whose pictures while in the process of partaking of cocaine, were plastered in magazines across the country. No formal charges were filed against her, if anything it seemed that the pictures added to her celebrity appeal. Another high profile woman who has been in the news for drug addiction is Cindy McCain, who is the wife of 2008 Presidential contender Senator John McCain. It is a well documented fact that, Cindy McCain had "battled" addiction. It is interesting to note that the term used by the media for the

---

65. Chambliss, 93.
66. Chambliss, 93.
67. Chambliss, 93.
68. Bush-Baskette, S.R. (1997). The war on drugs as a war against black women. In Miller, S. (Ed.), *Crime Control and Women: Feminist Implications of Criminal Justice Policy* (pp. 113-129). Thousand Oaks, CA: Sage Publications.
69. Bush-Baskette

most part to address her dependence on prescription drugs is "battling addiction." According to Wikipedia, Mrs. McCain became addicted in 1989 to opioid painkillers, Percocet and Vicodin, and subsequently in 1994 admitted that she was addicted to those.[70] She also admitted stealing those aforementioned drugs from the pharmacy of a charity that she helped found, the American Voluntary Medical Team. In fact she had solicited prescriptions for painkillers, from physicians who worked for the charity. She would have the prescriptions filled, by using the names of her staff.[71]

A former employee of her charity had contacted Drug Enforcement Administration, to report her crime, there was an investigation but no formal criminal charges were filed against her and neither did she serve jail or prison time for the crime.[72] She instead entered a diversion program.

According to Stanton Peele, Mrs. McCain's position can be contrasted from differing viewpoints. It is feasible that some will view her as a privileged wealthy lonely wife of a politician who turned to drugs for solace, and as such she should be pitied not punished.[73] Others might view her as a criminal that deserves the same punishment that is meted out to other lower socioeconomic street drug addicts that are caught within the criminal justice system. She has the means to enter drug rehabilitation unlike street drug addicts who usually end up in prison. Is her crime not greater (since she violated a position of trust, by stealing drugs from her charity) than that of street addicts who merely buy illicit drugs from the streets.[74] Cindy McCain admitted to being addicted to drugs from 1989 through 1992, while raising her children and she actually adopted a child while still an addict.[75]

Cindy McCain's circumstances can be contrasted with that of a street addict whom most assuredly would not have been granted the opportunity to adopt a child while addicted.[76] When the war on drugs is examined in detail, one glaring fact that stands out, is that enforcement is usually focused on lower income neighborhoods. A host of circumstances also conspire to ensure that lower socio economic women are disproportionately the ones in prison serving time for drug

---

70. Wikepedia. Cindy Hensley McCain, http://en.wikipedia.org/wiki/Cindy_Hensley_McCain, (accessed August 8, 2008).
71. Peele, S. 2000. McCain has Two Standards on Drug Abuse: *Los Angeles Times*, February 14, 2000, p. B5, http://www.peele.net/lib/mccain.html, (accessed August 8, 2008). Note : Stanton Peele, is a New Jersey psychologist, attorney and author of *Diseasing of America* (Jossey-Bass, 1995). He is a senior fellow of the Lindesmith Center, a drug policy think tank in New York and San Francisco.
72. Peele.
73. Peele.
74. Peele.
75. Peele.
76. Peele.

crimes.[77] This is despite data that would seem to indicate that drug addiction is proportional across all socioeconomic spectrums. Different studies have evaluated the relationship between socioeconomic status and drug use, but such studies have only found weak and inconsistent relationships.[78] Such studies appear to suggest that socioeconomic factors might have a positive correlation with drug use, only under extreme poverty and inadequate opportunities.[79] The 1997 National Household Survey on Drug Abuse reported that of the women they surveyed, 34.3% of Caucasian women, 24.9 % of African–American women and 19.2% of Latinas, reported having used illegal drugs in their lifetime.[80] There was no demarcation within the study along socio economic strata. But the study did indicate that drug addiction has been on the increase where women are concerned. The study also showed that women are usually more addicted to legally prescribed drugs than men, and through the period spanning 1992–1997 regular use of cocaine for women increased while that for men decreased.[81]

One of the most important characterizations of the above mentioned study is the idea that causes of addiction, its extent and effects on women's lives and bodies are not fully comprehended, simply because addiction has traditionally been treated as a male disease.[82] According to the Bureau of justice Statistics, there were about 5,600 incarcerated women in 1970, by 2006, that number had jumped to over 112,000.[83] This is an increase of over 2,000 percent. When these numbers are demarcated by race, the finding is that incarceration rates for African American women are currently higher than that for Caucasian men.[84] This is not withstanding the fact that these women are generally incarcerated for non violent and minor offences. African American women are thus the fastest growing sector of the U.S. population in state or federal custody.[85] This penchant for increased punitive incarceration for minor offences has serious policy implications. Increased incarceration rate imposes enormous burden on state and federal budgets, to the extent that states and federal government would have to allocate funding away from proactive and supportive public institutions to operate puni-

---

77. Some of these circumstances, would include, the fact that drug enforcement is disproportionately focused on lower income neighborhoods, lack of education/knowledge about the criminal justice system, lack of resources to hire a private attorney and public perception that street drug users are criminals, not victims and should be treated as such.
78. Davis
79. Davis
80. The Effective National Drug Control Strategy 1999 http://www.csdp.org/edcs/page14.htm. (accessed December 19, 2008).
81. Effective National Drug Control.
82. Effective National Drug Control.
83. Bureau of Justice Statistics 2006a, Prisoners in 2006. Washington, DC: U.S. Department of Justice
84. Pratt, T. 2009. Addicted to Incarceration: Corrections Policy and the Politics of Misinformation in the United States, Sage
85. Pratt.

tive incarceration systems.[86] This especially brings to bear when USA is compared with other first world countries. New Zealand, Finland, Sweden and Denmark earmark about 40–50 percent more of their GDP[87] on education than USA. Other first world nations spend more of their GDP on healthcare than USA does. Conversely USA spends a greater portion of their GDP on incarceration systems. This puts a burden on funding for programs, such as health, educational, scholarship and artistic programs for young children that will help generate more productive adults. Punitive and especially "Get Tough on Drugs" approach is turning the US towards being a nation of incarceration. If this trend continues, at some point USA as a nation will have a great proportion of their citizens incarcerated for minor non violent offences. These incarcerated individuals will thus be dependent on government while incarcerated for their livelihood. This will put a heavy financial burden on government, and money will be increasingly directed towards easing incarceration financial burden in lieu of proactive, progressive, social, economic and health programs. Without feasible policy changes with regards to "Get Tough on Drug" current policy mandate, mandatory drug sentences and tougher drug crime laws, will ensure that an increasing percentage of US population will be locked up and thus unable to be taxpaying citizens of US.

This research thus seeks to understand circumstances leading to addiction and subsequent incarceration of the women interviewed. Special emphasis is on processes and circumstances (as narrated by respondents) leading to contact and subsequent incarceration of these women drug offenders within the criminal justice system in Tennessee. In the United States, there appears to be a small but increasing consensus that current drug policy is not working, but there is a dearth of research pertaining to due process issues or circumstances leading to incarceration of women drug offenders. This research will attempt to address that, while focusing on women drug offenders in Tennessee. It must be noted that all the names within the research narrative were changed to fictitious names.

86. Pratt.
87. Gross Domestic Product.

Chapter 2

Voices from the Inside: Pain Killers and Addiction

> "There were women in prison that were serving less sentences and they had committed more heinous crimes, like killing their babies, or their husbands" Jane 3

> "Prison is not that bad, especially when compared with jail. In county jail there are no programs for inmates unlike prison where they have different programs." Jane 5

> "It is sad and bad that, the sentences for drug offenders are as long as sometimes longer than the sentences for the "murderers or baby killers." Jane 19

> "At the peak of my drug use, I could smoke about $1000 worth of crack cocaine in a day." Jane C

> "Prison is a sort of comfort zone, more so than a rehabilitative place. Though I would like not to come back." Jane C

This chapter compiles interviews that showcase how drug addiction can start from legitimate prescriptions for the relief of pain. What led these individuals to prison is that they often could not afford or legally obtain the opioids,[1] stimu-

---

1. Opioids have pain reliving properties and they are usually prescribed to treat and manage pain. When used responsibly and as directed they can be very effective in long term pain management, without necessary addiction. Some examples of opioids would include hydrocodone, oxycodone , OxyContin, Codeine, Dilaudid and morphine which is utilized for severe pain management.

lants,[2] and CNS[3] depressants or medications that they had gotten addicted to. As a last resort they turned to theft, prescription fraud or sale of illegal drugs to enable them to get money and or gain access to their drug of addiction. The acting Director for the National Institute of Health has testified that long term use of one of the commonly prescribed pain killer, OxyContin, changes the brain in fundamental ways that take over the user's motivations, which drives and leads them to actively seek out the drug.[4] According to National Institute on Drug Abuse (NIDA),[5] "an estimated 7 million persons, or 2.8 percent of the population, age 12 or older had used prescription psychotherapeutic medications non-medically in the month prior to being surveyed. This includes 5.2 million using pain relievers (an increase from 4.7 million in 2005), 1.8 million using tranquilizers, 1.2 million using stimulants, and 0.39 million using sedatives." This is the reality about pain medication and addiction, and it would be totally unfeasible and incomprehensible to incarcerate all these individuals that abuse such medications. The survey also indicated that, "among persons aged 12 or older who used pain relievers non-medically in the past 12 months, 55.7 percent reported that they got the drug most recently used from someone they knew and that they did not pay for it. Another 19.1 percent reported that they obtained the drug from one doctor. Only 3.9 percent purchased the pain reliever from a drug dealer or other stranger, and only 0.1 percent reported buying the drug on the Internet. Among those who reported getting the pain reliever from a friend or relative for free, 80.7 percent reported in a follow up question that the friend or relative had obtained the drug from just one doctor."[6] If both medical and nonmedical users can possibly become addicted after receiving this type of medication either from their healthcare provider or friends, then it would seem that a rigorous detoxification program should also accompany the prescription.[7] Likewise rehabilitation would be indicated for those addicted to such medications, regardless of their initial source of the medication. Prison is likely not the most effective alternative for the individual or society. This chapter compiles the narratives of such users.

---

2. Stimulants generally increase dopamine production in the brain which can lead to a sense of euphoria, increased energy and attention. Some examples of stimulants would include Concerta, Ritalin and Dexedrine

3. CNS depressants are Central Nervous System depressants, such as sedatives and tranquilizers which slow down normal functioning of the brain. Some examples of CNS depressants would include Valium , Xanax and Ambien.

4. Statement by Glen R. Hanson, Ph.D., D.D.S. Acting Director, National Institute on Drug Abuse on OxyContin: Balancing Risks and Benefits before the Senate Committee for Health, Education, Labor, and Pensions February 12, 2002

5. NIDA InfoFacts: Prescriptions and Over the Counter Medications. http://www.nida.nih.gov/infofacts/PainMed.html (accessed January 13th 2009).

6. NIDA

7. NIDA

Jane 4

Jane 4 was a Caucasian 33-year-old woman that grew up with a brother and two sisters. Her parents later divorced. Apart from her brother who had been in trouble with the law for drug related crimes, none of her other siblings had ever gotten into trouble with the law. Jane 4 was very uncomfortable with the questions asked of her. Her responses were very sketchy. According to her, she had no prior criminal history; she had a fairly "normal" childhood and graduated from high school. Soon after graduating she got married, had three children and worked at different jobs, but mainly as a waitress. A few months after the birth of her last child she injured her back on the job and could no longer work. After having surgery on her back, as a result of the injury, she was prescribed hydrocodone to help alleviate the residual back pain. Unfortunately, she got addicted to the hydrocodone and since she could not afford it she dabbled in theft and burglary to be able to buy the drug. She did not want to discuss the extent of the dabbling. About two years after her back surgery, she started selling hydrocodone to support her habit and to support herself and her three children.

One day, a buyer (who happened to be an informant) stopped by her house to buy 15 hydrocodone pills. Unbeknownst to Jane 4, he had a camera strapped to his wrist. She sold him 15 pills, and about three months later she was arrested for delivery of Schedule III drugs.

She was appointed a public defender and they negotiated a five at 30 (i.e. five years of which 30% must be served). At the time of the interview, she was incarcerated for a Schedule III drug charge as well as for a theft and burglary charge that she was disinclined to mention. She did admit that she was satisfied with the representation of her public defender.

Jane 4 stated that she did not like prison, and would never want to be back in prison after serving her time. When asked what she would do to make sure she does not recommit, she responded that she would go back to work when she got out and that she would live with her mother, which would make expenses manageable, thus alleviating the need for making extra money through drug sales. She had never been treated for any mental illness.

Jane 5

Jane 5 was a 29-year-old Caucasian American, from a working class family. Her father was a carpenter and her mother was a factory worker in a factory that manufactured bathtubs. She was raised with four brothers, one of whom had been in a lot of drug related trouble, and three other brothers who had never been in trouble with the law. All three other brothers have jobs.

Jane 5 graduated from high school and then got married. She had hurt her wrist and had to have surgery on her wrist. As part of her pre-surgery medical work-up she was diagnosed with bi-polar disorder, and was started on antipsychotic medication. She also was diagnosed with seizures. She used to work at a gas station prior to the surgery, but she had a seizure once in a while at work. The incident scared her and she thus made the decision to stop working at the gas station. She resigned prior to her scheduled surgery. After surgery, her physician prescribed Hydrocodone[8] for her. Her physician initially started her on 5 mg, two to three times a day to help alleviate the after surgery pain. After a period of time she acquired a dependence to the prescription medication. Her physician was not amenable to increasing her prescribed dosage. So with her continued dependence on the drug, she needed to and finally managed to find a physician who put her on 10 mg, four or six times a day. About a year after her surgery, she got divorced. In her words this "made money tight." She thus started selling some of her prescription hydrocodone to support her habit.

One day, on or around November 27, 2004, (about a year and six months after her surgery), her uncle's wife Anna stopped by her house and gave Jane 5 money for her to get her some Hydrocodone pills. Unbeknownst to Jane 5, her uncle's wife had turned informant,[9] and so she was wired. Later on, around the first of December 2004, Anna stopped by her house again and gave her money for some more hydrocodone, which Jane 5 supplied. A secret or silent indictment[10] was handed out on Jane 5 and on February 2005 she was arrested. She spent 16 days in jail because she could not make bail. She was appointed a public defender. About 17 days after her arrest, she appeared in court with her public defender. The judge sentenced her to four years house arrest. Her public attorney

---

8. Hydrocodone, is a semi-synthetic opioid that is manufactured from naturally occurring opiates, codeine and Thebaine. It is commonly available in tablet, capsule, and syrup form and is often compounded with other analgesics like acetaminophen or ibuprofen. It is marketed, in its varying forms, under a number of trademarks, including Vicodin, Symtan, Dicodid, Hycodan (or generically Hydromet), Hycomine, Lortab, Norco,, Hydroco, Tussionex, Gentex, Vicoprofen, Xodol, Duodin, Orthoxycol, Norgan, and Hydrokon. The drug is very addictive and in the U.S., pure hydrocodone and forms containing more than 15 mg per dosage unit are considered Schedule II drugs. Wikepedia http://en.wikipedia.org/wiki/Hydrocodone (accessed July 25, 2008).

9. Her uncle's wife, Anna is a crack addict, and she was arrested in a crack sale transaction. The police offered her a deal whereby she will not be prosecuted if she turned police informant. In addition they paid her a fee of $200 for every individual managed to get on tape selling her drugs. So every time Anna got an individual to sell her drugs, she will be paid $200 by the police. In such situations the state usually gets two tapings by the informant prior to handing out an indictment against the individual taped by the informant. Thus far, according to Jane 5, Anna had gotten 72 individuals on tape at least twice, leading to a payoff of 144X$200, and 72 indictments against the 72 individuals she had implicated on tape.

10. According to Wiki Answers, a secret indictment is "the basis in which the prosecutor brings the person giving the testimony before a grand jury to give a testimony so that the accused can be arrested with a warrant. Note that the person being accused of a crime is not aware that he/she is being charged with a crime because they have no idea they are being indicted. That is why it is called a "silent" indictment." http://wiki.answers.com/Q/What_does_secret_indictment_mean (accessed July 25, 2008).

explained to her, that if she had a steady job, the conditions of her house arrest were such that allowance would be made for her job. Thus with a job while under house arrest, she would still be able to leave the house in the mornings and come back in the evenings. Jane 5 said her defense by the public defender was okay enough.

Jane 5 said she was never home whenever the house arrest officer would stop by, thus less than three months after commencement of her house arrest she was violated[11] and rearrested. With her re-arrest, she now had to serve out the remainder of her four-year sentence in prison. She spent a year in prison and went on parole for the remainder of her sentence. About two months into her parole, she got into a fight, which caused her to violate the terms of her parole. She got arrested again and she stayed in jail for about six months, after which she went before a parole board and they decided to let her out again. Jane 5 described her time in jail as being hellish. According to her, jail was so much more horrible than prison. She noted that prior to going to jail, she had gotten a letter from the drug treatment clinic. The letter stated that she could die from methadone withdrawal symptoms if not properly managed. (She explained that methadone was utilized to wean morphine addicts, but that quitting methadone cold turkey was very tough and hard on the body. According to Jane 5, it was easier to quit morphine cold turkey than methadone). She took the letter with her to jail and showed it to the officers there and they told her they would make sure she saw a nurse and that they would work with her. Nonetheless she was left in her cell to withdraw cold turkey, a nurse stopped by once a week to check on her but that was the extent of the help they rendered her. She mentioned that prior to turning herself into the jail, she had decided to hide some of her bi-polar medication in her vagina. While in jail, she pled to see a health care professional such that she could get some bi-polar medication. She was ignored. Since she was never given medication for her bi-polar disorder, she decided to retrieve the medication she had stashed in her vagina. A cellmate saw her retrieve it and asked her to give her a pill otherwise she would report her. She gave the cellmate a pill, but the cellmate went ahead and reported her anyway. She was taken to the jail clinic and a physician retrieved the medication from her vagina. For that incident, she had a pending charge for introduction of contraband to a penal facility. She was yet to go to court for that charge.

Jane 5 also recollected a jail fight. She noted that she was moved to another cell after the medication incident. In her new cell she encountered a cellmate, Felicia, who would stay up all night crying and proclaiming her innocence. One day, Jane 5 asked her to be quiet, but Felicia ignored her, so she punched Felicia in the eye. She was moved yet again, but that weekend during visitation, apparently Felicia urged her mother to fight Jane 5's mother. Jane 5 was so mad at this, that as they were being moved back to their different cells after visitation,

11. This is the term respondent inmates utilize to connote violating the terms of their probation. Once an individual on probation violates the terms of probation, the probation officer can decide to have the individual rearrested.

she pounced on Felicia and they started fighting. For that incident she earned a simple assault/battery charge. When she went to court for that charge the judge sentenced her to the six months time already served in jail.

For a period of about two years after this last parole Jane 5 was doing relatively well with regards to conditions of her parole. Then one of her clients urged her to try morphine and she ended up being addicted to morphine in addition to her original methadone addiction. She attributed her relapse to the fact that her divorce became final around that period and she was just generally angry with her ex-husband and life in general. She re-started her sales of both methadone and morphine in order to generate money for her addiction.

Sometime around November/December of 2007, while her brother was visiting with her, she had two addicts come over to her house. They were both clients of hers. They implored her to sell methadone to them and she ended up selling to them 75 mg of methadone for $75 on two different occasions. Unknown to her they were informants. She ended up getting arrested in June of 2008 when there was only six months left of her original four year sentence, so she was in prison now to serve out or to flat line on her sentence.

Jane 5 said that prison was not that bad, especially when compared with jail. In county jail there are no programs for inmates unlike prison where they have different programs. She said she believed her prison stay would have a positive impact on her and help her in her determination not to be a recidivism statistic. She knew for sure that she did not want to come back to prison.

When asked what recourse she would take to ensure that she stayed away from prison, Jane 5 replied that she would keep away from her old acquaintances.

Jane 7

Jane 7 was a Caucasian woman in her early thirties. She was one of two children from a two parent family. Her older brother was a computer analyst, and her father worked for 30 years for a fiber glass company. Her mother worked as a medical coder prior to retiring. So she grew up in a pretty much working class family. According to her, there was nothing remarkable about her upbringing, it was adequate. She left high school and earned her GED. She then earned a certification in Medical coding/Office management.

She eventually interviewed for and landed her first clinic job. She worked at that job for a period of about 12 years. While at the clinic she noticed that Lindsey, the manager of the clinic, was ordering excess prescription medicine. She would then keep the excess medication for herself or for resale. Lindsey was addicted to Hydrocodone. Lindsey wanted Jane 7 to join her as an accomplice on the underhand transaction, but for the first two years of her job tenure there, Jane 7 was not inclined to join the manager. Then Jane 7 was diagnosed with

Cystitis,[12] ovarian cancer,[13] endometriosis[14] and ovarian cysts.[15] She had surgery to treat her ovarian cysts, and was subsequently prescribed hydrocodone for management of post surgery pain. She became addicted to hydrocodone and could not afford to keep buying it so she decided to collaborate with Lindsey in the ordering of excess prescription medicines for the clinic. This went on for a period of about five years. Then Jane 7 decided that she did not want to take part anymore in the fraudulent ordering of excessive medications. Lindsey continued on with the fraud for about five more years, till she was diagnosed with a malignant tumor. Lindsey thought she was going to die, so she confessed to the medical doctor who owned the clinic about what they had been doing for the past decade or so. The medical doctor decided not to prosecute, but he fired both of them, and brought in his wife to help manage the clinic. The wife, sometime in early 2003, discovered the unaccounted excess prescription medications when she took over as office manager. She called Department of Drug Enforcement (DEA). Lindsey and Jane 7 were indicted on two charges; (1) theft of property from $10,000–$60,000 and (2) trying to illegally obtain narcotics.

Jane 7 hired a private attorney, who negotiated a plea bargain of two years probation for each indictment, for a total of four years probation for the two indictments, in lieu of prison time. In addition Jane 7 was expected to pay restitution of $10,000 back to the doctor prior to the completion of her probation. Jane 7 did not think that she was going to be able to pay back $10,000 within four years of probation, so she instructed her attorney to ask for 10 years probation in lieu of four years probation. She eventually ended up paying off the $10,000 restitution within four years but since she had negotiated for a 10-year probation she had to complete the duration of her probation.

She went on probation in 2003, and in 2005, her probation officer violated her for being on medical patches. The patches were to help wean her off hydrocodone. Jane 7 and her lawyer were able to have the probation reinstated because, they were able to prove that there was no wrongful violation. Sometime in 2006, her grandmother died and burial was set for the weekend. Jane 7 called her probation officer on the Friday prior to the burial to ask for permission to travel to Indiana for her grandma's weekend burial. She could not reach her probation officer, so she left a voice mail message for the probation officer, and then traveled to Indiana for the burial of her grandma. Her probation officer violated her for travelling out of state without permission. Jane 7 was arrested when she came back from the burial. She was then put on intensive probation for the remainder of her 10-year probation. The conditions of intensive probation included reporting more often to her probation officer and she also had a curfew.

---

12. Cystitis is a urinary tract infection that can result in the inflammation of the bladder.

13. Ovarian cancer is cancer of the ovaries.

14. Endometriosis is a condition that can be quite very painful where tissue that looks and acts like the lining of the womb, grows outside the uterus.

15. Ovarian Cysts are blister like fluid containing sacs that adhere to the walls of the ovaries. Some are quite painless, but in some women they can cause a dull persistent pain.

She was still on the patch, when she met her current partner, an engineer who subsequently became her fiancé. She got pregnant, and made the decision to get off the patch, while pregnant. Her initial probation officer died during her pregnancy and a new probation officer replaced her. After the birth of her baby, Jane 7 decided to get back on the patch. She was prescribed Seboxin.[16] Jane 7 started using the Seboxin patch after the birth of her baby, and subsequently informed her probation officer that she was on the patch. About three weeks after sharing that information with her probation officer, her probation officer called her, and told her to come in for a face-to-face meeting. When she got there, two policemen were waiting for her in her probation officer's office and she was arrested. Her probation officer had violated her on account of the fact that Jane 7 had informed her of the Seboxin Patch.

Her attorney tried to reinstate her probation to no avail; she had to go through trial. Her probation officer stated in court that Jane 7 was a hard-core addict. Her doctor testified in court that Jane 7 needed the Seboxin patch to help her get through withdrawal from her addiction. The judge sentenced her to seven years at 30%. Jane 7 was not given credit for the one year she had been on intensive probation. That was sometime in May of 2008. Two weeks later Jane 7 was transported to the Tennessee Prison for Women. Jane 7 was hoping to go on parole in October 2008. She said that her lawyer performed adequately enough, with regards to her defense. She was never diagnosed with any mental condition.

When asked about prison, Jane 7 said that prison was depressing but it was much better than county jail. According to her, in county jail, the officers treat inmates like animals. She spent five weeks in county jail prior to being transferred to prison and while she was there, the sutures on her caesarean section ruptured and got infected. She was not treated for the resultant infection, till she got to prison. She said that these were a lot of beneficial prison programs and they seemed to her to be serious about trying to rehabilitate inmates. Prison administrators also have support programs, but at the same time you have to watch your every move so as not to get into trouble. But she knew she did not want to come back to prison once her time in prison was done.

When asked what she would do to make sure she does not end up back in prison, Jane 7 responded that she was scared of being released and of doing any small thing that might bring her back to prison; but, that maybe she should have been more assertive about getting her doctor to explain to her probation officer the need for her patches. She also said that she quit cold turkey while in jail and that she was not going to go back to using medications once out. She would focus on her baby and fiancé. Hopefully, they would get married soon after she gets out of prison. Her fiancé had been very supportive throughout the ordeal with her last probation officer.

---

16. Seboxin is the name of a drug that is utilized to alleviate opiate withdrawal symptoms.

Jane A

Jane A was a 30-year-old Caucasian woman that grew up in a working class family. Her mother died when she and her brother were young. When Jane A was nine years old, her father remarried. Jane A and her brother were then raised by her father and stepmother. Her father owned a trucking company and her stepmother was a stay at home mother. Her brother who was her only other sibling had never been in trouble with the law. He worked for a tire company.

Jane A dropped out of high school when she was 17 years old. She was dating an older guy who was 31 years old. Jane A said she got tired of school, so she dropped out. In her own words she hung out, "with the wrong crowd." They smoked and drank quite often. She then married the 31-year-old man she was dating. She had an ectopic pregnancy and her fallopian tubes ruptured due to the ectopic pregnancy. She had to undergo surgery to treat the ruptured fallopian tubes. After treatment for her ruptured tubes she was prescribed Percocet.[17] She quickly got dependent on Percocet. Jane A said that she could not readily fill her prescription to Percocet (which she was now addicted to) thus she asked her doctor to change her prescription. He changed her prescription to OxyContin. She started using OxyContin heavily. Initially she would grind it up and snort it up her nostrils. She subsequently graduated to diluting and then injecting it with needles. Throughout this period she was working at a Sonic fast food restaurant. When she was about 24 years old, her husband was arrested and imprisoned for methamphetamine manufacture and sales, so she decided to move to a smaller town. Shortly after her move to the new town, she got a new job working at a restaurant. At the restaurant she formed an alliance with the manager, who would as a side business/job bring OxyContin in to work and sell them to employees that were interested in buying. Jane A was a regular buyer. She worked at the restaurant for a year or two. Then the restaurant went out of business. Jane A was 26 years old then. With the closing of the restaurant, Jane could no longer get in contact with her manager supplier. Thus she had lost her steady source of supply for OxyContin. She was desperate. She did everything she could to get the money for the drug. She started sleeping with men on the side for money. She also started buying OxyContin in bulk from dealers. She would then sell the OxyContin to addicts for profit. One day the police showed up at her house. They had a warrant for her arrest. It appeared that there was a forged check in question. Jane told the police that she was not the one who forged the check, her boyfriend did. Her boyfriend said he was not the culprit, invariably Jane was charged with aggravated burglary. She hired a lawyer and eventually plea bargained on the aggravated burglary charge. She was sentenced to four years probation, as part of her plea bargain.

---

17. Percocet is a Pain medication that is comprised of active ingredients oxycodone and acetaminophen. The oxycodone is an opiate derived analgesic and thus has the potential for abuse. The acetaminophen is a non-opiate derived pain reliever.

According to Jane A, her friend Ann called her one-day on the phone. She wanted to know if Jane could possibly pick her up to run an errand at the neighborhood strip mall. Jane agreed to pick her up. She drove over to Ann's home, picked her up then drove her to the strip mall. It happened that Ann had a meeting at the strip mall to sell some drugs to a customer of hers. The customer turned out to be an informant. Because Ann arrived for the sale in Jane's car they were both indicted. She was remanded to jail, to await her court hearing, since she could not afford bail. She tried to escape from jail a total of three times. When she eventually got to court to answer for her pending drug charges, Jane A got six years for the sale of one 20 mg pill of OxyContin, and two years for sale of counterfeit hydrocodone. She also received three years sentence for her three jail escape attempts. All together she got a sentence of 10 years total at 30%, but her lawyer was able to negotiate a plea whereby she would go on probation in lieu of prison time.

Jane A was put on probation for 10 years. She had a Sugar-Daddy,[18] who was essentially supplying her with OxyContin. He called Jane one night and asked her to come over to his house for intercourse. Jane said that she was too tired for sex that night. Her sugar daddy got angry that Jane would not come over, therefore the next day he called Jane's probation officer and informed the probation officer that Jane was still using OxyContin. Her probation officer called Jane in for a drug test. She failed the drug test; she was retested twice and failed both retests. Jane's probation officer recommended that Jane be remanded to an inpatient rehabilitation program. The state then consigned her to inpatient rehabilitation program. About 26 days into the inpatient program, Jane A's sugar daddy came on a beautiful day in April to visit her at the rehabilitation center. She subsequently absconded from the rehab center with him. There was a warrant for Jane A's arrest since she did not complete her court mandated rehabilitation. There was also a $100 reward for information leading to her whereabouts. Jane A said she thought her sugar daddy called in for the reward and told them that she was at his house. The police came over to the house, picked her up in the police cruiser and took her to jail. That was April of 2006. When she got to court, the judge informed her that there would be no more probation for her; she was going to serve the remainder of her sentence in prison. He revoked her probation, and sentenced her to 10 at 30, but her sentence would include time already served on probation or her street time.[19] She was transferred from county jail to prison in May of 2006. Jane A went up for parole in May 18, 2008. She was granted parole on the condition that she completed her substance abuse program in prison. She was due to complete her substance abuse program by mid August 2008, after which she would be released. But she would be on parole for five years after release. Jane A said that she was not

18. A Sugar Daddy is a wealthy older man who usually in exchange for friendship or intimacy, provides financial and other support for a younger partner.

19. This means that the time or period she was successfully on probation will count toward the total time served for her sentence.

satisfied with the representation of her attorney. She said that the plea bargain he suggested was not a very good deal.

Jane A said that prison was rehabilitative, "It is a sort of lesson." She said, "When in prison it sort of brings the point home to you that you do not want to stay all your life in prison." According to Jane A, prison can sometimes be depressing and she hates it and would not want to be back. She did acknowledge that while in prison she had the opportunity to take a lot of classes. She said that hopefully these classes would help prevent the possibility of her reoffending and thus getting incarcerated again. She made a point of clarifying that she never abused any other drugs apart from OxyContin and morphine.

When she gets out on August 11, 2008, Jane A said that she would move in with her father and focus on raising her three children. Her children were three, seven and eight years old. She would also finish her GED and hopefully will be able to find a decent job.

Sally 4

Sally 4 was a 31-year-old Caucasian college graduate with an Associate's degree and a certification from American Payroll Association. When she was 14 years old her parents divorced and her father moved out so she lived with just her mother and her identical twin sister. So Sally 4 and her twin sister were raised by a single parent. Her twin sister worked in an office, but had previously been in trouble with the law. Her sister was charged with theft/burglary and had subsequently served time in prison. At 20, Sally 4 married but ended up divorced three years later. Shortly after, she re-married, had two children, and stayed married for eight years. When Sally 4 was sentenced, the State's Department of Children's Services picked up her daughter and son. Her nine-year-old daughter lived with her biological father, while her three-year-old son lived with Sally 4's mother.

The start of her journey to prison began when she was 25 years old. She was involved in a serious car accident in Arkansas. She was rushed to hospital after the accident and subsequently went in for surgery. Her doctor prescribed pain killers, Percocet[20] and hydrocodone, to help her manage the after surgery pain. She became addicted to the painkillers. When her husband became aware that Sally 4 was addicted to the medication, he informed her doctor who abruptly took her completely off all medications. This "cold turkey" end to pain killer use was physically hard on her. Thus Sally 4 decided to use her knowledge from her job as a Human Resources Director for a neurosurgical practice to call in fraudulent prescriptions and get more Percocet. She was able to fill her

20. Percocet is a narcotic (oxycodone) and acetaminophen combination. They are combined to get a synergistic effect on pain. Oxycodone is similar to other narcotics in terms of effect and addiction. Narconon Vista Bay http://www.drugrehab.net/index.php (accessed August 9, 2008).

fraudulent prescriptions this way for about three months, then her pharmacy became suspicious of the frequent prescriptions. The pharmacist suspected the prescriptions were fraudulent, and the pharmacy informed the police. When Sally 4, went to the pharmacy to pick up another fraudulent prescription, she was arrested by police. She was charged with felony prescription fraud and her bail was set at $35,000. She remained in jail for about two months until her court date, since she could not afford bail. She was assigned a public defender for her defense, but Sally 4 said she was not satisfied with the representation of her public defender. She felt she could have gotten a more lenient sentence with a private attorney than the six years of probation that she ended up with.

She was out on probation. About five months into her probation, Sally 4 reverted back to her use of painkillers. She claimed it was an emotional addiction. Again she started writing fraudulent prescriptions using the same method as before. She was able to get away with it for another seven to eight months until she was caught when the pharmacy called to verify the prescription and discovered that it was a fraudulent prescription. The pharmacy called and informed the police department. The police started investigating. The police came to her house one day to ask her some questions and ended up arresting her. She was later released on a bail bond. As a result of the charges she had to go to court. Her public defender was able to negotiate a plea deal of two more years of probation. Sally 4 was able to complete the two years of probation without incident, but shortly after that her six week old baby son died from SID.[21] Sally 4 said that she was so devastated by the death of her baby son that she went back to abusing pills. According to her the pills were her way of escaping the pain of the death of her son. Sally 4 still had a six-year-old daughter at home.

Although she knew of the consequences of being caught while involved in prescription fraud, her addiction overwhelmed her and she started calling into pharmacies and acting as a representative for a doctor's office to get more pills. This prompted another investigation in 2005 and after five months she was arrested at the pharmacy when going to pick up fraudulent prescription. This third arrest was based on just one isolated incident of prescription fraud. Her public defender obtained a plea deal of six months where she would get a day off her sentence for each day of sentence served on good behavior. Thus she was able to serve a total of three months incarceration, since she behaved as a model prisoner during her incarceration. At the end of her three months incarceration, she was indicted for only seven counts of prescription fraud which was all that could be proven from the police investigation. Sally 4 said she was really satisfied with her assigned public defender for the new indictments. She said he worked really hard on her case. The state offered her eight months in a county jail; four months in rehabilitation (which she graduated from), and 16–17 months in

21. Sudden infant death syndrome (SID) occurs in infants that are younger than a year old. It is likely due to a combination of some congential defect combined with an external stress. MayoClinic.com http://www.mayoclinic.com/health/sudden-infant-death-syndrome/DS00145 (accessed April 24, 2009).

community corrections. During the time she was in community corrections she went to a pharmacy to buy cough medicine for her daughter. According to Sally 4, coincidentally that pharmacy had received a bogus call for a prescription earlier that day and Sally was not aware of that fact. She said, she showed up at the pharmacy at around the same time the bogus caller claimed he/she would be arriving. The police had been called and she was arrested and charged with misdemeanor solicitation for being in the pharmacy. She posted bond and was released. She was scheduled to appear in court for the charge five months later which would be May of 2007. Her public defender recommended that she plead guilty. She pled guilty to the misdemeanor charge and was put on probation. Sally 4 said she did not bother to go check in with her probation officer. She felt like she was going to be in violation no matter what she did. She just spent as much time with her children and was afraid to call her probation officer until September 10, 2007 when her probation officer sent the police to pick her up at her house. Sally 4 was taken to the county jail where she served 9½ months of her sentence and was then transferred to TPFW. At the time of the interview she had been at the TPFW for about two weeks. Her earliest release date was in March of 2009 when she hoped to get parole in lieu of serving out the rest of her sentence.

She had lived with her grandparents for the past three years prior to her incarceration and she felt that she was not viewed as a person but as a statistic. Sally 4 said her prison experience had been positive and that there was a program for everything which she believed does rehabilitate more than half of the people there. It gave her hope when she saw rehabilitated inmates. A year before being locked up she was determined to stay off pills. She found out about medication to get off of opiates and the cravings. She said the medication was called Seboxin.[22]

When asked if she had ever been diagnosed with any mental condition, Sally 4 said that she was once diagnosed with depression and was subsequently treated as an outpatient. When she gets out of prison her plans were to start working and look for a job to "get her life back" in order to prevent the possibility of her reoffending and facing re-incarceration. Sally 4 indicated that she would get over her drug dependency, perhaps remarry and settle down. In the past she had worked as an officer manager for a real estate company and a purchasing supervisor for an automotive company. She was only a few credits away from earning her Bachelor's degree which she planned on completing. She said that in county jail there was no rehabilitation or mind stimulation and that prison was more rehabilitative than jail. Sally 4 said that she hoped to accomplish a lot while in prison while hopefully "bettering herself as a person."

---

22. Subutex and Suboxone are medications approved for the treatment of opiate dependence. Both medicines contain the active ingredient, buprenorphine hydrochloride, which works to reduce the symptoms of opiate dependence. Center for Drug Evaluation Research http://www.fda.gov/CDER/DRUG/infopage/subutex_suboxone/subutex-qa.htm (accessed August 23, 2008).

Sally 9

Sally 9 was a 37-year-old Caucasian female who was raised by her parents. Her parents have been married for 54 years. She was raised in a practicing Catholic household. Both parents worked. She had two siblings, an older brother and sister. The older brother was 16 years older than her, while her sister was 15 years older than Sally 9. Thus Sally 9 was practically raised as an only child. She was a high school graduate and earned a Bachelor's degree in science and nursing. She married a man who was in the Marines and had three children. Her 19-year-old daughter attended the University of Tennessee and was majoring in political science. Another daughter, who was 17 years old was a junior in High School and lived with her grandparents. Her third child, a son was 12 years old. Her 12-year-old son lived with Sally 9's husband who was stationed in Detroit, Michigan. She had an older brother, who was serving a 31 year sentence in prison for DUI and vehicular homicide.[23] Her sister was a hair stylist in Knoxville.

Prior to her incarceration, Sally 9 was employed by a plastic surgeon in Knox County. When she was about 26 years old, just after giving birth to her last child, she was diagnosed with endometriosis.[24] She needed to have a hysterectomy. As part of her post-operative pain management, she was prescribed Loretabs. Loretabs are usually prescribed for relief of postoperative pain. She became addicted to Loretabs. She was so dependent on the medication, and thus was using it more frequently than prescribed. She would go through her prescription quickly and soon enough her physician stopped prescribing the medication for her as frequently as she wanted. One day, feeling a desperate need for the pills, and knowing that her physician would not prescribe anymore Loretabs for her that month, Sally 9 called in a fraudulent prescription for herself. She was able to go to the pharmacy and pick up the fraudulent prescription without incident. She found the process to be so easy that she just continued to call in fraudulent prescriptions whenever she needed Loretabs. For three years, she was able to continue committing prescription fraud without incident. One day (about three years since she started calling in fraudulent prescriptions), Sally 9 called in a prescription, but she forgot to forward to the physicians answering service. When the pharmacy called the physician's office to verify the prescription, the physician picked up the phone. Of course the prescription was found to be fraudulent. Sally 9 was not aware of this state of affairs. The pharmacy notified Drug Enforcement Administration (DEA). Upon, further investigation the DEA

---

23. Vehicular Homicide is the crime of killing someone while driving under the influence of alcohol.

24. Endometriosis is a condition where tissue similar to the lining of the uterus (the endometrial stroma and glands, which should only be located inside the uterus) is found elsewhere in the body. Taken from endometriosis.org http://www.endometriosis.org/endometriosis.html (accessed September 5, 2008).

found 107 prescriptions total that had been called in this way. Sally 9 was the prime suspect. She drove to the pharmacy to pick up the prescription. She was arrested and read her Miranda rights while being escorted to the police car. She was taken to City-County Building at 4 a.m. and was interrogated there. Sally 9 said that she did not feel she had a choice in stopping the questioning, calling an attorney, or even leaving the room, despite the fact that she was read her Miranda rights,[25] Sally 9 responded to the questions asked of her during the interrogation. After the questioning, she was taken to Knox county jail and bail was set at $85,000. She stayed in jail for 2½ weeks prior to appearing in court to answer to her charges.

She was assigned a public defender and was charged with 47 counts of prescription fraud and 12 counts of attempt to acquire controlled substance by fraud. The public defender told her that the state would offer her 30 years at 30% with a chance to apply for probation. With this daunting information, she decided to hire a private attorney. Sally 9 later found out through her private attorney, that the wife of the public defender was a pharmacist at one of the pharmacies that Sally 9 had used to fraudulently obtain Loretabs. In the three years of perpetrating prescription fraud she had used a total of eight different pharmacies. Her hired attorney and the DA worked out a plea deal of 10 years at 30% without probation. Sally 9 accepted the plea deal and after spending four more weeks in Knox county jail she was transferred to TPFW. She had been in prison for 2½ years but she was scheduled to appear before the parole board sometime in December 2008. This incident was the only time in her life that she had ever been in trouble with the law.

She said that prison life was better than county jail and described time spent at county jail as "serving hard time." She said that she had been rehabilitated. Sally 9 said that the programs at prison have provided her with coping tools to better deal with her addiction than before. Interestingly, she said that she did not view prescription medicine usage as drug abuse. She also said that prison does not rehabilitate unless a person was pro-active and joined the available programs. According to Sally 9, "If all a person is doing is spending time with the other inmates they are only going to learn how to be better at committing other crimes." She felt that prison was more punishment than correction.

After leaving prison she planned to work as a counselor for drug and alcohol rehab. She was not sure that she would continue as a registered nurse. Based on her experience she wanted to help raise public awareness on the dangers of prescriptions of narcotic based medications. She felt that physicians should warn

---

25. Prior to a custodial interrogation, Police officers are required to inform suspects that they have specific constitutional rights relating to police interrogations and questions. They are expected to do so by reading the Miranda warning to the suspect. The Miranda warning consists of four specific information that suspects need to be aware of prior to responding to questions during interrogation. The gist of the four warnings are as follows: (1) you have the right to remain silent; (2) Anything you say can and will be used against you in a court of law; (3) You have the right to an attorney; (4) if you cant afford an attorney one will be appointed for you.

people of the dangers of becoming addicted. If she did not have access to call in her prescription she would have probably bought the pills from a street dealer and been exposed to the path that led some of the other addicts to prison. Sally 9 said that she did not ever want to be re-incarcerated again.

Sally 12

Sally 12 was a 35-year-old Caucasian female. She was raised with her younger brother and older sister in a two parent household. But her parents got divorced when she was 16 years old. After her parents' divorce, she lived with her mother, while her younger brother moved in with their father. Her older sister had already left home by the time of their parents' divorce. Suddenly, recounted Sally 12, she found herself living alone with her mother after her parents' divorce. Her younger brother worked in Charleston and her older sister was now married and a housewife. She moved out of her mother's house, when she was 17 years old. Her father gave her the money to move out. A short while after moving out of her mother's house, she graduated from high school. Upon graduation from high school, Sally got a job with a vending machine company. She worked for the vending company for six years. Sally met the man, who later became her husband while working for the vending company. She got married when she was 23 years old but divorced five years later. She had a nine-year-old daughter that lived with her mother and an 11-year-old son who lived with her father.

When Sally 12 was 28 years old she was involved in a bad car accident. She was rushed to the hospital and as part of her post emergency room visit she was prescribed a host of medications for pain management. Prior to the prescriptions, she had never tried drugs or alcohol. It was this exposure to drugs, through legitimate prescriptions, that was the start of her addiction to painkillers. During the ensuing three years her mother noticed her growing dependence and addiction to her medications. Her mother decided to report her to the prescribing physician. Sally 12 said that when her physician found out about her drug dependence, "he cut off the prescriptions abruptly without any ramp down period." Thus said Sally, she did not have the opportunity to gradually get used to living without the drugs in her body. This approach was very hard on her so she needed to find a way to obtain the painkillers again. The solution for her was to forge prescriptions. She was able to fraudulently fill 13 forged prescriptions prior to getting caught. She was charged with two counts of prescription fraud. She was appointed a public defender. The public defender was able to work out a plea bargain whereby she got one-year of probation, a fine, and ten days of community service. Sally 12 said she was very satisfied with the public defender's representation.

During the course of her probation she became very depressed. She tried to commit suicide by taking 50 pills. The pills "knocked" her out but did not kill her. The unsuccessful suicide attempt left her so scared that she decided not to take pills anymore. She was able to complete her probation without incident. Then she started hanging around the "wrong kind of people" and in 2000 they introduced her to methamphetamine (meth). She became addicted to methamphetamine. Shortly after getting addicted to methamphetamine, Sally 12 began to manufacture and sell methamphetamine, so as to be able to afford her habit. In 2004 she was charged with 26 counts of check forgery and sentenced to eight years. She served 16 months, and was released on parole. She managed to stay drug free for eight months. Then she had a relapse and started abusing methamphetamine again. Within a month she had started manufacturing and selling methamphetamine once more. She was caught when she sold meth to a wired informant. According to Sally 12, for every drug sale transaction (leading to indictment) that the informant was able to capture on tape, the police would pay him $200. On the basis of the recorded drug sale transaction, Sally 12 was arrested. She was charged with sale and delivery of methamphetamine. She hired a private attorney and received eight years at 30% which would run consecutively with her paroled sentence. She stayed in county jail from June 15, 2005 to January 10, 2008. On January 11, 2008, she was transferred to TPFW.

While in prison she joined the prison rehabilitation program. She was in the ninth month of the rehabilitation program. Sally 12 said that she felt like she was becoming rehabilitated. Prison had been a positive experience. She said that there were a lot of programs in prison for inmates who wanted or needed help and that the programs offered help and sought to help inmates. When released from prison, Sally 12 indicated that she would get her children back, find a job, and start life over clean and sober. She adamantly insisted that she would do everything in her power to ensure that she did not become a recidivism statistic. She was not planning to ever return to prison or to relapse again.

Sally 14

Sally 14 was a 59-year-old Caucasian female. She was the oldest of seven siblings. She said she had a traumatic childhood. According to Sally 14 she was given to a foster family when she was only three days old. Then at age seven she was taken back by her mother. She was abused at her mother's home from the age of seven till she turned 13 years old. From early preteen she started acting out as a result of the abuse, by the time she turned 13 her mother had made the decision to place her in a training school for girls. So she was placed in a training school for girls but she kept running away. She would escape back to her mother's house and a short while later her mother would take her back to the school. This pattern continued for a few years. To escape from this life she finally ran away from home in North Carolina and got married at 19 years. She moved with her new husband to Michigan. They lived together for about three years. Then her husband had to leave for a tour of duty in Vietnam. Prior to his leaving for Vietnam she told him that she would move back to her home town of

North Carolina while he was in Vietnam. Her husband did not approve of that idea; he responded that it would be the end of their marriage if she went back to North Carolina while he was in Vietnam. They eventually divorced after he came back from Vietnam. A few years later Sally 14 remarried when she was 30 years old. She and her new husband adopted three children.

In 1981 she was diagnosed with polymiositis,[26] and there was no apparent cure or standard treatment for the disease then, so she was put on pain medication by her physician. In 2004 her TennCare[27] benefits were cut off and she was thus unable to afford consultations with her physician. Without seeing the physician, it would be impossible for her to be able to get her prescriptions legitimately. At this point she was already addicted to her medications. So in order to maintain her addiction or habit, she started buying hydrocodone illegally from drug dealers and she would sell the excess for profit. Sally 14 said that she bought and sold hydrocodone illegally for about a year before inadvertently selling to an informant. She sold hydrocodone on five different occasions to the same wired informant. Based on the wired recording, a grand jury indicted her on charges of possession of controlled substance with intent to distribute and manufacture.

She was assigned a public defender since she could not afford an attorney. When asked if she was satisfied with the representation of the public defender, Sally 14 responded, "Why wouldn't I be? I was guilty." She made the choice to accept the plea bargain proffered by the District Attorney. In return for a reduced count, she accepted a three year sentence at 30%. That meant she had to serve at least 30% of her sentence before she would be eligible for parole. From December 14, 2007 through February 19, 2008 she was in a county jail. She was subsequently transferred to TPFW in February of 2008. Sally 14 was scheduled to go before the parole board on August 3, 2008.

Sally 14 said that prison had been a positive experience. She started on the GED program. Her plans were to finish her GED, and upon release from prison help take care of her grandson. According to her, some of the other prison programs helped her overcome her dependence on painkillers. She was diagnosed in 1990 with depression and was still taking medication for it. She also planned to spend more quality time with her children and husband. She was also looking forward to travelling and visiting with family. In order to stay off drugs she was

---

26. Polymyositis: is an uncommon disease that causes inflammation in muscle tissues. It leads to weakness in the muscles of the upper torso especially the shoulder muscles. The muscles of the hips can also be affected. This disease can make it difficult to carry out activities of daily living. For example individuals afflicted with this disease can find it difficult to brush their hair, get out of chairs or climb stairs. www.mayoclinic.com/health/polymiositis/DS00334 (accessed August 24, 2008).

27. TennCare is Tennessee's Medicaid managed care program that provides health coverage for 1.2 million low-income individuals, children, pregnant women and disabled Tennesseans. Bureau of TennCare http://www.Tennessee.gov/tenncare/ (accessed August 18, 2008).

also going to participate in narcotics anonymous with a sponsor. Hopefully a sponsor would help ensure that she makes it to narcotics anonymous meetings. Sally 14 was very clear and determined that she would not be coming back to prison, once released. She stated she had worked too hard to keep herself clean thus far.

Chapter 3

Voices from the Inside: Peer Pressure and Addiction

A large group of inmate respondents indicated that the circumstances leading to their addiction and sale of illegal drugs were mainly due to peer pressure or influence from their peers. Often these individuals started abusing drugs when they were adolescents. Studies and research indicate that adolescent period is a most vulnerable period, when individuals are most likely to engage in daring and thrilling behavior.[1] The stories suggest that there were family and community support breakdown that allowed this kind of dependence to occur. The dependence subsequently turned into full fledged addiction. In some cases older siblings and older family members provided negative influence in the respondents' lives during their teenage years. An individual can partake of a drug once without becoming addicted to the drug. Thus the first or initial drug exposure did not guarantee that the user will become an addict. But it is important to note that weaknesses in the external environment of the individual also have a role to play in the shaping and growth of dependence on drugs. The external environment would include socioeconomic environment as well as general educational level and background. External environment of an individual would also include friends, family, quality of life, stress, peer pressure, parental involvement, physical and sexual abuse.[2] Apart from external environment other facts can predispose to addiction. Such factors would include biology[3] and developmental stages of an individual. Teenagers are usually more susceptible to peer pressure because, during their teenage years, their brains are still developing in brain ar-

1. Drug Abuse and Addiction, *National Institute on Drug Abuse.* http://www.drugabuse.gov/scienceofaddiction/addiction.html (accessed January 10, 2009).
2. National Institute on Drug Abuse: NIDA InfoFacts: Understanding Drug Abuse and Addiction. http://www.nida.nih.gov/Infofacts/understand.html (accessed January 13, 2009).
3. Biological factors that would predispose an individual to addiction would include metal disorder or diseases, genetics, ethnicity and gender.

eas that govern cognitive decision making, judgment and self control. Likewise at this stage because teenagers are still in the process of developing self control, they are more prone to trying new things.[4] Using drugs can lead to drug addiction at any age, but the younger the age of initial drug abuse, the more the potential to progress to serious abuse.[5]

There was also a group of inmates who intimated that they had lost hope with life and did not see a future for themselves. Thus for those individuals there seemed to be no other legitimate avenue for making it economically or professionally and so they turned to drugs and subsequently drug business. For these respondents, drugs provided an escape from what seemed like a mundane existence. The drugs provided a high or gave them energy and power at the same time masking the routine of their admittedly non progressive life. These groups of respondents appear to mirror some of the socioeconomic conditions relating to drug abuse.

Jane 3

Jane 3 was a 31-year-old Caucasian female who grew up in a middle class Catholic family. Her parents had always been in the restaurant business and owned a restaurant throughout her childhood. She had six siblings. Her mother had seven children from two separate husbands. None of her siblings had ever been in trouble with the law. As a matter of fact her siblings had jobs ranging from a nurse, paralegal, general manager, realtor, manager of a parts company and Summit Hospital administrator. Her father was her mother's second husband and Jane 3 was second to youngest. She started working in her parents' restaurant when she was a child and enjoyed working in her parents' restaurant business. She was therefore very devastated when her parents sold the restaurant when she was 10 years old.

Her parents got divorced when she was 12 years old. According to Jane 3, she hung out with a wild group of children while she was attending Father Ryan High School in Nashville. She started smoking marijuana when she was 16 years old, because she saw a friend smoking it and decided to try it with the friend. A few months later she started selling marijuana while still in high school. She also had a job, working at a video store. At 17 she graduated to selling cocaine because she saw a friend who was making a lot of money as a dealer of cocaine. So she decided to start selling so as to make tons of money too. One day she went with her coworkers from the video store to a wild party that was hosted by the owner of the video store. She said the host gave her a drink that was laced with a date rape drug, and she passed out. She recalled waking up

4. NIDA
5. NIDA

with blood between her legs and on her legs. She did not tell anybody. A couple of months later she found out she was pregnant. She was only 17 years of age. She delivered a baby boy about nine months after the party. She graduated from high school, all the while living at home with her mother. Jane 3 met a woman when she was 18 and thereafter moved in with her while attending a two-year college, majoring in business. She graduated from college and joined the military. Thus from the age of 18 through 23 she barely used any illegal drugs and neither did she sell, mainly because in the military they had occasional drug testing.

At the end of her enlistment, Jane 3 left the military and got a job in the restaurant business. Her female lover left her and Jane 3 was so heartbroken, she started using drugs heavily. Her drug of choice was cocaine. Since she was spending so much money on her drug habit, she needed to make more money than her job at the restaurant was paying, so at the age of 24 years, Jane 3 started selling cocaine. A year and half later, when Jane 3 was 26 years old, she sold five grams of cocaine to an informant, who was wired. She was arrested, and posted bond. She hired a private attorney, and they agreed on a plea with the assistant District Attorney. In lieu of prison she was to serve three years on probation. Some of the terms of her probation were: drug tests two to three times a week; four classes a week; and being expected to see her probation officer once a week, while working her 40-hour-a-week job. She violated the terms of her probation less than two months after starting probation, because she did not go in to see her probation officer. She was arrested shortly thereafter for violation of probation. She had to go before the judge to answer to her charges. According to Jane 3 she also had a prior theft charge. The judge doubled her initial cocaine and theft charges from one year for theft and three years on the initial cocaine charge to two years for theft and five years for the original cocaine charge since she had violated probation. These sentences were to be served consecutively.

Jane 3 served two and half years and was released on parole. She started dating a new woman and got a job at Chili's. She had a very laid-back parole officer, so she only had to report in about once every two months. Thus she was able not to violate parole for about 18 months. Her parole officer retired and one day the new parole officer called her on the phone and asked her to report that day for check in. Jane 3 decided just not to go in because she knew she was going to fail the drug test. She was cognizant of the fact that her new parole officer was going to call in a warrant for her arrest since she did not show up. According to Jane 3, she laid low for a while and also moved to a new apartment. Then one day, sometime in mid 2007, she was out riding with her girl friend and a police officer pulled behind their car, which had expired tags. The police officer turned on his siren such that Jane 3 and her girlfriend would pull over, but her girlfriend who was the driver refused to do so. She led the police on a high-speed chase. Their car finally crashed and she and her girlfriend were arrested.

The judge sentenced Jane to prison to serve out the remainder of her seven-year sentence. She also received a sentence of two years for being a fugitive from justice, but the sentence was to be served concurrently with the remainder of her seven-year sentence. Jane said her attorney did a good job with her defense.

When asked of her impression of prison, Jane 3 said that she was mad that she got such a long prison sentence for merely being addicted to cocaine. According to her there were women in prison that were serving less sentence and they had committed more heinous crimes, like killing their babies, or their husbands. She said that women in prison play the system to get parole and that the programs in prison were jokes. She hated prison. She did admit that Therapeutic Counseling in prison helped her with her anger management, though she had never been diagnosed with any mental illness.

When asked what she would do to ensure that there was no recidivism on her part, Jane 3 responded that she would do everything within her power not to get into trouble again. She said that she had hit her lowest point and once a person had hit their lowest point there was no place else for them to go but up. Not having been in contact with her son was very hard for her and she recognized that she had an ongoing addiction to marijuana and cocaine. Thus when she had served her time in prison and was released, she would continue to attend narcotics anonymous. She also said that her father died and left her one third of $250 million, so she would use that money to open a recovery house for drug addicts. That would keep her busy long enough to stay out of trouble.

Jane 12

Jane 12 was a 46-year-old African American woman, from a working class two-parent family. She was the second oldest of seven children. Her father worked as a driver of an oil tanker for a construction company. He also trained Tennessee walking horses part time. Her mother worked as a factory worker. Of all her siblings, five had never been in trouble with the law, but her youngest brother was incarcerated for auto theft. He was the only other one in her family, apart from Jane 12 that have had an encounter with the criminal justice system.

Jane 12 got pregnant at the age of 15, when she was in 9th grade. The school hired a tutor for her such that she could continue with her schoolwork. After passing 10th grade she made the decision to quit high school in-order to take care of her baby. [6] After dropping out of high school, she worked odd jobs while taking care of the baby. Jane 12 mentioned that after quitting school, she occasionally used marijuana and alcohol. Around her early 20's she met a guy and started dating him. He introduced her to crack cocaine and she became addicted to crack, so much so that she became a dope runner[7] for crack dealers.

---

6. Jane 12 is currently trying to earn her GED.

7. A dope runner is a slang term for someone who traffics in illegal drugs. In Jane 12's case she would take the order for the drugs from addicts and get the order filled with the drug dealer. The drug addicts will give her some drugs as fee for her procuring the drugs

While on drugs she got pregnant again with her boyfriend's baby. She delivered a baby girl. She later had another baby girl for the boyfriend. She said she lived to get high, and her children spent a lot of time with her mother.

Eventually Evelyn, who was one of the ladies she was supplying with crack, was arrested and became an informant, unbeknownst to Jane 12. Evelyn told the police that Jane 12 was a dealer. Sometime in late 2003 and early 2004 Evelyn called Jane 12 on two separate occasions and ordered $100 worth of crack on each occasion. Jane 12 made the delivery each time. In early 2004, two police officers showed up at her house with a search warrant. They searched her apartment but did not find anything. She was not arrested at that point, but the police search of her apartment cost her the public housing apartment she was living in.

Sometime in 2007, she was in her car, and a police officer stopped her for a broken taillight, when he came up to her car, he noticed marijuana joint in her car ashtray. She was arrested for a drug misdemeanor possession charge. She served four months in jail and on the day of her release, Jane 12 was told that according to NCIC,[8] she had a hold in another city, meaning that there was a warrant for her arrest in another city. That was when she discovered that there were two indictments for her, stemming from the drug transactions she made with Evelyn in 2003/2004. She had a public defender, who suggested that she plead guilty since they had her on tape for the two transactions. Thus in March 2007, she pled guilty to two counts of sale of Schedule II drugs, and she received a sentence of 12 years at 30. She was at the county jail for about nine months prior to being transferred to Tennessee Prison for Women. She had been at the prison since January 2008. When asked about the representation by her public defender, Jane 12 responded that she was not really satisfied with his representation.

According to Jane 12 prison had been a learning experience in that being incarcerated had taught her that drugs are not worth the consequences of being in prison or being without her family. She was being rehabilitated in prison to an extent, because incarceration had helped her learn how to live with herself and in the process find out whom she really is. She did not feel she had the opportunity to discover who Jane 12 really was prior to incarceration. She dropped out of high school, had a baby and then met the man that introduced her to crack cocaine; according to Jane 12 she never really had the opportunity or the lull in her life prior to incarceration to be introspective. She said she missed her family. They would not visit her in prison. She had never been diagnosed with a mental illness, though she said that prison can be quite depressing.

Jane 12 said that she would probably parole out to a halfway house and that she would do everything in her power not to re-offend. She would try to get a

---

for them and the drug seller will also give her some money and drugs as fee for helping with sales. So she got free drugs both ways.

8. NCIC means National Crime information Center. According to their web site, NCIC, is an index of criminal justice information, that provides information regarding criminals, fugitives, missing persons. This information can be shared across federal, state and local jurisdictions.

job, and likewise attend narcotics anonymous meeting. Hopefully she would get a sponsor, who would be able to talk her through things when life hits her hard. That way she would be able to talk issues through in lieu of turning to drugs.

Jane 14

Jane 14 was a 44-year-old African American woman that was born into a single parent household. She was the oldest child of her mother. Her father was a landscaper and Jane 14 had some contact with him since her father had moved in with her mother and her stepfather. All three of them lived in one house. Her mother was sixteen years old when she met her father, got pregnant and gave birth to her. Her grandma at that time adopted Jane 14. Her mother then met and married another gentleman and had two children with him; a boy and a girl. Thus Jane 14 had two half siblings. Her half brother was incarcerated and her half sister was serving an eight year prison sentence for drug and other offences.

Jane 14 graduated from high school and got accepted into nursing school. She dropped out of nursing school two weeks prior to her final exams. She said she dropped out because she was on marijuana. She used up the remainder of her student loans and Pell grant on drugs. After dropping out of school, Jane 14 worked a number of odd jobs and fast food restaurant jobs while maintaining her drug habit. Sometime in her thirties, she met a much older man and began dating him. One day they were having an argument and he punched her in the face. He busted her nose and Jane 14 was bleeding profusely. He apologized repeatedly afterwards and helped her staunch her bleeding nose, but thereafter he would beat her up whenever he felt like it. One day, sometime in 1995, they were having another argument in the kitchen, (Jane 14 cannot remember what the argument was about), and he pounced on her. Jane 14 was pressed against her kitchen counter. With her back pressed against the kitchen sink, she managed to grab a butcher knife and stab him with it. He died and she was charged with manslaughter. She pled guilty and was sentenced to 55 days in jail and five years unsupervised probation. Prior to serving her jail time she found out that she was pregnant. She gave birth to the baby. After the birth of the baby, Jane 14 began to feel that she could raise the baby. But Jane 14 subsequently left the bulk of care for the baby up to her aunt. When it became clear to her aunt that Jane 14 was not inclined to care for the baby, her aunt decided to have the baby put up for adoption. According to Jane 14, when the baby was around 14 months old, her aunt took the baby to welfare to be adopted out. Jane 14's baby was adopted out, while Jane was serving her five years of unsupervised probation. She served her five years unsupervised probation without any incident. Then in February 2007 she got arrested for selling half a gram of crack cocaine in a school zone. She got a public defender. The public defender negotiated a sentence of six years at 30 but in lieu of serving time she was to stay in a halfway house for six months after which she would be on enhanced probation for six years. She accepted the offer, and moved into the half way house. Around June 2007, about four months into the halfway house program, Jane 14 said that, she panicked and left the program with the clothes on her back. When asked why she did that, Jane 14 said, "I was afraid that I was not going to make it through the enhanced probation." In hindsight she ruefully agreed that it seemed somewhat ironic for her to have escaped from the halfway house (which in itself was a violation of the conditions of her probation), because she was afraid of not being able to meet the conditions of enhanced probation.

She was on the "lam," till February 27, 2008. On that day, two of Jane 14's friends picked her up on their way to a restaurant. En route the driver decided to stop at a friend's house.[9] The driver left Jane 14 and her friend in the car while he went into the house. Jane 14 and her friend were talking and suddenly they found themselves surrounded by police officers with guns drawn. The police officers asked for their IDs and Jane 14 gave them her driver's license. Since there was an arrest warrant pending[10] on Jane 14, she was read her Miranda rights and arrested. She was taken to jail. She was assigned a public defender. She said that she appreciated the effort the public defended put into her case. He explained to her the details of her arrest. He suggested that she serve out her time, since she was not too keen on enhanced probation. So on February 2008 she was sentenced by the judge to serve out her six years at 30 without any credit for street time.[11] She was transferred a few weeks later from jail to TPFW to serve out her sentence. Her red date[12] was June 10, 2009. On that day she would have served 30% of her time and thus be eligible for parole. Jane 14 had never been diagnosed with a mental illness.

She found prison to be a rather interesting experience. According to her prison was not that hard, it depended on what you wanted to make of it. Some of the programs were alright. Jane 14 said that after release, she would do whatever it takes to make sure that she did not re-offend such that she would never go back to prison. When asked what she would do to make sure that she did not re-offend, she responded that she would stay away from her old friends, especially the ones that were part and parcel of the drug culture. She wanted to maybe get a job in dry cleaning, when she gets out of prison.

---

9. Jane 14 said that probably the friends were all involved with drugs.

10. The pending warrant was because Jane 14 had violated the terms of her probation by escaping from the halfway house.

11. In some cases when violation of probation occurs, judges will discount from the defendant's total time, the period the defendant had successfully served their probation, without any violation. For instance if a defendant served one year (of a 6 year sentence) on probation without violation, and then violated probation on the second year of probation, the judge might have the defendant serve only five years of the original six years in prison because one year (street time) was completed successfully in probation.

12. Red date is the term used by inmates to connote the date or time when they will be eligible for parole. Usually they must serve a percentage of their sentence prior to being eligible for parole. For instance, a sentence of six years at 30 means that the inmate must serve at least 30 percent of the six year sentence before they can be eligible for parole.

Jane 15

Jane 15 was a 48-year-old Caucasian woman from a single-family background. Initially Jane 15's mother was married. Her parents had four children, all of them girls. Her father worked as a carpenter but then was arrested for manufacturing of drugs. Her mother was a housewife but then when her carpenter husband got arrested she became a waitress. Jane 15's mother worked as a waitress for a while prior to meeting Jane 15's stepfather and marrying him. He had a daughter from a prior marriage whom he brought with him to the union, bringing the total combined number of children to five girls. Of her four siblings, three graduated from high school and one of the siblings earned her GED while in prison for robbing a check-cashing place. The oldest sister served time at Tennessee Prison for Women for theft at different houses and at Wal-Mart. Jane 15 said that oldest sister was now "worse off," after having served time in prison. The implication being that her oldest sister was now a more hardened and better criminal than prior to serving time in prison.

When her father got out of prison, Jane 15 moved out of her mother and stepfather's house to move in with her biological father. She was 12 years. Her father always had a stash of weed[13] in the house while Jane 15 was growing up there. One day Jane 15 decided to experiment with the weed and she rolled up the weed just like she had seen her father do. She enjoyed the feeling she got from smoking the weed and hence thereafter she would regularly steal some of her father's weed to smoke. After a couple of years getting high on weed she dropped out of high school at the age of 14 because she no longer liked school. She got a job at a "taco place" and it was while working there that she fell in love, with a young carpenter that worked for her father. She was only about 15 years old. She married him after she turned 16. They were married for a few years and then her husband decided to join the Navy. They did not have any children, so Jane 15 traveled easily with her husband to each subsequent Navy station. Throughout this time she was abusing weed and cocaine. Her husband was eventually stationed in San Diego and they moved to the city to live. While her husband was stationed in San Diego, Jane 15 got involved in the transportation of drugs across the border from Mexico to California. She said she made a ton of money doing that and thus it was very lucrative for her. One day she was transporting weed and cocaine from Mexico to California, and she got caught at the border. Jane 15 said that she thought they got caught because the driver of the truck was wearing a long sleeve shirt whereas the temperature, that particular day was over 100 degrees Fahrenheit. The truck driver was also acting nervous. The customs agent searched their truck and found five ounces plus 18 grams of mushrooms[14], one handgun, a box of 32-caliber shells and a whole

---

13. A colloquial name for Marijuana.
14. Mushroom is a colloquial name for an addictive hallucinogenic compound.

backseat of weed. She said that they had removed the truck's backseats and padded the hollows with weed. They then had put back the backseats in the truck. Upon seeing the cache Jane 15 and the driver were arrested. Jane 15 hired a private attorney to defend her. Jane 15 said her attorney was very good and the fact that her husband was then an airport carrier in the Navy helped her get only five years for her offence. She got out after three and a half years for good behavior,[15] since there was no parole for federal sentences.

After she was released from prison, Jane 15 and her husband moved to Norfolk, Virginia. They lived there for nine years without incident, though she was still smoking weed and using acid, periodically through out that period. Then they both moved to Alabama in 1992, because her husband was stationed there. She stayed there for three months but she could not stand living in Alabama, so she left and moved to Memphis, Tennessee to be with her father. While staying with her father she learnt from him the process of making methamphetamine from ingredients commonly bought from the store. After about two years, she got tired of staying with her father in Memphis, so she traveled to Virginia, to stay with the friends she made back when she was living there. She lived in Virginia for almost two years. She then decided to move back to Tennessee in 1996. She got a job in Tennessee working as a hospital cook and then started her own catering company, all the while using weed periodically. The money was not sufficient for her, especially with her escalating drug habit, so in 2002, she began manufacturing and selling methamphetamine. She bought a concrete building in Cleveland, Tennessee, that was for the sole purpose of manufacturing and distributing methamphetamine. She had the building outfitted with cameras, and hired paid security "guards" that she armed with guns. According to Jane 15 you could not get into the building without clearance. During the course of her "enterprise" she fell in love with John, a customer of hers and they began dating in 2004. John was addicted to methamphetamine but that did not diminish the affection she felt for him.

Sometime in 2005, John was arrested for buying methamphetamine paraphernalia, and in order to have his sentence mitigated, he agreed to serve as an informant. He thus took pictures of Jane 15, while she was in the process of manufacturing methamphetamine in the building. He also took pictures of the inside of the methamphetamine building she had bought. This was all done without her knowledge.

Later on during the year she went with a friend to another county for a visit and on their way back, the truck they were in, broke down. They were in the car trying to call somebody to come pick them up when a police officer happened to stop by. The police officer called in the car license and discovered that it did not belong to the truck. That gave the police officer probable cause to search the

15.Despite the fact that there is currently no parole provision at the federal level for prison sentences, an inmate at a federal prison can still get the so called "good time" provision. This is whereby a well behaved federal inmate can subtract 54 days of each year off the sentence for good behavior.

truck and he found marijuana at the passenger side where she was seating. She and her friend were arrested.

She hired a private attorney and he got her two years probation in lieu of serving time for the marijuana charge. Jane 15 said that after that incident, she noticed that police officers would follow her at times. Sometime in September 2006, the police knocked on her door and when she opened the door they had a search warrant for her house and her building. They searched her house without finding anything, and then they took her to her building and she let them in to execute the warrant for the building. The police discovered the two methamphetamine laboratories she had inside the building. She was arrested and her bail was set at $30,000. She paid $3,000 bond and was released to await her court date.

Her private attorney suggested that she should plea bargain, since the police had all the evidence against her. Jane 15 agreed to plea, and her attorney was able to "secure" a plea deal of six at 30 which would be served concurrent with the rest of the time left on her violated probation. Jane 15 said that she was very happy with the representation she received from her private attorney. She said that she was surprised she only received a plea sentence of six at 30, especially considering the fact that she was a big time manufacturer and distributor of methamphetamine. As a contrast Jane 15 pointed out that a former client of hers[16] received a sentence of 10 years for sale of one half gram of methamphetamine.

Jane 15 thought that being in prison was an interesting and educational experience. She did not think that prison was depressing at all since there was so much to do. According to her, she had always been busy in prison, although in her opinion state prisons are much harder than federal prisons. She qualified this by saying that in federal prison there were much less restrictions like they have at Tennessee Prison for Women. She used to work in the kitchen of TPFW as a cook but during the research interview period she was participating in Therapeutic Community (TC).[17] She knew for a fact, that she did not want to come back to prison, ever again.

Jane 15 said she was officially retired from the drug business. She made enough money, which she thought would last her for a pretty long time. She elaborated by providing specifics of her past "drug business." Jane 15 said that it cost her about $67 to buy ingredients to make seven grams of methamphetamine. She said that she used to net (after all expenses) about $600 per batch of methamphetamine made. She used to make two batches a day, seven days a week. So she made quite a lot of money. The money was in "safekeeping." She

---

16. This client used to buy methamphetamine from Jane 15 and sometimes she would work for Jane 15 in manufacturing of meth in return for methamphetamine crystals. This former client of hers was also interviewed during the course of this research.

17. Therapeutic community is a program inside Tennessee prison for women that is based on counseling, the end goal being to help former offenders deal with issues that led them to prison. It is discussed in greater detail later on in the book.

said she never really thought about the individuals she sold methamphetamine to. "The people on methamphetamine are not right," said Jane 15. She did not have any qualms selling to them. "Nobody put a gun to their heads and told them to use methamphetamine," she said. But she did add that if she had children maybe she would never had gone the route of manufacturing and selling drugs. Jane 15 also made it clear that she never wanted to have children, as a matter of fact she had a hysterectomy in her late twenties to preclude her from ever having children, or having to go through her menstruation any more. Jane 15 did not respond to the question about having ever been diagnosed with a mental illness.

After serving her time in prison, Jane 15 said that she would go live in a cabin that she owns in the hills of Tennessee, and be there for her mother. Her nest egg would be sufficient for her. In addition, her husband (whom she never divorced) had a life insurance policy with her as the named beneficiary. Likewise her male friend had a life insurance policy whereby she was also the named beneficiary. She said she never officially ever used methamphetamine, though she was sure she inhaled a copious amount by default, simply because as a manufacturer she was exposed to the fumes. Thus she did not think that drug addiction would be a problem for her upon release. Up there in the cabin she would stay out of sight and would not manufacture anymore. That would keep her from re-offending.

Jane 16

Jane 16 was a 35-year-old only child initially from a two-parent Caucasian working class family. Her parents were married and her father was an alcoholic. Her mother used to be a stay at home mother, but had to go back to work making shoes for Genesco, since father was too much of an alcoholic to hold down a job. Her mother finally kicked her father out of the house, when Jane 16 was four years old, because her father would most usually come home drunk every night. Thus from the time she was age four, Jane 16 was raised in a single parent household, by her mother. Her mother worked long shifts and invariably Jane 16 had her grandparents (from both her father's and mother's side of the family) as her caregivers and babysitters.

While in high school, Jane 16 hung out with smokers and drinkers. Finally in 1990, she dropped out of high school at the age of seventeen. After dropping out of high school she, in her own words, went "wild." She partied hard with her friends and smoked weed. She also had an assortment of odd jobs, for instance she worked as a telemarketer, then worked as a disc jockey for a long time. She met her future husband while still working as a disc jockey. She was 20 years old and he was nineteen when they met. She stayed off weed and alcohol after meeting him. They got married in 1996, and her mother attended the wedding but her father did not bother to show up despite the fact that he was invited. After getting married, they decided she should be a housewife and she therefore resigned from her job. Her husband worked training Tennessee walking horses. A year after the wedding, they had a baby.

In February of 2001, when Jane 16 was 28 years old, she was diagnosed with non-Hodgkin's lymphoma.[18] She was started on treatment and was also prescribed several strong pain relievers, e.g. morphine, OxyContin, Loritab. Jane 16 said during that period she was always on some form of pain medication. While she was going through treatment for the non-Hodgkin's syndrome her mother died in 2003. About a year later, her husband died in a car accident. He was involved in a car accident on July 20, 2004 as he was leaving work. He died at the scene of the accident. Jane 16 was devastated since she was suddenly left husbandless, jobless, with a young boy to take care of and she had no marketable skills. Her family church helped out initially with food, but pretty soon, they stopped bringing food regularly to the house. Jane 16 and her young son were also receiving $600 a month death benefit, but that was not sufficient to cover her expenses, so sometime in December of 2004, she ended up getting a job as a waitress. She then also started selling prescription pills, in her own words "here and there" to make a little bit extra money.

She worked as a waitress and sold her prescription pills in her spare time without incident till March of 2006. According to Jane 16, her friend Alex had been in trouble with the law, so he turned informant in order to mitigate his judicial penalty. So one day in March of 2006, Alex came over to her house and asked for five pills of methadone. He said that he was in so much pain and that he needed just a few pills to help alleviate his pain. He asked for five pills and Jane 16 told him that she did not have much pills to spare but that since he was in so much pain she would give him three methadone pills. Alex asked her how much she wanted for the three pills of methadone and Jane 16 replied "Whatever you can give me, you are a friend and I am not trying to make money off of you, I just need a little bit of money to buy a birthday present for my son." So Alex gave her $30 for the three pills, and he left with the three pills. Soon after he left, Jane 16 took her son to Wal-Mart, to buy him the toy he had been asking her for his birthday, with the $30.

On their way home from Wal-Mart, as Jane 16 turned the corner into her street she noticed three police cars behind her. She pulled into her driveway and when she got out of her car they stopped her and said that she had to go with them to the police station. Her son was crying in the background. Jane 16 called her neighbor to keep her son for her and she went with the police officers to the station. Her bail was set at $20,000 her neighbor paid the bond which was $2,000. After a series of court appearances with her public defender, Jane 16 was sentenced, on August 11, 2007 to eight years at 30 for sale of Schedule II drugs. She spent two weeks in county jail prior to being transferred to Tennessee Prison for Women. She recollected going through withdrawal symptoms

18. This is a type of cancer of the lymphatic system. Radiation, chemotherapy and sometimes surgery is usually the treatment of choice.

while waiting at the county jail for a spot to open up at the prison. She had to quit cold turkey because there was no assistance whatsoever at the county jail to help inmates going though withdrawal symptoms. She said, she suffered through the chills, shivers, diarrhea and sweats associated with withdrawal without any attention from county jail officials. Jane 16 said, "I could have died there and none of the officials at the county jail would have cared." She had been at the Tennessee Prison for Women since August 28, 2007.

Jane 16 said that she believed her public defender did a fair job in defending her. She also indicated that her public defender suggested the plea bargain. Her public defender told her that eight at 30 was the best that she could get without a trial. Her options were either to plead out and accept eight at 30 or go through a court trial. There was the possibility that she would receive a longer sentence if she was found guilty at trial. So Jane 16 accepted the plea bargain.

Jane 16 stated that she had never been diagnosed with a mental illness. According to Jane 16, prison "is rehabilitative, though very horrible." It was rehabilitative in that she knew that she despised it and she would do everything in her power never to come back. She felt harassed, threatened, bullied, degraded everyday, and also felt like she was at the whim of the correction officials. They could search them anytime and after every outside visit they were strip-searched. It was a very humbling experience. She loathed it at the prison. Jane 16 said that it seemed to her that her past usual everyday morning habit of taking her pain pills with an early morning cup of coffee brought her to prison.

When she is released, Jane 16 said that she would steer clear of narcotic pain medications. She would focus on raising her young son. She would also have to get a job. That she hoped would keep her from re-offending.

Jane 17

Jane 17 was a 47-year-old Caucasian American that started life in a two parent household in Tennessee. Her parents were married but her father was an alcoholic, and very abusive, so her mother divorced her father when Jane 17 was four years old. Her mother then moved with her and her younger sister to Delaware. A few months later, her mother, brought Jane 17 back to Tennessee such that she could stay with her grandmother, on her father's side of the family. Her mother then took her younger sister back with her to Delaware. Her mother shortly thereafter remarried a reasonably well to do man and had two sons with her new husband. Jane 17's mother raised Jane's younger sister and brothers with her new husband, while working as a seamstress, and Jane was left in Tennessee to be raised by her grandparents.

Jane 17's grandparents were poor and old. Jane 17 said that she believed it must have been a serious readjustment for her old grandparents to be suddenly thrust with a rambunctious four-year-old child to raise. Jane indicated that it was very tough for her growing up with them. They were not very warm people and she was usually hungry, had ill fitting or no suitable clothes and the grandparents were very strict. They did not believe in sparing the rod. Jane 17 started using weed when she was 14 years old. She happened to find a roll of weed in her aunt's purse one day and decided to try it. Thereafter she would sneak weed from her aunt without her aunt's knowledge. She dropped out of high school at the age of 17, though she later earned her GED. After dropping out of high school, she started working in a restaurant. She started partying and drinking with older co-workers, but when she turned 19 she decided to move to Delaware to be with her mother. Her mother was by now divorced from her stepfather. She then wanted a relationship with Jane 17. She moved to Delaware in 1980 and started looking for a job. She saw an advertisement in the newspaper that read as follows "Good Money, Great Hours, and No Experience Required." So she applied for the job and when she went for the interview, she found out that the job was really a stripper job. But the amount of money the manager of the club told her she could make each week, overruled any misgivings she might have had about the job. She called her mother and her mother encouraged her to take the job, especially after she heard the possible amount that Jane 17 would be making every week. So Jane 17 took job.

While working as a stripper she was introduced by her co-strippers to cocaine, mushroom[19] and methamphetamine. At the strip club she had the opportunity to try and experiment with those drugs for the first time. She worked at the strip club for two years as a stripper and made lots of money. She made her mother the manager of her money. She said she would come home from work early in the morning tired and sleepy (after having worked all night at the strip club), with sometimes up to $1,000 cash and she would give it all to her mother to deposit in the bank for her. Her mother wrote her checks and balanced her accounts for her. When asked why she gave all her earnings to her mother, Jane 17 replied that she felt the money was guilt money and thus she did not want to have much to do with it. After about two years of stripping she segued into prostitution. Then she met a man and started dating him. She stopped working to spend more time with her lover, and her mother did not like that. Her mother kicked her out of the house when she stopped stripping. Jane 17 then married the man, so as to have a place to stay. Jane 17 and her new husband began using drugs heavily especially methamphetamine. They decided to move to Tennessee to try and get off methamphetamine. She got pregnant when they moved to Tennessee, and Jane said she stayed clean while pregnant with her son but started back using after the birth of her son. She eventually divorced that husband. Throughout the ensuing years she tried to stay off drugs, and worked odd jobs. She said it was difficult to stay off drugs because she was raising her then young son by herself and he was getting into a lot of trouble with the law. She

19. This refers to a particular kind of mushroom that is usually found in cow pastures after a rain, but they can be cultivated, and are available at illegal drug market. Mushrooms contain Psilocybin, which generally produces a hallucinogenic effect on the user.

utilized drugs to cope with the stress. He was sent to Taft Juvenile home, and a few months after he got out of the Juvenile home, he was charged with aggravated rape. He spent a year in jail awaiting trial. Jane 17 did not have the money to bail him out. In desperation she went to talk to a well-known criminal defense attorney in her town, Mr. X, about possibly taking her son's case. She ended up having an affair with Mr. X who was married. He agreed to defend her son and waived his attorney's fees. With the help of Mr. X, the aggravated rape charges pending against her son were later dropped. Her son was released from jail, and about five months later he was arrested for battery and assault charges. In despair Jane 17 resorted to smoking crack cocaine, and in order to sustain her habit she started selling crack too. She sold crack to a wired informant and was arrested for sale of Schedule II drugs. Mr. X. bailed her out. While she was out on bail, she was still engaged in selling crack cocaine, and she unknowingly sold crack to another informant. She then "forgot" to appear in court for her hearing. Her bond was revoked and she was rearrested in September 2006. At this point, she had indictments for a drug delivery charge, a failure to appear and the initial Schedule II drug sale charge. Mr. X did not offer nor attempt to bail her out this point. So she was in jail till November 2007, when her case was settled.

Mr. X advised her that she should accept a plea of 14 years at 35 for the three charges. She was not happy with the plea but Jane 17 said she grudgingly agreed because Mr. X told her that was the best that he could do. She was sent to Tennessee Prison for Women in December of 2007. While at Tennessee Prison for Women, Jane 17 had time to research and ruminate about her case. She wrote Mr. X several times but he never responded nor visited her. She decided that Mr. X did not quite handle her case well. Jane 17 indicated that she believed that Mr. X wanted her to be put away for a long time[20] and that was probably the reason he came up with such a lengthy prison time for a plea bargain. So she wrote him, and told him in no uncertain terms that she was going to go before the board of ethics, and let them know that she had an affair with him. According to Jane 17, it must have worked because her 14 years at 35 sentence had been amended to eight at 35, with six years probation after she gets out.

According to the respondent, prison had been very rehabilitative. She knew she did not want to continue within the drug culture anymore. Jane 17 said it was a personality "thing." "You stop when you are ready to stop." Cocaine in her own words, "Is mentally addictive, you dream about using it . . . it is all in the mind. Prison helps you get to that point, where you are ready to stop faster, if you are inclined to." She had seen people lose their homes, cars and fortune to drugs. "Crack is so addictive," she said. She also implied that there was an inherent addiction to the selling and moving of drugs. The whole danger and illegality tinged business was filled with adrenaline. She did not want to come

20. Jane 17 believed that by the time of her last court appearance, Mr. X was tired of the affair, thus he effectively did not want her around. Thus he offered her a long sentence as part of her plea bargain.

back again to prison though. She had had enough. She had a disability, due to mental illness.

When she is released from prison, she was going to work hard in order not to re-offend. She would move away from the city that she used to live in. She was going to go through vocational rehabilitation. She believed it would be possible for her to get into school because she was disabled. The key for her would be to stay busy. She had been in inmate counseling in prison.[21] She would like to get into recycling when she gets out and hopefully would find a way to make money legally from recycling products. She also hoped that being with her new boyfriend would help her stay off drugs.

Jane C

Jane C was a 44-year-old Caucasian woman from a working class family. In her earlier years, she was the only child of her single mother. When she turned four, her mother ended up marrying the man that Jane C would come to regard as her father. He brought with him to the marriage, seven children of his from his two prior marriages. Their respective mothers could not take care of them so they were in state custody, but upon getting married to Jane C's mother he brought all seven children to live with them. One of the seven children was mentally ill. Jane C's new father worked as a plumbing supervisor at University of Tennessee at Knoxville. Her mother worked at Levi's jean company during the day and as a waitress at Holiday Inn in the evenings. Her mother was very protective of Jane C, and took her everywhere she went. Jane C's mother gave birth to her baby brother when Jane was 13 years old. A few months later her "father" got involved in a motorcycle accident. He was hurt very badly. He clung to life for about a month at the hospital prior to finally dying. At the time of her father's death there was only one of his seven older children still living at home. Her mother enrolled Jane C in various different programs, such as swimming, gymnastics and piano, with the hope that the activities would help Jane cope with the devastating death of her step-father. Despite all those activities, Jane C was still having a hard time coping with the loss of her father. At about 14 years old, she started dating an older boy named Eric. She also started dabbling with drugs, using marijuana, and injecting quaaludes.[22] Her boyfriend introduced her to them. When she was 15, she ran away with Eric to Florida. He was 22 years old. Her mother managed to bring her back from Florida. Her mother put Jane C in juvenile home for 24 hours, after which she took Jane C back home. Jane lost contact with Eric. During that time, according to Jane C, there was a statute in

21. An inmate counsel is a liaison between inmates and the warden.

22. Quaaludes used to be utilized prior to 1984 in USA for the treatment of anxiety. It is a nervous system relaxant, used to help induce sleep. But it can also cause euphoria. As such it was abused for such purposes. Since the risk of abuse was so high, it was taken off the United States prescription market.

Knoxville, Tennessee that allowed students to be able to quit high school so long as they were 17 years old. Jane C took advantage of that law, and therefore dropped out of high school at the age of 17. She was still using marijuana and injecting quaaludes.

One day her father's brother approached her and asked her if she was interested in selling drugs for him for money. She jumped at the idea. She started selling illicit drugs for him and he introduced her to powdered cocaine. Jane would also transport cocaine, quaaludes, and marijuana, from Houston to Knoxville for her uncle. During that period, Jane started dating a male friend that she knew when she was in high school and eventually had a baby daughter for him. When she turned 18 and she married him. The marriage lasted only six months because he was very abusive. Jane delivered her second daughter after the divorce.[23] Shortly thereafter Jane met a 43-year-old man and married him. She had two sons with him, but he was also very abusive. He beat her up once so much that he broke her jaw. She had to have her face rewired. She had 26 surgeries on her face.

Jane C had been to jail about seven times for drug offenses. She had been charged in the past with prescription forgery. She would call in the prescriptions or fill out the prescriptions and she would always go to the pharmacy to pick them up herself. She had also been arrested three times for possession of marijuana. She was on probation for those counts. She started making and writing counterfeit checks. Whenever she was low on money for her drugs she would write fraudulent checks and cash them. Jane C said that she would dress up real nice and go to Wal-Mart or Food Lion. She would tell the available clerk at the store that she wanted to cash her paycheck. They would usually cash it for her. She made sure she always told them that they had to key in the numbers of the checks because the scanner would not recognize the numbers. She would habitually tell the cashier that her workplace had been having problems with scanners reading the checks. They always fell for it and they always cashed her checks. Sometimes she would cash three checks all at one store or place. She would ask the cashier if it was okay to cash her paycheck, her bonus check and her vacation check. They usually agreed to let her cash the three checks at once. Jane C said she had a cardinal rule and that was to never cash a check at a store more than once a month.

One day Jane C was with a friend of hers. The friend went with her when Jane cashed three fraudulent checks. They used the money to buy some cocaine. They went to Jane C's house and used the cocaine. Jane C then fell asleep. While she was asleep her friend took some of the blank checks that she saw in Jane's pocket book and went back to the store to try and cash another $495. She used Jane's ID card since her name was on the fraudulent check.

---

23. Her two daughters have had problems with drug addiction. Her oldest daughter Shannon had a drug overdose but survived and her younger daughter lost her house, because she spent all her money on drugs.

Jane was subsequently arrested for one count of forgery for that on the 31st of July 2007. That arrest violated her current probation. She went to court to answer to the forgery charge and was sentenced to intensive probation. Thus she was expected to check in with her probation officer regularly. One of the conditions of her intensive probation specified that she had to report to work everyday, but since Jane had an earlier suspended license she was not supposed to drive to work. She said that sometimes she would have a friend drive her to work, but it was not possible everyday. On those days when it was not possible, she would drive her car to meet with her probation officer prior to going to work. She always made sure to park a distance from the probation officer's office, because the probation officer would usually stand outside waiting to see if Jane C drove there or used public transportation. Jane said it was impossible for her to use public transportation because it would take "forever" for the bus to get her to the probation office and as such she would never make it to work on time. She said that on enhanced community corrections, she had to meet with her probation officer everyday; she also had to give them her land phone line. That way they could call whenever inclined during her curfew to make sure that she was at home. She had to fill out a questionnaire upon commencement of her probation that was to be used by the probation officer. Whenever the probation officer called her land line, the probation officer could choose any question randomly from the questionnaire Jane C had filled out, to ascertain that it was Jane C that was actually on the land line phone and not a substitute.

According to Jane C, enhanced community correction was too tough for her to be able to keep up. She had to work to pay the $290 monthly probation fee that was required. She also had to meet just about everyday with her probation officer. She also had to be on time for work, despite the fact that she had a suspended driver's license. So technically and legally she was not supposed to drive. The probation officer also made sure to stand outside every time Jane C showed up, so as to verify that Jane C was not driving to the appointment on her suspended license. Jane said it got too much for her. Thus on January 17, 2008 she went on the run. She just did not bother to show up for the meeting with her probation officer and neither did she show up at work. From January 17th through March 6th 2008, Jane C stayed in motels and cashed forged checks to pay for her expenses. Then on March 7' 2008 she moved in with her daughter Shannon and helped Shannon with taking care of her baby.

One morning late March 8 around 9:30 a.m. Jane C had her grandchild in a high chair and was feeding the child cereal. There was a knock on the door. Shannon went to the door, and asked, "Who is it?" Jane C said the police kicked the door in and arrested her. Someone must have called the police to report her said Jane C. She had a public defender and was sentenced to 10 years. Jane said her public defender was "OK", with regards to his legal defense of her. Jane had never had a mental illness diagnosis.

To Jane C, prison was home away from home. She worked in the recreation department of the prison and helped set up tournaments. She liked the job but she did not like the prison environment, because she would rather be at home. Nonetheless prison had been a sort of comfort zone for her, more so than a rehabilitative place, though she was clear to state that she would not like to ever come back again to TPFW upon her release.

When she has served her time and is released, she would continue to attend church services and hopefully get a job at Marriott. She used to work at Marriott when she was on enhanced probation. Jane C said she had not injected any drug now for about 20 years and she did not ever want to go back to injecting herself with drugs. As a matter of fact she said she did not want to sell or use drugs anymore. Jane C confided that at the peak of her drug use, she could smoke $1,000 worth of crack cocaine in a day. She stated that she was a compulsive person, thus when she was involved in something she tended to go overboard. She would overeat for instance or overindulge. Hopefully, by attending church and working, she would be able to resist going down the route of using and selling drugs.

Jane G

Jane G was a 52-year-old Caucasian woman that grew up in a dysfunctional family. Her mother was a bookkeeper who abused alcohol and pills. Her father was an alcoholic firefighter. Her parents were married, but they got divorced when Jane G was seven years old. Jane was the youngest of four children. She had a brother and two sisters. One of her sisters died as a result of cirrhosis of the liver[24] at the age of 44 years. She was an alcoholic and a drug addict prior to her death. Her only brother was living in a veterans assisted facility. He was a Vietnam era veteran. In his 20's he used to work as a tree trimmer, one afternoon while trimming a tree he fell off the tree. He was paralyzed from that accident and subsequently had to use a wheelchair. He was doing well, and getting around in the wheel chair. But that changed one afternoon when he was riding his motorized wheel chair and got hit by a car. He was only 35 years old at the time of the car accident. He almost died and was resuscitated. According to Jane G, since then his mental faculties had not been the same. He had been living in assisted living since then. He was 52 years old. Jane G's only surviving sister was a private financial planner and owned a large nursery.

She had a pretty good childhood. Her mother raised all of them with the help of her father. Her father was always present, although he was divorced from her mother. When Jane G was 16 years and in high school, her mother gave up custody of the children to her ex-husband. Her mother did that because she was too addicted to alcohol and drugs to take care of the children. Since Jane G moved to live with her father, she had to change schools in her senior year of

---

24. The most common risk factor for cirrhosis of the liver is chronic alcoholism. Other less common risk factors include hepatitis and genetic diseases.

high school. She was unhappy at the new school so she dropped out of school shortly thereafter at the age of 17 years. Jane G said that upon quitting school she immediately checked on taking a GED[25] test. She took the GED test soon after dropping out of high school, and passed. She then went to work for a music store in Knoxville. While in Knoxville she started drinking, smoking marijuana, and doing LSD[26] with her friends and co workers from the music store. Jane G said that she loved her job at the music store and likewise loved getting high. She said, "I did not do drugs because I had a problem, I had problems because I loved doing drugs." She got pregnant at the age of 19, and while pregnant her physician found out that she had cancer of the uterus. Her understanding was that the cancer was a direct result of her mother taking DES[27] when she was pregnant with her. Jane G told her mother about the cancer and what the doctor had said. The mother was very distraught about the news. She could not get over the fact that the medication she took during her pregnancy had resulted in her daughter getting cancer of the uterus years later. Her mother committed suicide. According to Jane G, her mother shot herself clean through the heart and died. Her mother was remarried at the time of her suicide.

At 19 years of age, with her mother dead, Jane G then decided to marry the father of her baby. They got married and 19 months later, they had another baby. She stopped working at the music store when she found out that she was pregnant with her second child. She said she wanted to have the two children prior to submitting to a hysterectomy, which was recommended for the treatment of her cancer. About three months after the birth of her second child, she found out that she was pregnant with a third child, but her doctor informed her that her cancer was growing. He recommended the termination of her pregnancy such that she could start medical treatment for the cancer. The pregnancy thus was terminated at six months, at the same time that she had the medically necessary hysterectomy. She had been fine till the medical abortion and hysterectomy. She took the termination of her pregnancy hard. Jane G said that she blamed her doctor for killing her unborn child. She stopped going to see the doctor for her medical checkup. She felt she could not trust anybody anymore especially the

---

25. GED stands for General Education Development or General Equivalency Diploma. This test is for individuals who for various reasons did not have the opportunity to graduate from high school. The GED diploma indicated that the individual has the required criteria for graduating from high school. More than 90 percent of, employers, colleges and universities will accept the diploma in lieu of a high school graduation certificate.

26. LSD has the scientific name of lysergic acid diethylamide. It is a man-made hallucinogenic drug that is abused for its hallucinogenic properties.

27. DES stands for Diethylstilbestrol, which is a synthetic estrogen that was prescribed for pregnant women during the 50's through the 70's. It was supposed to prevent complications of pregnancy such as diabetes, and high blood pressure, but it was chiefly used to prevent miscarriage in pregnant women. Studies have shown that children, especially daughters of women that took DES while pregnant have a higher than normal chance of developing a rare cancer of the uterus or vagina. Such children also have the propensity to be born with birth defects of the reproductive system.

doctor, whom she felt killed her baby. During that period of trauma within her life, her husband, Joe an auto-mechanic, got into trouble with the law. He broke into a drug store and was arrested. He was sentenced to serve time in prison. So Jane G got divorced. She let her two young children go to foster care, but as soon as they were sent to foster care, Joe's parents took custody of the two young children. When Joe got out of prison, he and Jane G remained amiable towards each other. He tried to be a part of his children's lives, despite the fact that the children were living with his parents. Over a period of time Jane G switched her drug of choice from LSD and marijuana to cocaine. She worked odd jobs while selling cocaine occasionally on the side.

Coincidentally it happened that her next door neighbor Alice was a drug dealer. Sometime in 2001, Alice moved out. About a month after she had vacated her house, Jane G saw three men in a pickup truck parked in front of Alice's vacated house. She observed them for about 20 minutes. They seemed to be waiting, so she finally decided to go and see what they wanted. Jane G walked up to them and asked them if they were looking for anyone. They said that they were looking for Alice. Jane G informed them that Alice no longer lived there, but that she could help them. They said they wanted cocaine. Jane G told them to come back a few hours later. They did. She gave them the cocaine and they paid her for it. They subsequently came back twice more and each time, Jane G got them cocaine in exchange for money.[28] She never saw them again, after the three instances whereby she acquired had drugs for them.

One day, in 2003, she went over to another neighbor's house to visit. According to Jane G while she was there visiting she had three shots of whiskey. They then decided to walk down to the nearest phone booth down the street to make a phone call. As they walked down the street Jane G said that they were stopped by two policemen in a police cruiser. They were arrested for public drunkenness because the police officers said that they could smell the alcohol on their breaths. When Jane G got to jail and was being processed, the police officer processing her informed her that she had three indictments for sale of cocaine.[29] She got a court appointed attorney, John D. She met with him while still in jail and the attorney informed her upfront that she would not receive a favorable judgment from the court because the District Attorney that was over her case hated John D's guts. That said, John D represented her with regards to her drug charges. Jane G said that she was not satisfied with the defense rendered by her public defender. According to Jane G, she asked her lawyer to show her the evidence against her. But her public defender only showed her a laboratory analysis report, and informed her that it was in her best interest to plea bargain, which Jane G did.

---

28. Unbeknownst to Jane G they were undercover agents of the Tennessee Bureau of Investigation.

29. The sale of cocaine indictments were for sale of one fourth an ounce of cocaine, worth about $300.

Despite the fact that she plea bargained, she still received sentences for three different counts of facilitated sale of cocaine. She received a sentence of seven years for each count, for a total of 21 years, but two of the sentences were to be served concurrently, while the last sentence was to be served consecutively.[30] Therefore Jane G was to serve a total of 14 years at 35. It was a multiple offender sentence. A multiple offender sentence was usually imposed on multiple offenders. In lieu of serving her sentence in prison, her lawyer negotiated for her to serve 14 years of probation. That was in 2003. She complied with the stipulations of her probation for a few months. One day she just decided she was not going to show up for her meeting with the probation officer. She went into hiding at the house of her then current boyfriend's sister. The boyfriend's sister Amy was also into drugs. She paid Amy money or drugs for the use of her house as a hideout. The arrangement worked till October 2006, when Jane G went out for a visit to a friend. She had some drinks at her friend's house. On her way back to Amy's house, she was stopped by police for erratic driving. The police officer walked to her car and asked for her driver's license and registration. Jane G said that as she handed her identification and registration over to the police officer she knew with a sinking feeling in the pit of her stomach that it was over, she was going to be arrested. Sure enough when the police officer went back to his car to check her license and registration, he found that she had a warrant out for her arrest, for violating her probation. When she went back to court the judge said she had to serve out her sentence in prison. So sometime in October or November of 2006 she was transferred to Tennessee prison for women to serve out the rest of her 14 year sentence. Since she had already served a year in jail, when she was transferred in to the prison in 2006 she had a net 13 years of the original 14 at 35 sentence left. She had been in prison for almost two years and she already served one year in jail, so she would be eligible for parole in March of 2009. Jane stated emphatically that she was not happy with the representation of her public defender. She said that she wished she could apply for a modified sentence. She wrote to her public defender for a copy of her sentence but thus far had not heard back from him.

According to Jane the prison experience had been enlightening, in that it "opened" her eyes in different ways. Some aspects of the prison experience she said were positively educational. She also indicated that incarceration had also helped her on a spiritual level; they had so many spiritual programs, and she found God in prison. She had no mental diagnosis. She was adjusting well to life on the inside but she was having problems with one of her vocational teachers. Jane G said that there were sexual implication and verbal abusiveness in her

---

30. When a person is serving two or more prison sentence concurrently, that means that each year served counts towards each of the concurrent sentences. But when the sentence is consecutively, that means that the convicted person finishes serving one sentence before starting to serve the second consecutive sentence. Therefore consecutive sentences are longer because each sentence has to be served to the fullest before the next sentence can begin to be served in prison.

dealings with him. She gave an example to buttress her statement. She was in the dining room a few months ago, and was having lunch when according to Jane G, he walked over to her and said to her, "What if I lay my dick on the table?" Jane told him to stop it, that should not be the way to talk to a woman. She added that she had been "ostracized" for the past few months, but on a bright note, he was not working the week of the research interviews.

Jane G clarified that she did not want to be in prison, but in her own words, she "will not dwell on the injustice of her long sentence." She had been taking pre-release, Therapeutic Community classes and she also started substance abuse classes in the fall of 2008 that would last for about five months. She was trying to do things with a different outlook than in the past.

When asked what she would do to ensure that she did not come back to prison after she was released, Jane replied that she would seek out a support system probably at church. She would also find employment. Jane G said that she knew that she's an addict. Accordingly, statistics dictate that there was the probability that she would relapse, but she was not looking forward to that. She hoped that knowing what she "knows now" and with the help of her support system she would not relapse. She was looking forward to "Celebrate Recovery." It was a Christian centered 12-step program. She would also not go back to her old neighborhood upon her release. She said that her best friend Judy wanted her to move in with her upon her release. Her best friend had never used drugs nor ever been in trouble with the law. Judy was a nursing assistant but had been off work for a few years, although she was going to go back to being a nursing assistant.

Jane G said that she was looking forward to being released and working on getting her life back together again.

Jane H

Jane H was a 22-year-old Caucasian woman that grew up in a two parent household. Her parents were married. Her father was a landscaper and her mother was a housewife. She had an older brother and a younger sister. Her older brother was in jail for stealing and her younger sister was a stay at home mother with three children. Jane started smoking marijuana, using Xanax and drinking moonshine at the age of nine. The Xanax was from her father's prescription medication for his anxiety disorder. The moonshine was his drink of choice. Her mother knew that Jane H smoked marijuana, but she could not stop her. Her mother even had her sent to juvenile hall for a while when she was nine years old. At the age of 13, Jane started abusing cocaine and methamphetamine. Her parents actually tried methamphetamine with Jane H. According to Jane H, she was abusing methamphetamine with her mother one day, when they ran out of the drugs, her mother wanted Jane H to bring out some more methamphetamine from her stash, but Jane H told her mother that she did not have any more left. Her mother thought Jane H was lying about not having any more methamphetamine and got mad at her. She screamed at her to move out of the house. In her fit of anger, her mother told Jane H that she did not want to see her again. Jane H was 13 years old, when her mother kicked her out of the house. She took her methamphetamine with her and left her parents house, with her 26-year-old boyfriend Rick. Rick was a methamphetamine dealer. He was also mentally, physically and emotionally abusive. Jane H was with him till she turned 18 years old. She tolerated years of abuse from him. Jane H said that she did not think she deserved better. She recounted incidences of abuse that occurred when she was dating Rick. For instance, Rick would have her put her head down in the car whenever they drove through town, because he did not want Jane H to look at any man. Rick would take her everywhere with him, including when he picked up women. He would have sex with these women in exchange for methamphetamine. Jane H had to remain in the same room while he was having sex with these women, simply because Rick could not stand for her to be out of his sight. He would have sex with these female methamphetamine (meth) customers without condoms. After sex, he would give them some meth for their "services," and drop them off. He would subsequently have sex with Jane H without condoms. Rick kept Jane H with him at all times. He would not let her out of his sight, even to change her sanitary pad or to have a bowel movement. He accompanied her even when she was undertaking the most private of her grooming. She had to shower with him. They lived a very transient lifestyle. In the summer months they would live in a tent in the woods of Tennessee, and in winter they would stay with different people.

Once when Jane H was 17 years old, she decided to run away while Rick was "occupied" cooking up some meth. She stealthily opened the door of the trailer home they were staying in and ran out. Rick ran after her and brought her back to the trailer. He put a short gun to her forehead and accused her of having sex with his best friend who was then serving time in prison. He told her that must be the reason she wanted to run away from him. Rick informed her, that if she ever tried running away again, he was going to shoot her.

Once, they had their truck and trailer hitch on Rick's grandmother's property. Rick kept berating Jane H for something that she had supposedly done. Jane H said she suddenly snapped and "beat the crap out of him." The grandma called the cops and Jane H was taken to jail. She was booked on domestic assault and criminal trespassing charges. The domestic assault charge was for beating up Rick. The criminal trespassing charge stemmed from the fact that Rick's grandma had informed the police that Jane H was not wanted on the property and was therefore trespassing.[31] Rick was arrested because the police found drugs on him. Jane H served 11 months and 29 days in jail. She was released when she was 19 years old. After release, she got addicted to injected

31. According to Jane H, Rick's grandmother was being mean because she knew all along that Jane H was on the property because she would come out to give spending money to Rick all the time.

morphine, and she would buy morphine to inject into her veins. One day she ran into Rick at the neighborhood corner. Jane H told Rick that she wanted nothing more to do with him. In her discussion with him, she also subsequently told him that she was a morphine addict and she was injecting. Jane H said she informed him of this fact to "turn him off." Rick did not believe her. He told her that if he saw her injecting morphine with his own eyes, he would leave her alone. So she took out her needle, syringe and her vial of morphine and proceeded to inject herself, right there on the corner in front of him. Rick dragged her into his car, and drove her to the nearest woods. They got into an argument because she did not want to go with him. While they were in the truck in the woods, he raised his leg and kicked her in the face with his boot, he then pulled out a knife. Jane H ran out of the truck, with her hand to her bleeding nose, and as she ran she would turn back to see if he was catching up on her. She was not paying attention to where she was running to and she ran smack dab, into a tree. Rick was so close on her heels that he collided into her and the knife he was holding in his hand cut her rear. She passed out. The next thing she felt was Rick punching her, all over her body. She was very bloody. Rick then dragged her to his truck, started the truck and drove out of the woods into the main road. For some reason unbeknownst to Jane H, Rick was pulled over by a police car. When the policeman saw the condition that she was in, he called for backup. Rick was arrested and Jane H was transported to DeKalb hospital. She was at the hospital for two days.

Upon release from the hospital, Jane H, went to the home of a friend. In the meantime she was trying to get into a shelter and was babysitting to make money. She would take her babysitting money during the weekends to go buy pills, and that was how she met Luke who was then 39 years old. He was the dealer she bought from. He sold pills. They started dating. Jane H subsequently started selling with him. She sold pills with him for a few weeks before getting caught.

Jane H recounted how she was arrested for selling pills. A childhood friend of hers came over to the house where she lived with Luke.[32] He wanted five pills of Dilaudid. Jane H, sold him five pills at $25 a pill for a total of $125. Jane H was not aware of the fact that there were indictments against her for the sale of the five pills. Coincidentally Jane H happened to get into a fight with one of the girls in the project. The police were called and when they showed up, they arrested Jane H on assault charges. She was in jail for 90 days for the assault charge. On the day Jane H was supposed to be released from jail after serving her time for her assault charges, she got dressed up and was waiting for the correction officer to open the jail cell but she was told that she could not be released because she had a sealed indictment against her.

32. Unknown to Jane H, the childhood friend had turned informant, because he was caught buying drugs, so in order that he not serve time he agreed to be police informant. He was wearing a minute camera when he bought the five pills of dialadid from Jane H.

Jane H met with her public defender while she was still in jail. Her court date was 89 days later. She was sentenced to 180 days in jail including the time she had already served while awaiting trial. She served about two and half months in jail and was released to intensive four year probation. Jane H said that for three months she was able to meet the requirements of her probation, but then she got back on drugs. She was always strung out so she never made it to any of her probationary appointments. She knew there was a warrant for her arrest for violating probation. She was on the run for about two months and during that time she met Rick's best friend, Don. Don was out from Jail[33] and he was then a hardwood floor installer. They started dating and he helped her "get her life back on track."

They were driving back one day from a fast food restaurant, when Don was pulled over for speeding. There were two police officers in the police cruiser. They walked over to Don's car. The police asked for her name and social security number. Jane H gave it to the police officer. The second police officer pulled her out of the car upon hearing her name and slammed her on the ground. She was handcuffed and taken to jail. She appeared in court to answer to her criminal drug charges and was sentenced to four years at 30. She was transferred to the Tennessee prison for women after five months at the county jail. Jane H was represented by a court appointed attorney. She said that she was satisfied with the legal representation of the court appointed attorney.

Prison had been a learning experience for her. She had been taking different classes since she got to prison. It was while she was in prison, sometime in June of 2008, that she was diagnosed as being bi-polar. She was on medications for her bi-polar disorder. Jane H believed that she had rehabilitated herself while in prison and to that extent she believed prison had been rehabilitative. She said that she had been taking Therapeutic Community classes. During the classes she had learnt about what other people go through in life. The classes had also taught her anger management, how to open up and how to express her feelings. According to Jane H, the majority of time at prison had been full of positive experiences, but she definitely did not want to come back to prison.

When asked what she would do to change her actions to help ensure that she would not reoffend, Jane H replied that she would try and stay out of trouble. She would continue to be "spiritual." She started going to Christian services when she got to prison. She was determined to take the GED again. She had taken it twice already. She was going to move in with Don when she was released. She really wanted to go back to school and be a nurse as well as a counselor for abused women. If she could get to these goals she believed she just might be able to make it without reoffending.

---

33. Jane H said that Don was in jail pending charges for wrongful concealment of information about a murder case. When it was found out that it was not so, he was released and since then he had been working legally installing hardwood floors.

Sally 1

Sally 1 was a 34-year-old white female. She was raised in a small house by her grandmother and mother. After she got divorced from her husband, Sally 1's mother moved in with her grandmother. The divorce had been hard for Sally 1 and her sister. Then when she was 15 years old her grandmother died. This left Sally 1, her sister and her mother living together in their deceased grandmother's house, but the bright side was that Sally 1 started to see more of her mother. Eventually her mother relinquished her duties as "mother" to go out on dates and left Sally 1 to raise her sister who was ten years younger. While her mother did not abuse drugs Sally 1 recalled that her father was always drunk and he also abused drugs. Partly due to the lack of a father figure she became close to her boyfriend and had two children with him prior to turning 18. She then broke off with her boyfriend and started a relationship with another man,[34] whom she married at the age of 18. She had two more children from that marital relationship. Her two children from that relationship were 12 and 14 years. After ten years of being married to her childhood sweetheart, she divorced, remarried then had another child who was six years old. Her husband worked at X-Ray Boats and she worked at Durand Inns before being incarcerated. She did manage to complete high school but did not continue on to college or trade school. Sally's younger sister was an assisted living nurse. On her grandfather's side of the family, all the "girls" have been in trouble with the law.

Sally was no stranger to trouble with law enforcement. She had several prior run-ins with the law, prior to being charged with misdemeanor petty theft. The petty theft charge was as a result of a wild night "messed up" on drugs and alcohol. She was with some friends and they were high on alcohol and drugs. In their drug induced bravado they stole some property from a house on her street and brought the property to her place. Unfortunately, for Sally 1, the day before the stolen goods were brought to her house she had tried writing a fraudulent check while at Target. When the police arrived at her place to follow up on the fraudulent check, they noticed some stereos and furniture piled up in her living room. Since they had received a report about some stolen property in the neighborhood, they were suspicious about the piled up furniture. The police held her responsible for the stolen property and the stolen checkbook. Sally 1 claimed to no avail, that her friends were the ones that stole the property and that she was in a stupor when she wrote the check at Target. According to her, since she was in a stupor at Target when she wrote the check, she was unsure of what was going on. Ultimately she was indicted for writing fraudulent check, receiving stolen property and for theft over $10,000.

Her first criminal drug offence was in 2004. The criminal drug offence was for two counts of prescription forgery. One count was for attempting to obtain prescription drugs with a forged prescription. The second count was for obtain-

---

34. He was her childhood sweetheart.

ing prescription drugs with a forged prescription. She was arrested and was in jail for 21 days prior to her court appearance. She received probation for the two counts of prescription forgery. According to Sally 1, prior to her drug arrest in 2004, she had been involved in a "two year pattern of forging prescriptions." Her conviction did not just occur based on one incident of prescription forgery, but was rather based on a "series of prescription forgery." The first time she was caught, she had gone into the pharmacy with the prescription "cut funny" which tipped off the pharmacist to notice that it was a forged copy. The pharmacist however took it and acted like the prescription was going to be filled, but unbeknownst to Sally 1, the police was called. When the police arrived she was questioned but was not arrested so she figured she could continue to make the prescriptions on her computer and have them filled at different pharmacies.

The second time she was caught for illegally trying to obtain prescription drugs, occurred when she was driving and was stopped by a police officer in a cruiser, for running a stop sign. The officer approached her and asked for her license and registration. She gave them to him. He then asked her if it was "ok" for him to search her car. She gave the officer consent to search her car. During search of her car, the police officer found two bags of pills in the vehicle and fraudulent prescriptions. The police officer took a report, gave her a citation, but she was not arrested at that particular time. Unbeknownst to her, an investigation was launched. During the investigation the police department in conjunction with office of the District Attorney looked over her record of petty crimes, the prior prescription forgeries and theft of over $10,000 (class C Felony) and decided to press charges. She was then tried for all three offenses; the burglary, and two counts of prescription fraud.

During her initial court appearances, she used a public defender but did not feel that she was represented well, stating that "people get less time for a homicide." Based on their assumption that Sally 1, was not getting a fair and equitable representation, her family decided to pay for consultation with a private attorney. They hoped that with the representation of a private attorney, she might be able to stave off being incarcerated. After the initial consultation with the private attorney, Sally 1 decided to keep the public defender. Regardless, she was sentenced to a total of five years (one year for each of the prescription counts and three years for the theft). Her public defender arranged this as a plea bargain which included a recovery program called CAPP (Community Alternative Prison Program). The first five months were spent in Knox County jail; the next 16 months were spent in community corrections; and the next three years were served as regular state probation. While on probation, she was diagnosed and treated for depression. Sally also attended and graduated from CAPP during her 16 months of community corrections.

Then during a routine meeting with her probation officer she was "violated" for failing a drug test. According to Sally 1, that was despite the fact that she was not on any illegal drugs at the time and was well aware that she was going to be screened every time she saw her probation officer. She was however taking a prescription nerve medication called Benzo,[35] but did not make her probation officer aware of her medical use of the nerve medication, when she tested positive for drugs. The probation officer submitted record of the violation to the probation commissioner. The probation commissioner had the authority to decide what sanctions if any to take, when there was a probation violation. Actions for violation can range from simply continuing the supervision to issuing a warrant for arrest of the violator. In order to try to keep her from going back to prison her family hired a private attorney. However, during court room proceedings, her probation officer told the court that Sally had failed the drug test, because she was on "all kinds of drugs." Sally 1 also said that, two days prior to the hearing a law was passed that prevented anyone who had violated probation from going back to community corrections. So she had to serve out the remainder of her sentence in prison. She hoped that her incarceration time would be flattened out with good behavior. At the time of the research interview, she had served 21 days in prison and had about 10 months left.

During the period of the research interview Sally 1 was being held in classification. New inmates are usually placed under classification, while TPFW officials decide where to place them.[36] The placement was based on a host of criteria. Her general impression of prison was that, it was like assisted living with free medical treatment; nurses; "big huge meals"; free dental; and free "you-name-it". She asked rhetorically, "What kind of punishment is that? The tax dollars are paying for all this too." She said that prison was alright but she did not understand what the objective was.

As for "in prison" rehabilitation programs, she did not think that they were working because the inmates kept coming back and she did not see any kind of rehabilitation. Sally felt that inmates should not be sent to prison for just 30 days because of the high cost. She said "too many tax dollars are being spent on the inmates here." In her view, ideally the system should give people every opportunity to be rehabilitated and help them before they come to prison. "Some women like it here so much that they commit offenses just to be able to return to their girlfriends or friends and it was easy to get into this prison."

She was still trying to get over the initial shock of being in prison so she did not know what to do or how long she was going to be there. She was also not sure, whether she would be spending all 10 months at TPFW or if she was still expected to eventually serve out the remainder of her three years of street probation or just have the years added as more prison time. Sally 1 did not appear to be cognizant of the terms of her incarceration.

As for her thoughts on jail and prison she said that prison was not much different from being in the county jail since they were on lock down most of the

35. Benzo is the colloquial name used to refer to benzodiazepines. Benzodiazepines are psychoactive drugs which can be used to treat anxiety and depression. They also have a tendency to be addictive.

36. The process of classification involves sorting inmates by possible likelihood of misconduct. During this process officials also ensure that the charges from court for the specific inmate are correctly recorded.

day. She would try to flatten her time while in prison so she would not ever have to come back. After receiving these charges she had not been in trouble since and did not plan to again.

Sally 2

Sally 2 was a 52-year-old African American female that initially grew up in a two parent household. She grew up with four brothers and four sisters. She was the eldest of the nine children and the only one of her siblings that was in "trouble" with the law. In her own words, she had a normal childhood. She had some diverse interests while in high school. She played clarinet in the high school band. She was also on the cheerleading squad in her senior year. While in high school she worked hard and was on the B-honor role. She earned a high school diploma. Her parents divorced prior to her final year of high school. She and her siblings ended up being raised in a Christian home by her paternal grandparents, so her mother could work. After graduating from high school she enrolled for a year in a business college. She dropped out of the business college prior to graduating and moved around a lot. At one time she left Tennessee and moved to Ohio. In May 1974 she decided to return to Tennessee when she found out that she was pregnant. She gave birth to her daughter, Alice in Tennessee. She needed to work, so as to be able to support her daughter, but it was difficult for her to maintain a job with a baby in tow. So she left her daughter Alice with her grandmother. In July of 1983 she had another daughter, but this time she made the decision to keep the child with her in lieu of having her stay with her grandmother. The decision did not last. When she got entrenched into the drug lifestyle, Sally 2 also left her second daughter with her grandmother.

Sally 2's first exposure to drugs and alcohol was in high school. While in high school, she started drinking alcohol (beer) and smoking marijuana with friends. She noted that she only "did" acid[37] two times in her whole life and never "did many pills". After a year of smoking she started to sell a little on her own. She sold marijuana for four or five years but only sold about one-pound of marijuana in aggregate.

Sally 2 had no juvenile record but she was arrested shortly after turning 18 years for assaulting a girl. A few weeks after the assault charge, she went in to a clothing store and shoplifted some clothes for which she was charged. When asked why she did that, Sally 2 responded that she felt that she did not have enough money to buy clothes. She subsequently stole a check. She received a

37. Acid: The street name for LSD Lysergic acid diethylamide which produces unusual psychological effects which include time distorting and the loss of the users identity. The US Army Biomedical Laboratory at one time administered LSD to subjects without consent and then perform a battery of test to investigate the effect of the drug on soldiers. It is a Schedule I drug in the US. LSD en.wikipedia.org/wiki/Lsd (accessed August 21, 2008).

charge of theft of a check but did not receive any jail time for that particular criminal infraction. Around this time she decided to stay in Tennessee. She got a job at Pizza Hut and ended up befriending a woman at work named Sarah. Sarah was from Washington, D.C. and introduced her to Preludin. Sally 2's introduction to Preludin,[38] commenced the start of her increased drug use. She initially started getting high on Preludin. Then she was approached by a woman who offered to buy some of her Preludin pills, and thus progressed to dealing. When she saw the potential to make some money selling Preludin, she went to her doctor and got a legal prescription for Preludin. She filled the prescription and sold all the pills for a healthy profit. She concluded that selling Preludin had a real potential for easy profit, so Sally 2 then decided to start forging Preludin prescriptions. She would forge prescriptions for Preludin and have the prescriptions filled at various pharmacies. She would then sell the pills on the street for profit. She carried on with this illegal enterprise for about 11 or 12 years without getting apprehended.

Then sometime in 1991 she started dating a man who asked her to go to Knoxville with his cousin to pick up cocaine for him. She did. Likewise on several subsequent occasions she would drive to Knoxville to pick up cocaine for him as well as his friends. The easy access to cocaine was too much temptation for Sally 2, thus she started using cocaine. She would ask for some cocaine after each Knoxville trip. Her boyfriend was very generous with cocaine, as reward for her trips. Initially she was able to constrain her cocaine use to weekends only since she worked at a factory on week days and needed to be alert when at work. Eventually she progressed to injecting coke. Almost a year after she started dating him, her boyfriend, John got a contracting job in Florida. She moved to Florida with him. During the move she brought two new needles that she was going to use to inject cocaine. She made a vow to herself that once the needles were used up, she would quit injecting and using powder cocaine. However, after the needles were worn out, Sally 2, went straight from injecting cocaine to smoking cocaine. She did not work the first year she was living in Florida with her boyfriend, John, but she ended up getting a job in a restaurant during her second year in Florida. She then progressed to smoking cocaine during the week as well as on the weekend. They had a supplier in Florida that sold them cocaine readily and at a low price. The whole time Sally 2 was in Florida she was working as well as using cocaine, but she claimed that her cocaine use did not interfere with her work. She stayed in Florida with John until 1993 and then they decided to move back to John's home town of Knoxville, Tennessee. They dated for 11 years.

John did not have a steady job in Knoxville and neither did Sally 2. Without steady work they turned to making money from crime. She began to sell drugs

---

38. Preludin: Phenmetrazine is a stimulant of the central nervous system sold under the name Preludin. The weaker analogue Bontril is rarely prescribed due to abuse. It is considered to have a greater potential for addiction than amphetamines. The US classes it a Schedule II drug. Source: en.wikipedia.org/wiki/Preludin (accessed August 21, 2008).

intermittently, steal, write bad checks; and engage in other criminally fraudulent behavior. During the decade from 1983–1993 she had vacillated from to using needles and smoking cocaine again. In 1997 she was arrested because she had sold rock cocaine to an undercover cop.

During court room proceedings for her charge on sale of rock cocaine, she had a public defender who convinced her to enter into a plea bargain. She plea bargained and was sentenced to eight years at 30%. She was incarcerated from 1998 through 2000. She was released on parole in 2000, but she violated parole after one year and was sent back to prison where she completed her sentence. She got time off her sentence, for good behavior and participation in prison programs/educational classes. She spent a total of 24 months in prison.

After prison she returned home. Shortly after her return from prison, her grandmother passed away in April of 2001. By that time her two daughters were old enough to be relatively self sufficient. Fortunately, her grandmother willed her house to her father and brother, so Sally 2 was able to move into the house and live there.

About a month-and-a-half after Sally 2 came back from prison, she started selling drugs. Sally's daughter Andi brought home a friend Carl, and he rented a room in the house. Carl was a drug dealer, but Andi, had informed him that her mother, had a problem with drugs and thus made him promise never to sell drugs to Sally 2. He promised. Since he would not sell drugs to her, Sally 2, would usually ask him to take her to Knoxville so she could buy drugs. After a while Carl, finally decided to start selling to Sally 2 since she was obviously getting the drugs from Knoxville. He figured it was not rational for her to go all the way to Knoxville to get the drugs, when she could buy them from him. Carl and Sally 2 eventually became close friends. Then in 2005 Carl was in a massive car wreck that left him paralyzed.

One day she went to a party and after the party, some of her friends stole some things from the party and hid them in her house. As a result the police searched her house and coincidentally found crack rocks (rock cocaine). Her public defender plea bargained with the judge and got her out on a misdemeanor charge with a sentence of probation.

Despite the fact, that she was on probation, Sally 2, still continued to use drugs and likewise sell them. According to her, sometime in 2005 the Drug Task Force set up a confidential informant who was paid $200 to watch her and ultimately purchase from her. The informant was someone she had partied with. Since she had a social relationship with the informant, she did not suspect that he could possibly be an informant. Over the subsequent few months he bought drugs, a total of three times from her. Based on this evidence she received two indictments for sale and delivery of Schedule II crack-cocaine. She was once again defended by a public defender, but this time Sally 2 said she was not satisfied with representation provided by the defense attorney. Initially, he informed her that she was not going to be able to get a sentence of less than 20 years at 30%, but then convinced her to plea bargain. She plea bargained and received a sentence of eight years at 30%. She was remanded to county jail, and stayed there from August of 2006 through October of 2007. From county jail, Sally 2 was directly transported to TPFW. She had been at TPFW since October of 2007. She would go before the parole board during the later part of summer of 2008.

Sally 2 attributed her life of crime, as being directly related to her interest in being with "bad people" and in particular drug dealers. She claimed that prison programs geared towards rehabilitation were not effective. She also claimed that, "prison takes away so many privileges and punishes inmates based on the actions of one person." There was more freedom at the prison Annex. Sally 2 said that inmates at the Prison Annex were treated more humanely but she could not be transferred there because of her rheumatoid arthritis. She had been diagnosed with diabetes and high blood pressure prior to coming to prison. She had been taking medication for her chronic conditions.

Being in prison was a learning experience for her although it was depressing to be there a second time partly because of her new found spirituality. Sally 2 recalled that when she was initially incarcerated at TPFW, she thought it was refreshing and rehabilitating, but once she was released she had a relapse due to the lack of a support system in her community. In order to find a better support system when she is released after serving her sentence, Sally 2 planned to go to a halfway house and join a church. Hopefully she would be able to work on contemporary gospel music by singing and writing songs. She would also love to go back to school to earn a computing certificate or diploma. She eventually would like to be able to set up a mail order greeting card sales business. She was really enthusiastic about the prospects of being involved with music and selling cards, specifically humorous cards. Sally 2 intended to focus on how to gain better control of what motivated her. She would especially like to work on controlling her "bad" motivations while channeling positive motivation. This would help keep her from reoffending. Sally 2 did not intend to continue with drug sales and use after serving her sentence. She stated that she was "off" drugs and only took a mild pill to help her get to sleep.

Sally 10

Sally 10 was a 25-year-old Caucasian who was raised in a two parent family till she turned eight. She grew up with three older sisters. Of her three older sisters the eldest was a homemaker with three children; the middle one had a professional out of state job and, the last of her sisters was a homemaker with three young children. She was the only one of her siblings that had gotten into trouble with the law. Her mother and father separated when she was eight years old. Upon separation, her parents decided the girls should live with the mother. So Sally 10 lived with her mother but her father saw her regularly. Her father was a "beer" alcoholic. When she was ten, he remarried. After the re-marriage he saw her less frequently. She graduated from high school despite the fact that she had gotten pregnant while in her senior year. Her steady high school boyfriend was the father of the baby. Upon graduation from high school she got a job and moved in with her high school boyfriend. She subsequently had two more daughters with him. They were five and two years old at the time of the interview.

Though she claimed never to have had any addictions to drugs or alcohol, Sally 10 admitted to using methamphetamine a few times in the past. She claimed that she wanted to become a confidential informant, so she started trying to figure out who sold drugs and what kind of drugs they were. During her subsequent investigations she became acquainted with a couple Dan and Daria. Dan told her he had been indicted on child pornography charges. Then at some point the couple called her and asked her if she knew someone that sold meth. They offered her twenty five dollars for the "hook up." The money seemed very appealing since she was on state benefits. They also offered to let her borrow their car so she could go get the meth. The offer was very tempting so she agreed. As planned, Dan arrived at her house in one vehicle with his wife Daria following in another. They dropped off one of the vehicles and the agreed upon amount. They later came back that day to pick up the drugs as planned. Two days later Dan, came back and made the same request, which she complied with, again. To her surprise after about nine months after the fact, two police officers showed up on September 24, 2007 while she was at a cousin's house. They served her with a warrant for her arrest and arrested her. She was taken to Wayne County jail for an hour and then sent to Giles County jail. While in jail, she was not questioned, nor read any rights, nor shown any documentation until she saw her public defender. She ended up firing her public defender because she thought he was not supportive. According to Sally 10, her public defender thought she was lying when she told him her story. She also did not appreciate the fact that he brought up an incident that had happened two weeks prior. She had gotten into a car wreck and was placed on probation for leaving the scene of a car accident and not paying fines or fees. After firing her public defender she hired a private attorney and paid him $1,500. He said he could get her credit for time served and kept putting off the court date. Five months later, the private attorney informed her that he did not think he could get her credit for time served. He advised her that based on the facts of her case, the District Attorney had offered a plea bargain of six years at 20%. It was either that or go to trial, he informed her. According to him that was the final offer from the DA since it was the fourth time he was negotiating a plea deal with them. She took the plea bargain on March 6, 2008 and was sent back to jail after the court hearing. She was transferred on March 31, 2007 to TPFW. She said while she was in jail she was denied a 72 hour furlough to spend time with her children.

During her stay in prison she received counseling. She was also diagnosed as not having depression anymore. She had previously been diagnosed with depression and was on medication prior to getting arrested. Sally 10 said she had not had the opportunity yet to join the prison programs, but she had no plans to come back to prison once she had served her time. This was the first and last time she would be in trouble with the law. She said, "Once I get out I'm not even going to go out and buy a pizza for anyone, I've learned my lesson." She said prison was a good experience but at the same time a very bad experience.

Sally 15

Sally 15 was a 30-year-old Caucasian female that was raised in a single parent home, for part of her childhood. Her biological father left when her mother was pregnant with her. Her mother already had a young baby by the time she gave birth to Sally 15. She was thus raised with her sister by her mother in a small town. Her mother was just 16 years old when she gave birth to Sally 15. Her mother never abused drugs or alcohol. When Sally 15 was nine years old her mother remarried a retired man from the military. Her new stepfather brought his two daughters into the marriage. He had two more daughters with Sally 15's mother. Thus growing up, Sally 15 had five other siblings, a sister, two step sisters and two half sisters. Apart from her immediate sister, none of her other siblings had ever been in trouble with the law. Her life as a child in the small town was stable; they ate dinner together and went to the church as a family.

Yet somehow, she hated that lifestyle and hated her parents. So she turned rebellious and started doing drugs when she was 13 years old. Her friends introduced her to marijuana, and she subsequently started smoking it with her friends daily. They also introduced her to cocaine and she became addicted to cocaine too. According to her, she would smoke marijuana daily, punctuated by consuming cocaine. She dropped out of school and thus did not graduate from high school. Three days after turning 18 years, she moved in with a cocaine drug dealer. About, one year later, she was arrested for simple possession of cocaine. She received an 11 months and 29 days suspended sentence and fines of $750. Afraid that it would come out in court that she had sold cocaine to a minor, she hired a private attorney and paid off the father of the child such that he would not attend courtroom proceedings. Sally 15 did not go into details about that particular case but suffice to say that her attorney was able to get the charges reduced to a simple possession. When she was 20 years old she had her first child and at the age of 22 she had twins. She smoked marijuana and occasionally used cocaine while pregnant with her children. Her drug habits changed shortly after the birth of her twins. She segued into using morphine. By the time she was 25 years old, she was abusing morphine even more than cocaine.

In 2002 an informant wearing a wire[39] purchased cocaine on 12 separate occasions from her and her drug dealer boyfriend. Based on the recorded evidence they were charged with 12 counts of possession of cocaine for resale. They weighed their options in trying to decide how to proceed with their defense.

39. A wire is the colloquial term for recording devise, which is utilized by informants to tape illicit drug transactions.

Sally 15 was afraid that if she indicated that she was an addict, there was a real possibility the state would take her children away from her so that was not an option for her. Ultimately she was tried separately from her boyfriend and both of them accepted pleas. Her boyfriend accepted responsibility for eight of the charges while, she accepted responsibility for four of the charges. That way he would not have to serve seven years and he would be able to care for their children sooner. They both hired private attorneys' and the end result was her boyfriend received probation for eight counts. The stipulation to his probation was that if he violated probation he had to serve 90% of the eight years suspended sentence. Sally 15 pled guilty to four charges and received three years at 30% , but the sentence was to be "suspended to probation."

During her first initial meeting with her probation officer she informed him that she was an addict and that she needed to go to the Methadone clinic for help. He simply refused to help her and told her to show up in two weeks to take the drug test. Without the methadone it was not possible for her to wean herself cold turkey from cocaine. Thus she continued to use cocaine prior to the meeting for her drug test. Sally 15 knew she was going to fail the drug test, so she never showed up for the meeting with her probation officer and subsequent drug test. Her probation officer immediately violated her. With the violation in the system she was wanted by the police and on October 18, 2006 she was picked up at an Arby's. The police had been called because she had a seizure while buying roast beef sandwich at Arby's. When they arrived they checked her ID and saw that she had a record and warrant for her arrest. They took her in. On November 6, 2006 she went to court. She informed the judge that she did not want to go back on probation; she just wanted to serve the rest of her sentence. Sally 15 said she told the judge that, because she knew her drug addiction was such that she would easily violate probation again. The DA however wanted to keep her on probation and add two more years to her sentence as well. Knowing that she was going to be violated easily if she went on probation again, she pressed the judge and the district attorney to let her serve out her sentence. She informed them that she was a cocaine and morphine addict and that there was no way she could be on probation for all that period of time without any violations. Please, she begged, "Just send me to prison." The judge wanted to know if she was willing to waive probation. She responded in the affirmative. She subsequently signed a paper to waive her probation and was transported back to county jail. On November 2, 2007, she was then sent directly to the prison for women.

Sally 15 said that her life had changed at TPFW. Since being at the prison, she had been clean for two years. She was also learned sign language through their "Hands of Grace" program. She felt she was not ready to leave yet. "I want to be able to bring something back to my children out of this experience." While she was in prison she took advantage of the programs. She believed that the programs at TPFW could be rehabilitative, "if one chooses to take advantage of them." She would like to utilize the prison programs to help her learn skills, that would help preclude her from reoffending and being incarcerated again. Once she has completed her sentence she hoped never to be incarcerated again. Though she felt rehabilitated enough to leave prison, she still felt it was important for her to serve out her sentence, such that she could "get more" out of her prison experience. She had not been diagnosed with any mental condition, but she was on medications for her seizures.

Her plan after leaving prison would be to go to a halfway house. She said a half way house would help her ease back into life. Finding a job would be of utmost importance for her, especially considering the fact that she had never worked at a real legal job. The only job she had ever had was selling drugs, except for the few jobs she had in prison. Education would also be an important new influence in her life. To that end, she had been laying the ground work by taking the GED. According to Sally 15, "right now I am going through a process and so I do not want to jump straight back into life and overwhelm myself and get high again." In her own words, "I know my location, and that location is bad right now; but I do know my direction, and my direction is good."

Sally 17

Sally 17 was a 34-year-old Caucasian female that grew up in a single parent family. She grew up with seven siblings, and she was the oldest of seven siblings. They were raised by her mother who was divorced from her father. Her siblings do not have arrest records except for one brother who was serving time in prison for murder. She was rebellious and liked going over to stay with her father. She said she preferred being with her father more than being with her mother. She ran away from home when she was 13 years old and stayed away for 15 months. She never went back to school after that and thus did not graduate from high school. About a year later, when she was about 15 years old she met a boy, Chris who was a year older. They started dating. She would usually stay for extended periods at his mother's house where he lived. When she was not at her boyfriend's house she would be found at her father's house. Her boyfriend eventually became abusive so she moved in permanently with her father. Chris would stop by, to implore her to move back in with him, but she would always resist. Eventually Chris, in a fit of anger and insecurity, drove to her father's house. He got out of his car and banged on the door of the father's house all the while yelling for Sally 17 to come out. She yelled out that she did not want anything more to do with him. While she was still inside yelling out at him, in an act of desperation Chris shot himself in the stomach on her father's front porch during their heated exchange. She screamed out to her father in horror when she saw blood pouring out of him, and rushed out of the house with her father to drive him to the hospital. He survived. Chris claimed he could not live without her. She decided to try and make the relationship work. About a year later she married him when she was only 17 years old. They separated when she was 23-years but she never got divorced from him so technically she was still legally married to him. When she was 24 she met another man and started dating him. He was a crack cocaine drug dealer. Prior to meeting him, Sally 17 said that she had never been exposed to crack cocaine. She had used marijuana (weed) and alcohol when she was a teenager. Her uncle used to let her have some of his drinks or try out his weed when she was in her teens. Thus she had developed a propensity for alcohol and weed during her youth, but she had never tried cocaine till she met the crack cocaine dealer. They moved in together. She gave birth at 27 years old. The baby turned out to be a stillborn child.

The tragedy of the stillbirth was a catalyst to the beginning of heavy drug use and one suicide attempt. A doctor diagnosed her with major manic-depressive disorder. Around then she had her first arrest, which was for selling cocaine and forgery. She paid the bond, and thus was released from jail. She appeared in court with her public defender and ended up being sentenced to 10 years. She was sent to TPFW but she paroled out. Part of the conditions of her parole included community corrections, which she said was to be completed at the end of 2006. Shortly before the completion of her community corrections, Sally 17 received a new charge for drugs and forgery. She also got a 10 year sentence for this, to be served consecutively with her prior sentence. Instead of serving time her attorney managed to get her on probation. But her probation was conditional upon her completing 30 days inpatient rehabilitation. She completed the rehabilitation program at the rehabilitation center. She was then sent to a half way house. While at the half way house Sally 17 violated the terms of her probation by leaving the halfway house. She was rearrested and sentenced to serve out the remainder of her sentence, including the remainder of the earlier 10 year sentence. She claimed that she had already served six calendar years at TPFW.

Prior to being sent to TPFW, Sally 17 thought her public defender, did a good job of defending her. In retrospect she was ignorant of the law. Based on what she had learned in prison, she had revised her opinion of her public defender. She felt that her sentence was severe considering she was serving 20 years for some "crazy charges'. She said she got caught with a couple of grams of cocaine and for forgery. For those charges, she was serving 20 years at 35%. She did not feel her charges were comparable to the 20 years that most people at TPFW were serving for murder. She felt that the outcome of her case would have been totally different and much better if she had been represented by a private attorney. According to her, she would not have been serving 20 years for those charges. She claimed that her incarceration was directly related to the fact that she violated parole for a misdemeanor and auto theft charge. In total she had three drug convictions and more than 30 convictions for forgery since they counted each check separately.

When she got to TPFW, she participated in therapeutic community. After completion of therapeutic community program she began to realize that most people's addictions "come at an early age." Her addiction, she said, came from men. Because her father left her at an early age her subsequent relationships consisted of being in unstable situations where she would go from one man to another. Overall Sally 17 felt that she was treated fairly by the criminal justice system, apart from her long sentence.

She felt that her incarceration at TPFW had been positive. She felt that prison was much better than county jail which did not rehabilitate as well as in prison. At the time of interview, Sally 17 said that she needed surgery on her shoulder. Thus she could not work in prison, till her shoulder had been operated on. She claimed the first time she went to prison she was rehabilitated and did not use drugs when she got out. If she had not been incarcerated the first time for her drug charges, Sally 17 said, she would have been dead already. Her hope was that the courts or criminal justice system would come up with a structured place for drug offenders to go to instead of taking them first to prison or jail. That in her opinion would make a world of difference for drug offenders. Before leaving prison she hoped that she would be able to earn her GED and subsequently obtain a license to be a drug and alcohol abuse counselor.

Sally 19

Sally 19 was a 52-year-old Caucasian female who was raised mainly by her grandparents. Her parents were never married; however her mother got married about three to four months after Sally 19 was born. Her mother had three more children after getting married. It happened that her mother only knew her stepfather for all of three weeks prior to getting married to him. They were married for 44 years. She never knew who her real father was. She did not live permanently with her mother. Growing up, her living arrangement was such that she alternated between her maternal grandparents' house and her mother's house. Of her three siblings, one was her half sister who was a 51-year-old lab technologist supervisor; another half-sister was a 46-year-old who had Turner's syndrome[40] and lived alone in an apartment; and, she had a 50-year-old brother who was a truck driver. None of her half siblings had ever been in trouble with the law. Sally 19 graduated from high school and she noted that she earned a Bachelor of Science degree in business. Prior to her charge and subsequent incarceration, she had an Internet transcription business, whereby she would transcribe notes for doctors. After high school she attended a cosmetology school and earned a cosmetology license. She then went back to school to earn her Bachelor of Science degree.

One day while at an army recruiting office, she ran into a young handsome man and ended up marrying him. She was 26 years old at the time of her marriage. Prior to that marriage, she had been married before. Her first marriage was

40. Turner syndrome (TS) is a chromosomal condition that describes girls and women with common features that are caused by complete or partial absence of the second sex chromosome. Taken from the Turner's Syndrome website http://www.turnersyndrome.org/index.php?option=com_content&task=view&id=40&Itemid=63 (accessed September 8, 2008).

when she was 19. She had one child from that marriage but divorced four months after the birth of the child. The second marriage lasted for 25 years. It ended when her husband died of a heart condition and left her as a widow. She had two biological born children with him and an adopted one. So she had a total of four children. The oldest daughter, Wanda, was 32 years old and was in jail for check fraud and theft. Her adopted son Stephen was 27 years old and was an electrician and a sergeant in the army. Her daughter Suzie was 24 and was also serving time at TPFW for forgery, theft, and obtainment by fraud. Her youngest daughter Carla was 23 years old and a stay at home mother. Sally 19 was married. Her present day husband was a superintendent at a construction company.

Her first arrest was the sole reason she was incarcerated at TPFW. Sally 19 said it was her first and only felony charge. The tale of how she became involved with illicit drugs, started when her daughter Suzie's husband stole ten Xanaxes[41] from her. When the theft occurred, Susie and her husband Kirk were living in Sally 19's house. Kirk was then pulled over for a traffic violation. Somehow he allowed the police officer to search his car and the police officer discovered the drugs. The police informed Susie that if she "busted" someone for selling drugs they would let her husband go. So Susie put on a wire and went back to her mother's house. She walked into the house and saw her mother in the kitchen. Susie casually asked her mother if she could have a Percocet.[42]

Sally 19 had been using Percocet since the age of 19, when she was diagnosed with breast cancer and had to have both breasts removed. After her double mastectomy, she had silicone implanted, but the silicone implants burst and leaked into her body. She said as a result of that she ended up getting lupus when she was 36 years old. So it was normal for her to have Percocet in her medicine cabinet.

So when Susie asked her if she could have a Percocet for pain, Sally 19 told her daughter she could have one pill. Susie took not just a Percocet but three Xanax pills as well. She then left and a little while later she returned and said "here mother, here is $65." Sally 19 said she did not want the money but her daughter kept arguing with her so she told her to just lay the money on the counter, which her daughter did. When Susie left the house the police came in and arrested her. It turned out that her daughter had captured the "transaction" on wire. The police took her immediately to jail. She spent the night and the following day in jail before being bonded out for $400.

---

41. XANAX® is in a class of drugs called benzodiazepines. Approved by the FDA in 1981, controlled clinical trials have demonstrated that XANAX is effective in the treatment of Generalized Anxiety Disorder, anxiety associated with depression, and Panic Disorder with or without agoraphobia. Pfizer Xanax web site http://www.xanax.com/content.asp?id=4&sid=1 (accessed September 7, 2008).

42. Percocet is prescription medication that is utilized to manage pain. It is comprised of a combination of opioid oxycodone and analgesic acetaminophen. So it has a propensity to be abused.

She was given a public defender and charged with one count of sale of Schedule II (Percocet) and three counts of sale of Schedule IV (for the Xanax). She was not satisfied with her public defender because, according to Sally 19, he did not do anything to help her out of the charges. She said that first of all she was not and had never been addicted to drugs and; secondly, her medication was legitimate. Regardless her public defender convinced her to take a plea bargain. So she took the plea bargain. She received four years at 30% to be served as community corrections. Two years into her community corrections she had a heart attack. Because of the heart attack, the judge took her off of community corrections. She was then placed on state probation by a different judge and after a year her probation officer was changed. A month after she received her new probation officer she was violated for failure to report. Sally 19 had informed her new probation officer that she was in the process of moving and thus would not be able to make it to her probation meeting. The month following her move, she was admitted to the hospital for pneumonia, thus she could not appear for her meeting with the probation officer. While at the hospital, Sally 19 urged her doctor to let her probation officer know that she was at the hospital. Her doctor faxed her probation officer a notice. Nonetheless the probation officer violated her and a warrant was issued for her arrest. She was arrested for violating the terms of her probation. She met with the same public defender prior to going to court. She implored the public defender to "do something." He told her that she would be out in three months anyway. Instead she was sent to county jail in July 2007, and was then transferred to TPFW in December of 2007. She completed 30% of her sentence, in February of 2008 but she had to stay and finish a 25-week program called "Serenity" which deals with substance abuse. She had just completed the program a week prior to the research interview. At the time of the research interview she was waiting for her certificate of completion. Upon receipt of her certificate of completion she would be released on parole. Sally 19 said that while on parole she would not be credited for the year she had spent on state probation, she would only get credit for the time she had spent on community corrections. She spent a year and seven months on community corrections. She was credited for the year she spent in prison. She was neither impressed nor satisfied with the representation of her public defender.

She felt that the incarceration time spent at TPFW had been rehabilitative. One thing she did learn in prison was how to "wash a check'. Washing a check, she explained, meant putting a written check in a bath of alcohol. The alcohol would remove the original written ink on the check, thus leaving it blank. Anybody could then write in any amount on the now blank check. She had been diagnosed as bi-polar and generalized anxiety disorder. She took medication for bi-polar disorder and for the generalized anxiety disorder. She was also taking various other medications for her diabetes, heart trouble, lupus and rheumatoid arthritis. She said she also had growth masses on her left and right lung.

Her plans after leaving prison would include looking after her grandchildren and re-starting her internet business. She had operated the business for six years prior to incarceration. For personal time, she planned on traveling with her grandchildren with the money she won from a class action lawsuit against the company that made the defective silicone implants. The settlement came in April of 2008.

Sally 27

Sally 27 was a 27-year-old black female who was partially raised by her mother and step-father in a subdivision in Lebanon, Tennessee. She was raised from the time she was very young till she turned 12 years old by her mother and stepfather. She said she lived a good life as a child and was well provided for. Her mother was a flight attendant and her stepfather worked at a glass plant where he was still working. Between her mother and her step-father Sally 27 grew up with 14 siblings. Out of her fourteen siblings, two of her brothers were incarcerated at the federal penitentiary for non-violent drug charges.

She got pregnant at 15 and dropped out of high school to be home schooled. She had her baby while still being home schooled and she graduated from the home school program despite the birth of her baby. Her family supported Sally 27 and her baby. She had a total of four children; a 12-year-old son, a 10-year-old daughter, an eight-year-old daughter, and a three-year-old son. She also worked part time at her uncle's auto detail shop.

Her mother died during the birth of Sally 27's younger sister. She was still in her teens, when her mother died. Her parents got a divorce just a few months prior to her mother's death. Sally 27 moved in with her brothers after her mother's death. Her sisters went to live with her aunt in an apartment. She said that if she had chosen to live with her aunt, like her sisters did, she would probably not be incarcerated at TPFW.

Her brothers exposed her to drugs. One brother was the "weed man." He bought and sold marijuana. Another brother bought and sold crack cocaine. Her brothers asked her one-day if she wanted to become a chemist. She responded "yes." So they showed her how to bag and weigh marijuana. Likewise they taught her how to cook dope. She had smoked marijuana and popped ecstasy pills prior to that but she had never abused crack cocaine. Her brothers showed her how to do everything in their drug business and that was how she began making money. She also had a job at a Hardee's fast food restaurant but since she was making much more money selling drugs than working at Hardees, she resigned. After she resigned from Hardees her only source of income was derived from sale of illicit drugs. She met the father of her second child, through her brothers. He was also a drug dealer.

When she was 18 years old she moved out of the house she had lived in with her brothers. She moved into the projects with her boyfriend in order for them to have their own "spot" where they could sell drugs. They stayed in the projects all summer of her 18th birthday, making money from drug sales. Her oldest son was spending the summer with his father. When her son got back from visiting his father, she moved with her boyfriend to a nice apartment complex right next to a subdivision. They both started selling drugs from the apartment. About a year and some months later when she was twenty, she got into a fist fight with a friend in a store. The police were called and she was arrested. She was charged with battery and assault charge. She hired a private attorney. The private attorney was able to reduce the charge to simple assault. Sally 27 got one-year probation for the simple assault charge, which was considered a misdemeanor. Throughout her one year probation, she was still selling drugs and she managed to pass all of her drug tests. She successfully completed her probation.

When she was 21 she was arrested for her first drug charge. She was outside her apartment in the parking lot "chasing cars" with her boyfriend. She would approach cars and ask the occupants what they wanted. She sold to an undercover cop that day. One month later the police came to her aunt's house to look for her since it was the address she listed when she was arrested for the simple assault misdemeanor charge. Her aunt notified her that the police were looking for her. Thus she turned herself in, with the expectation that she would be bailed out immediately. She was bailed out quickly enough by her boyfriend. She was charged with selling half gram of rock cocaine. She hired the same private attorney that she had originally used. She said he was an excellent lawyer. In her opinion he was the best lawyer to have for a "dope" case.[43] She received four years at 30%.

A year later while she was still on probation she got arrested on another drug charge. She was in a van with some people when they were pulled over for having bad license tags. The officer asked them if it was okay for him to search the car. They consented to the search of the car. The police officer also searched them, but the officer did not find anything so he let them all go. Later on that night, one of her customers called her for an eight ball[44] of powder cocaine ($150 worth). Sally 27 told the client to come to her house to get the eight ball, since she did not feel like driving. Her client eventually convinced her to drive over to her house to deliver the drugs. She drove up to her client's house. On her way to the house, to make the delivery, she passed by a police officer that was parked at the T-junction road to her client's house. On her way back the officer pulled her over for expired tags and informed her, that she was driving through a heavy drug trafficking area. He asked, her if she was hiding anything. She responded no. So he said, "In that case you don't mind my searching your car." Sally 27 responded, "Go ahead." During the research interview, Sally 27 said that she gave her consent because she had managed to work the cocaine into her underwear. He did not find anything in the car and so he asked if he could search her. She let him search her because she was so sure that she had gotten all

43. A dope case, is the slang or street term for a drug charge case.

44. Eight Ball: A quantity of cocaine or methamphetamine that weighs an eight of a ounce. Urbandictionary http://www.urbandictionary.com/define.php?term=eight%20ball (accessed August 28, 2008).

of the drugs into her underwear. He found a "leg and a half" (i.e. $50 worth) of powder that she had forgotten was in one of her pockets. She was placed under arrest and put into the police car. During the drive to the police station she managed to work the remaining drugs into her vagina (a quarter gram of cocaine). Once she got to the county jail she was booked, searched, and placed into a holding cell. Once she was in the cell she managed to work the drugs farther into her vagina. At this point she was so panicked, that she was not focused at all on her discomfort. She knew that it was a felony to bring drugs into jail and she did not want to be caught. She called her brother and told him to bail her out as soon as possible but she could not let him know about her situation. She then waited a few more hours until her brother and boyfriend obtained her release by paying a bond.

Once home she went to the bathroom and squatted and tried pushing the drugs out and ended up physically removing it with her fingers. Because of that incident her probation was violated and she received four more years to be served concurrently with her previous charge. She was sentenced to a work camp for a year in Lafayette, Tennessee and then on to TPFW. She paroled out soon after. She said she had earned two years credit for the year she served at the work camp for good behavior. Parole was granted in August of 2007. She got a job at Media Mail. At that point she was no longer selling drugs to supplement her income. She already had a house, car, and furniture. During this period, she was also regularly seeing her probation officer every Friday, but one Friday her work did not permit her to leave because it was during their busiest season. She couldn't just leave because if she lost her job she would violate the terms of her probation, but at the same time if she failed to report she would violate her probation as well. She was in a quandary. She decided to miss that one meeting with her probation officer. So she did not report in. She was violated for failure to appear and also for moving into a different house without permission. She had moved in with her sister that lived in the same town. She paid off her court fines. She had decided to turn herself in, but prior to doing that, she made arraignments for her children to be taken care of. She figured once she turned herself in, she would just go back to county jail. Instead she was sent to prison November 17, 2007. She would be eligible for probation in November of 2008.

Her plan after finishing her sentence was to get into a halfway house[45] so that she could have some kind of structure in her life. She said she would go crazy if she were just on probation with "no papers." After six months in a halfway house she would go to Nashville to stay with her sister. She had the intent to subsequently attend Remington College to earn a nine month nursing certifi-

45. Halfway House: a residential center where drug users or convicted felons are placed immediately after release from a primary institution such as a prison…to allow the persons to begin the process reintegration with society. Wikipedia http://en.wikiperdia.org/wiki/halfway_house (accessed August 28, 2008).

cate. Sally 27 said that her sister was a registered nurse and was doing well, so she would like to do well too, in a job that was legal.

She felt she had been more rehabilitated by listening to other inmates' stories. She commented that she felt that she did not belong in prison. She had never been on the main compound except for the 30 days in Classification. She was taken straight to the Annex. She said prison had helped to rehabilitate her, as well as showed her that there was a better way to make it in life. She did not plan on ever coming back. In order to be placed in the Annex on a long-term sentence, an inmate had to be five years from their red date. She had never been diagnosed with a mental condition and neither was she on any medications. Sally 27 stated that she was not stressed or depressed because she knew her children were being taken care of. She said it was important for her to make goals and to project to where she would like to see herself in five years time. This projection was necessary in order to prevent her from relapsing.

Sally 28

Sally 28 was a thirty seven-year-old African American female with a grade ten education. She had dropped out of high school when she was in grade ten. She grew up with a twin sister. She and her twin sister were raised by their grandparents, because her mother was a single mother and could not take care of both of them. When she turned sixteen she moved in with her mother. Sally 28 lived with her mother till she got married. She was still married despite the fact that she was incarcerated. But she was legally separated from her husband. She had four children. Her oldest child was a 19-year-old daughter, who lived with her boyfriend; her 18-year-old son lived with his aunt in Kentucky; her 17-year-old son lived with his cousin; and, her 16-year-old son lived with a legal guardian. During her life she had worked in many different factory jobs simply because she needed to have a job while on probation or parole.

Her initial exposure to drugs occurred when she started dating at the age of 17 years. Her boyfriend was a cocaine dealer. Soon after they started dating he introduced her to selling drugs. She began selling drugs with him. When she was 18 years old unknowingly she sold to an undercover police officer. She was arrested and indicted on sale of Schedule II drugs. That was her first drug based arrest. She was provided a public defender. She appeared to indicate that his representation was adequate enough. She received eight years at 30% with six months jail term imposed. She served only four months of her six month jail sentence, because she was on good behavior. So she got released early for good behavior. The same day she got out of jail she was served with an indictment for another drug charge. She went to court to respond to the charges. She also had a public defender as her defense attorney. She ended up getting a five-year sentence that was to be served consecutively with her prior sentence. She was on house arrest at the time. Thus her house arrest was to be extended for the duration of her second sentence. She was under house arrest for about 2½ years until she violated it with another cocaine charge. She sold cocaine again to an informant. She had had a total of eight charges of sale of cocaine and one criminal facilitation charge just for being around cocaine. She had served time in prison previously as well for drug-related crimes, but she flattened out on all her prior prison sentences (which meant she served and completed her sentences).

Sally 28 claimed that she had only "done" powder cocaine but never crack. She started doing powder cocaine when she was 34 years old, prior to that she had only sold it and she only started using it because as she stated "I did it because of a guy I was with." She said she was addicted to selling cocaine but not to using it.

Her current incarceration was due to the fact that she sold cocaine to an informant in a school zone sometime in mid December of 2005. At that time she had just been released from prison. She had been incarcerated for violation of parole on another drug charge. She had been out of prison for only a few months when she was arrested for selling drugs in a school zone. The state provided a public defender for this charge. The public defender worked on negotiating a plea bargain with the District Attorney. The first plea deal she was offered was for 31 years. The second plea deal was for 31 years as well so she asked for another public defender. When she was assigned a new public defender, he was able to negotiate an initial plea deal for eight years. Sally 28 asked him to see if he could negotiate a better deal. Her public defender came back with a second plea deal for six years. She accepted the plea deal for a six year sentence, because she knew she was a multiple offender. Also the public defender had informed her that he did not think that he would be able to get any sentence lower than that, especially considering the fact that she was a multiple offender. She pled guilty to the negotiated plea. She was sentenced on June 9, 2006. After the court appearance for the plea, she was transported back to jail.

She was in county jail from May to early September of 2006 and in September of 2006 she was sent to TPFW. She spent time in Unit 3, since she was then in classification. On December 14th upon completion of her classification she was sent to the Annex. She worked at THP (Tennessee Highway Patrol) every day. She felt that since being incarcerated, she had had the opportunity to be rehabilitated. She was a multiple offender so she was doing six years at 35%. She said that upon her release if she gets indicted for one more offense, the criminal justice system of Tennessee would classify her as a habitual offender. That meant that she would have to serve out the full time of any new subsequent sentence. She claimed that this sobering fact was her motivation not to go back to selling, once she was released. She did not want to be re-incarcerated again, once she was out.

When asked what plans she had to prevent her from re-offending, Sally 28 responded that; "As long as I stay away from town, I know that I would be okay. If I ever go back to my hometown, I know for sure that I would relapse and go back to doing what I used to do." She said that she felt she had been rehabilitated this time. "This time is just it." She also noted that it was not the prison programs that helped with her rehabilitation, instead it was the fact that for her it gets worse every time she was re-incarcerated. According to Sally 28, "It just isn't worth coming back here anymore."

Interestingly, Sally 28 stated that she was satisfied with all of her public defenders because she was guilty of all of her charges and she did not have to pay them for their services. Her plans after leaving prison included entering a halfway house program in Knoxville. She would be at the half way house for up to six months if need be. She said she had chosen Knoxville because she did not know anyone in Knoxville. It was important and necessary for her to go to a place where she knew she would not find anyone from her past. She would not stay at her family members' houses because they all have had drug offenses on their records. She noted that the GED classes in prison "are not worth it" because they only had the classes once a month. She preferred that the classes were scheduled everyday. According to her the classes would be more effective that way. She would also get a job once she left prison, because it was one of the requirements for being on parole. She was not going to move back home neither did she plan on going back home, soon after release. She would only return home occasionally to visit her children. She was trying to secure an apartment in Jackson, Tennessee near her sister who was the only one with out a criminal record. Hopefully her sister would help her secure the apartment after she had completed the halfway program. Sally 28 was diagnosed in prison with high blood pressure and depression. She had been taking medication for both the depression and her high blood pressure.

While in prison she had taken "Better Decision" and "Substance Abuse" classes. She had graduated from both programs. Both programs had been helpful to her. She said that the classes on "Better Decision" especially helped her more because it focused on a "one on one" approach. That in her view was more effective than group sessions. She was scheduled to appear before a parole board on October of 2008, but she said that she would like to serve out her sentence in prison. That way when she leaves prison, she would have her sentence "all flattened without any papers."[46] So she said that it did not matter to her if her parole was granted in October of 2008 or put off. She was indifferent either way.

Sally 29

Sally 29 was a 22-year-old white female. She was raised with her four siblings in a two parent family. She was the oldest of five children. She had two brothers

46. In prison, the term "without any papers" connotes completely serving out the sentence, such that upon release the inmate would not have to worry about paper condition of release, like is necessary when the person is released on parole. Usually "with papers" means that the inmate is released on parole. Release on parole is conditional release and the inmate has to fulfill all the conditions of parole otherwise they could be "violated" and rearrested.

and two sisters. She said her early years were normal enough but that changed after she turned seven years old. Her parents got divorced when she was seven years old. After the divorce, the children were split up between the two parents on a rotating basis. She lived with her mother for about two years and then she moved in with her father. Her mother worked at the Bridgestone factory and her father was a truck driver.

When she was 15 years old Sally 29 was introduced to methamphetamine, by her friends. She had older friends, who used drugs and she liked to "hang out" with them. She started using methamphetamine when they were hanging out, and pretty soon, she started using it even when she was not with her friends. At 16 years old she got a job working in a grocery store. She also worked on the family farm. She had always worked with plants.

When Sally 29 turned 17 she started selling methamphetamine. She also began to stay over at her friends' houses regularly, despite the fact that she still resided with her father. She ended up dropping out of high school, though she later earned her GED. Sally 29 also helped manufacture meth a few times; however, she mainly sold it. She claimed that she had used meth every day from the time she was 15 years old to when she was 19 years old. When she was 19 years old she applied for a job at Waverly Health Care. She ended up getting the job and she worked there for seven to eight months.

Her first arrest occurred when she was 18 years old. She had one and a half grams of meth that she was going to deliver to a customer, in order to complete a sale. On her way she picked up a man who was a friend of her friends and gave him a ride. Unfortunately for her, she was stopped by two police officers. Apparently they had received an anonymous phone call tip that someone was going to steal anhydrous ammonia[47] from a plant. Coincidentally, she happened to be driving down the road that passed the anhydrous ammonia facility. The police told her about the "called in" tip but that was the only information they gave her. When she was stopped, she was high on meth and was not carrying a valid driver's license. The police asked to search the vehicle. She gave consent because she did not think she had anything in the car, except for the passenger and some aluminum foil that she had hastily stuffed under the driver's side seat. The police told her and her passenger to step out of the car such that they could search her car. After the search they asked her to empty out her pockets. She turned out her pockets, and the police officers found a "tutor" amongst the content of her pockets. A "tutor" is an empty pen that had been cut off from both ends. Drug users use this empty tube to smoke meth with. Since she had drug paraphernalia with her, she was placed under arrest. Prior to being placed inside the police car, she was also asked if she had anything else on her. She paused for

47. Anhydrous ammonia is used as a low cost, highly effective nitrogen based fertilizer. However, drug dealers have discovered that it can also be used to manufacture the illegal drug, methamphetamine, and have targeted tanks for this material. Ohio State University Fact Sheet "preventing Theft of Anhydrous Ammonia" Stephanie Simstad http://phioonline.osu.edu/aex-fact/0594-1.html (accessed August 26, 2008).

a second, because she was trying to decide in her mind the best response to the question. She knew that she had the one and a half grams of meth, but she was afraid that she might get another felony charge if its existence was declared, so she responded that she did not have anything else on her. She was taken to jail. Her car was impounded and she later found out that the guy riding with her was a fugitive from Texas.

When Sally 29 got to jail she made a call to her father, to let him know that she had been arrested and was in jail. She informed him that she needed him to bond her out. She was in county jail for two days. She was then released when her father paid the $50,000 bond secured against his property. A public defender was assigned to her case. He showed up for the first time, during her initial court appearance. She was charged with possession of a Schedule II drug. However, her public defender did not show up on the day of the actual court proceeding in General Sessions court. Despite the fact that her attorney was not present in court, she decided to continue on with the proceedings without her public defender. She said she made that decision because she just wanted to get the whole process over with. The judge and the DA gave her two options; (1) She could do 11 months and 29 days in a county jail or (2) she could bond over to circuit court. She chose circuit court because she did not want to go back to the county jail. In circuit court she hired a private attorney to represent her on the felony charge. Her lawyer got it dropped from a Class B Felony[48] to a Class C misdemeanor,[49] which included the paraphernalia (tutor and aluminum foil) as well as driving without a license. She accepted the plea bargain because she was informed by her attorney, that it would be a waste of time if her case was taken to trial. She received three years at 30%.

She was sentenced to state probation three months later in lieu of serving time in prison. She violated probation by failing a drug test after a New Year's party. She said it was a surprise drug test and it was the first drug test ever administered during a probation visit. She tested positive for meth. After she violated probation, her probation officer informed her that she had a warrant out for her arrest. Therefore, she turned herself in to the county jail on January 2006. She was 19 years old at the time. She was at the county jail for 69 days. Afterwards, she was sent to rehab in Davidson County drug court. She was in the program for 14 months. Sally 29 then asked to be transferred to the Dixon County drug program. She remained in that program for three or four months. Upon completion of the program she was placed on house arrest. She broke the conditions of her house arrest by visiting a friend. She was rearrested and sent to Dixon county jail for four months. From there she was transferred to the Hum-

48. A Class B felony in Tennessee is punishable between eight and thirty years incarceration. In addition you could be fined up to one hundred thousand dollars ($100,000) Tenn. Code Ann. 39-17-417 (c)(1)(2007) Truth in Sentencing http://www.attorneygeneral.org/truth.html (accessed May 2, 2009).

49. A Class C misdemeanor in Tennessee is punishable by not greater than (30) days in jail or a fine not to exceed fifty dollars ($50.00), unless otherwise provided by statute. Truth in Sentencing http://www.attorneygeneral.org/truth.html (accessed May 2, 2009).

phrey's County jail where her charge originated from. She spent four more months there. On December 4, 2007 she was sent to prison. Her sentence had just expired at the time of the research interviews and her release date happened to be scheduled the following Monday, a few days after she was interviewed for the research.

Sally 29 said that the programs at TPFW were rehabilitative enough, but Judge Norman's[50] program with the Davidson county drug court had the best positive impact on her rehabilitation. She learned how to stay clean as well as how to manage the situations that might lead her back to drug abuse. She never abused drugs while at the county jail. She clearly stated that the rehabilitation programs at TPFW had helped her, but what had the most influence on her was the fact that she was locked up and away from her family. She had never been diagnosed with any mental condition, and neither was she on any medication.

Upon completion of her sentence, Sally 29 said that she planned to have her felony expunged so she could get into a decent college. She never provided the details regarding how and why her felony charges would be possibly expunged. She took and passed her GED while incarcerated. She also had a valid driver's license. She had made the choice to serve out her complete sentence in prison without parole such that her sentence would be completely finished upon release. She had every intentions of not re-offending. Once she leaves prison, she planned on getting a job. But the first thing she was going to do as soon as she walked out of the gates of prison would be to go swimming in the family creek with her sister.

Sally 30

Sally 30 was a high school graduate who grew up in a single parent family. Her parents got divorced when she was only three years old. Her father had custody of her for the first 12 years after the divorce. He was in the air force, so they moved around a lot. He soon remarried after the divorce and had three more girls. Sally 30 began to act out shortly after her father remarried and had more children. Her father then threatened to put her into a girl's home if she did not behave, so when she was 13 years old she moved in with her mother. She was the only child living with her mother. Out of all the five children of her father, she was the only one with a criminal record.

Sally 30 had two children while she was in high school. She had her first child when she was still a sophomore in high school. After the birth of her first baby, she got a job at McDonalds. While she was still working at MacDonald's,

---

50. Judge Norman presides over the Davidson County Drug Court Program, which is committed to providing quality therapeutic community to promote positive change in criminal addictive behaviors for the purpose of reintegrating adult offenders into society. Davidson County Drug Court http://drugcourt.nashville.gov/portal/page/portal/drugCourt/purpose/ (accessed February 3, 2009).

she got pregnant with her second child. She lost her MacDonald's job just one month prior to the birth of her second child. She lived with her two children in her mother's house. When she was 19 years old, she moved out of her mother's house and into a low-income housing apartment. She was also able to apply and be approved for Aid to Families with Dependent Children (AFDC).[51] As such her subsidized rent was only $30 a month plus electricity payment. When she moved out of her mother's house, she decided to leave her oldest son with her mother, but she took her youngest son with her to her new subsidized apartment. Her boyfriend also moved in with her.

She was charged with theft of property, shortly after moving out of her mother's house. Sally 30 recalled not having any money, so she went to her oldest son's grandmother's house and took some jewelry. She pawned the jewelry at a pawn shop. About a month later someone recognized the jewelry and she was charged with theft. She was sentenced to month in jail and probation. That same summer her boyfriend introduced her to marijuana and her boyfriend's best friend introduced her to ecstasy and painkillers. She began to abuse ecstasy and the painkillers, but she completed her probation without incidence. She later on ended the relationship with her boyfriend and she moved in with a new guy that she met on her block. She opened a checking account with her income tax refund. With this new account she wrote a series of insufficient fund checks. She was arrested and charged with check fraud. She served four months in jail for check fraud and the rest of her sentence was on probation. Prior to completion of her probation, she was caught shoplifting, but the charges were later dropped, nonetheless she had to spend another four months in jail for violating her pending probation on the check fraud charge.

Shortly after serving her jail sentence, she left her boyfriend for another man. This new boyfriend was a cocaine dealer. He taught her how to sell cocaine, but did not teach her how to make crack cocaine. One Super Bowl Sunday, she rented a hotel room with her new boyfriend, and they took an eight ball of cocaine to the hotel room. While in the room, Sally 30 discovered that she had forgotten to bring her cell phone battery charger with her. Her cell phone was on low charge. She made the decision to drive back to the apartment to get the battery charger, but on the way back to her apartment, she was stopped by the police for not using her turn signal in an area known for high concentration of heavy drug users. One of the police officers from the police cruiser walked up to her car during the stop and asked for her license and registration. She gave both to him. He checked them out and handed them back to her. As he handed her back the papers he asked if she would mind his searching her car. She responded, "No go ahead." He told her to step out of the car. As she stepped out of the car, he asked for permission to search her as well. She gave him the permis-

51. AFDC: Aid to Families with Dependent Children is a grant program that enables states to provide cash welfare payments for needy children who had been deprived of parental support. AFDC http://aspe.hhs.gov/HSP/abbrev/afdc-tanf.htm (accessed August 24, 2008).

sion. The other police officer walked up and both officers `proceeded to search her and subsequently search her car. The officers did not find anything but they kept coming up with excuses to detain her. Finally according to Sally 30, they told her, she had two options, (a) they would follow her to her apartment or (b) they would follow her to her hotel room to conduct a search. Somehow during this whole sequence of events, she had managed to let them know that she was coming from a hotel room that she had just rented. Sally 30 acknowledged in hindsight, that she should not have agreed to let them go with her back to her hotel room. But then she had figured that there was no real problem with letting them go with her to the hotel room, in lieu of having them search her apartment. She had felt she did not have a choice in the matter. It was either take them to her apartment or to the hotel room, and she had felt that taking them to the hotel room posed less of a risk for her, than taking them to her apartment. After all, she had called her boyfriend on the cell phone to warn him that the police were following her back to the hotel room. So she was under the assumption that her boyfriend would have been smart enough to leave, especially considering the fact that he had a pending warrant out for his arrest for violation of probation.

Thus, she informed the police officers that she would take them back to her hotel room, so that they could conduct a search of the room. They followed her back to the hotel room. When they got there, her boyfriend was still in the room. The police found the eight ball of cocaine and Sally 30 and her boyfriend were both arrested. She was taken to jail. She had a public defender assigned to her. In retrospect, she said the public defender fought hard for her. In court, she was only sentenced to four months in jail and eight years of probation.

After serving time in jail she moved in with her best friend and continued visiting her boyfriend in jail. Her mother and boyfriend were both pressuring her for money. She was in dire need of money. She knew one of her friends, Eve was a prostitute. It had seemed to her that Eve always made a lot of money from prostitution. So Sally 30 decided to become a prostitute. She would "work" the streets with Eve. She did this for a year, before her boyfriend got out from jail. She would give the money she made from prostitution to her mother and to her jailed boyfriend. During that period, Eve also introduced her to cocaine, marijuana, ecstasy, and powder cocaine. When her boyfriend got out of jail he became very abusive and controlling. Sally 30 had thought that she would stop being a prostitute after her boyfriend got out from jail, since he would then be able to help financially. But he loved the fact that she was making good money from prostitution, and thus would not let her quit the trade. He made her consistently give him the money she earned from prostitution. Sally 30 claimed that he was the only man she was ever afraid of.

Eventually, she became pregnant. So she stopped drinking and doing all of the other drugs except for marijuana. She also stopped prostituting and her boyfriend eventually got a job. She was on probation all the while. Then one time she failed to report to her probation officer. Her probation officer subsequently violated her, and a warrant was issued for her arrest. Sally 30 went on the "run."[52] She was on the run while pregnant. Three months after giving birth she was finally caught and arrested. She was taken to jail but she was bonded out. She had left her former boyfriend when she went on the run. While she was on the "run" she had met a new boyfriend. He bonded her out from jail.

Her new boyfriend had a job, but shortly after bonding her out, he lost his job. Since money was very tight Sally 30 resorted to selling cocaine again. She was mainly the "middle man" but inadvertently sold three times to a confidential informant. Around the third time she sold to the informant she was also getting over a toothache and was given a prescription for Hydrocodone and Penicillin. The temptation of the prescription was too much for her, so she had a friend alter it, such that refills were included in the original legal prescription from the doctor. She was caught and arrested while trying to fill the prescription at the pharmacy. She bonded out. She was assigned a new and different public defender. She went to trial. In February 2005, she appeared before the court on charges of obtainment by fraud and three counts of sale of a Schedule II drug. Sally 30 said that her new public defender was nicknamed "11/29 Stevens," because people said that a person was guaranteed to get time with Stevens as their public defender. Her public defender advised her, that it was better for her to plea bargain, especially considering the fact that all of the charges against her, were obtained within a four-year period. That fact, would possibly have earned her more prison time if she were to choose trial. So she decided to accept the plea bargain. She was sentenced to 10 years for the three counts of sale of a Schedule II drug, and eight years for fraud. The sentences were to be served concurrently.

According to Sally 30, her time in prison had been rehabilitative. She participated in Therapeutic Community and "Transitions Programs." Through the "Transitions Programs" she learnt job skills which would hopefully provide her with opportunity to obtain an outside job, once she had completed her sentence and was released. The two aforementioned programs were also instrumental in helping her deal with some of the issues that she had prior to being incarcerated. She noted that she was rehabilitated from drugs and had no further desire to go back to using drugs. In Therapeutic Community and Transition Programs, she also learned how to confront some of the situations in her past that had led to her drug use. She was diagnosed with manic depression when she was incarcerated at the county jail. Since being incarcerated at TPFW, she had been diagnosed with general anxiety disorder and depression. She was taking Zoloft.

Her plans after leaving prison involved continuing with the mental health drugs and treatment/therapy programs. She also planned on going back to school in a few years to become a paralegal, which had always been a point of interest. With this new focus she envisioned working and spending time with her children. She felt that being with her children would help keep her motivated and

---

52. On the "run" is a colloquial term utilized to describe the concept when a person has a pending arrest warrant and does not want to turn him/herself in, but instead moves or changes location to evade arrest.

focused on staying clean. Her overall prison experience had thus far, been positive. Sally 30 indicated that she would say that prison had helped her deal with unresolved issues and in the process thereby resolved them (especially her self-esteem issues).

Sally 31

Sally 31 was a 25-year-old African American female. She was raised by her single mother, in conjunction with her grandmother, and great grandparents. She was an only child of her mother. She had half siblings on her father's side of the family, but she had never met any of her half siblings. Her mother worked at the National Pen and Pencil factory. Her mother was not married to her father. Her father owned his own business. His business involved auto detailing and audio installation. Sally 31 dropped out of high school when she was in eleventh grade, but later on obtained her GED in 2005 while in prison.

Sally 31 was 13 years old when she was introduced to marijuana, by an older friend. From then on, she smoked marijuana on and off, but according to her, she never "formed" an addiction to marijuana. She got a job at Sonic when she was 15 years old. She dropped out of high school shortly after getting the Sonic job. She ended up working at Sonic for three years. When she turned 17 years, she moved out of her mother's home and moved in with her aunt.

Her first arrest occurred when she was 16 years old. She was at a party in Tullahoma and was hanging out with the wrong crowd. At that party she picked up a pipe to use later to smoke marijuana. After the party as she was driving home, she was pulled over by the police. When the policeman walked over to her car incident to the stop, to ask for her license, Sally 31 did not have it. She tried to explain to the police officer that her license was taken away when she dropped out of high school. The police man asked her to step out of the car and he ended up searching her car. He found the marijuana pipe Sally 31 had picked up from the party. She told the police officer that the pipe was not hers, but he arrested her. She appeared in court, with a public defender. The charges were dropped after she passed a drug test and proved that the pipe was not hers. Two weeks after that arrest she got her drivers license back.

A few months later she met Eric, the man whom eventually became the father of her baby. She met him when she was 17 years old. Eric was a drug dealer. He sold cocaine, crack, weed[53] and pills. They dated for a while and then she got pregnant. She had her baby daughter when she was about 18 years old. At the time of the interview her baby daughter was almost seven years old.

One night, about a year and half after they had started dating, she was with Eric at her home, and they got into an argument. They were yelling at each other, suddenly Eric hit her. When she screamed at him to stop, he seemed to

53. Weed: vernacular for Marijuana

lose control and he really started pummeling her. He beat her so much that the police were called and she had to be admitted to the hospital. While the police were at the house finishing up their report, they noticed a $20 crack rock on the table. Eric informed the police that the "crack rock" was for Sally 31. He told the police that she had sold drugs to him. Eric called her while she was still at the hospital receiving treatment for his physical abuse, to inform her that she should accept that she sold the rock to him. She agreed, to take the blame for him. She was charged with sale of Schedule II drug. According to Sally 31, he was selling drugs out of her house without her knowledge. She got a private lawyer to defend her on the charge. She went to court with the attorney to answer the charge. Her attorney worked out a plea bargain and the charge was dropped down to a misdemeanor. She, however, felt that her lawyer did not believe her when she told him, that she did not know that Eric was selling drugs out of her home. Her lawyer told her that any Tom, Dick, and Harry can go on the stand and say that they never sold drugs, but that would not necessarily be the truth. Sally 31 reiterated that her lawyer was "no good" and made little effort to help or defend her. She was sentenced to 49 hours in jail and 11 month and 29 days probation. Twenty-five days prior to her probation being over, she "caught"[54] another charge. She was arrested and spent 48 hours in jail in February. In March, of the same year, she lost her apartment because of the charge. Thus she decided to move in with a friend named Twanda. Twanda was also a drug dealer. She sold cocaine. Upon moving in with her, Sally 31, also started selling cocaine, though she claimed that she made sure they never sold drugs around her daughter. She sold on and off for a year while concurrently working sporadically at Magic Pen (which was a factory that makes markers).

At some point, she unknowingly sold cocaine three times to a wired informant. She was arrested when she went to sell a 4th time. The police followed her and pulled her over for a burnt out taillight. When the police officer walked over to her car, incident to the stop, he asked her if it was alright for him to search her car, (at this time she had indictments already, though she did not know it). She informed the police officer that the car was not hers. Nonetheless the police searched her car. The police officer found cocaine in her car and her car was impounded.

She was subsequently arrested, and indicted on charges of three counts of sale of Schedule II and one possession of Schedule II drug for resale. She hired a private attorney whom according to Sally 31, only asked her stupid questions. She said that the day prior to court date she listened to the informant tapes provided by her attorney. She figured out who the informant was but her lawyer did not want to listen to her. Her attorney was supposed to work out a reasonable plea with the District Attorney, but instead her first plea bargain was 10 years at 30%, when she turned that down, her attorney came back with another plea bargain. This plea bargain was worse than the initial plea; it was for 24 years at

54. "Caught a charge" is a colloquial term used by respondent inmates to indicate that they were arrested for a criminal offence.

30%. She turned it down. Her attorney came back with a third plea bargain deal, which was 18–20yrs at 30%. At this point her attorney informed her, that if she took it to trial the judge would end up giving her 35 years in prison. Her lawyer never told the D.A. she knew who the informant on the tapes was. Sally 31 somehow imagined that if the District Attorney had known that she knew the informant, that bit of information might have garnered her a better plea bargain. She also told her lawyer that the informant kept in contact with her after the drug sales were completed but the lawyer would not "listen to her." Sally 31 still believed that her attorney should have brought up the fact that the informant kept in contact with her after completion of the drug sales. She even insisted during the research interview that the information would have made a difference with regards to the plea offer she received from the District Attorney. According to Sally 31, when she went to court for the indictments, the judge did not read her post conviction rights and she was put on the stand instead of her lawyer. Her post conviction was denied because of the statute of limitations, which was expired. She had filed too late, despite the fact that she had an attorney.

She was transferred straight to prison after sentencing. Her lawyer informed her that the District Attorney wanted to see her go to prison. Thus the District Attorney was not interested in including community corrections as part of her plea bargain. She got to TPFW on April 25, 2005, which was her birthday. She stayed on the main compound for two years and on April 25, 2007 she was transferred to the Annex. She went before the parole board in August 13, 2007. The parole board denied her parole and she would try again two years, from August 2007.

Sally 31 articulated that the reason she sold drugs was because she did not have her GED. Thus, it was difficult for her to get a good job. Since her incarceration, her young daughter had been living with her grandmother. She said her attorney did not do a good job at all with regards to her defense. In her opinion, her attorney "screwed her," especially considering that he couldn't handle post conviction cases. In her own words, "He did not bother to tell me, when I hired him, that he did not do post conviction cases."

She did not like being incarcerated. At TPFW she felt that she did not have autonomy over her life. She did not like having prison officers tell her what to do. She had had negative experiences with inmates at the prison. She had met women with child murder charges or murder charges. She was upset at the duration of her sentence for drug charges. According to Sally 31, she was serving a longer prison sentence for her drug charges than another woman inmate, who had stabbed her husband 17 times, killing him in the process. That in her opinion was a miscarriage of justice.

Sally 31 inferred that prison programs only help those people that want to be helped. She did not necessarily think that prison was rehabilitative. She had never been diagnosed with any mental health illness. She was diagnosed with high blood pressure in prison. She was not taking any other medications, apart from medication for her high blood pressure. She said that in prison, a lot of women "fake stuff" so as to get prescription medications.

Her plans after serving her sentence would include attending a two-year radiology program at Nashville General Hospital. If that did not "pan out", she would hopefully register for an eight month course to become certified in Phlebotomy[55] at the Tennessee Technical Center in Shelbyville. Sally 31 said that she was determined and hopeful that she would improve her education, upon release. With education she could have a legitimate improved lifestyle. That would hopefully prevent her from becoming a recidivism statistic.

55. Phlebotomy: the letting of blood for transfusion, diagnosis or experiment. Merriam-Webster Dictionary http://www.merriam-webster.com/dictionary/phlebotomy (accessed August 24, 2008).

Chapter 4

Voice from the Inside: Escape from Abuse and Tragedy

The series of interviews compiled within this chapter elucidates the circumstances leading to incarceration of respondent inmates who were either physically abused or unable to deal with a significant loss in their life. As part of their coping mechanism they turned to drugs. They did not appear to have other structurally adequate mechanisms for dealing with the loss or trauma in their lives. It is well documented that physical and sexual abuse can lead victims to try to shut off these encounters and memories in some way.[1] Some victims' "shut off" mechanisms for traumatic experiences in their lives, can involve the use of drugs or even acting out, which could result in criminal manifestations. Often these individuals delve into a cycle of trauma, drug use and crime that could lead to imprisonment.[2] The cases documented within this chapter, range from childhood rape to being beaten while pregnant. The traumatic circumstances of the inmate respondents appeared to have formed the basis for their drug abuse as a means of escaping their individual realities.

Jane 1

Jane 1 was a Caucasian that was initially raised with her brother in a two parent dysfunctional family. When asked her age, she noted simply that she was in her thirties. Jane 1's parents were on disability. Her father had always been on marijuana as far back as she could remember. Likewise, her mother had always used prescription pills and had been on prescription pills as far back as Jane 1 could

---

1. Pollard, J.,. "An Analysis of Coping Resources, Trauma and Significant Life Events in a Sample of Female Prisoners". Paper Presented at the Women in Corrections by the Australian Institute of Criminology 2000 http://www.aic.gov.au/conferences/womencorrections/pollbak.pdf (accessed January 9, 2009).
2. Pollard.

recall. Her parents divorced when she was a little girl, she could not exactly remember how old she was when her parents got divorced. She had a brother that was a diver and he had never been in trouble with the law. As a matter of fact Jane 1 was the only one in her family that had ever been in trouble with the law.

Jane 1 moved in with her mother and brother after her parents' divorce. She recounted being molested shortly after her parents' divorce. According to Jane 1, she remembered being sexually molested by a male cousin when she was 12 years old, but she did not want to talk about details of the sexual molestation, but it was clear, it visibly affected her to mention it. Her eyes started to water as she mentioned the molestation. She also recollected not mentioning the incident to anyone, because she felt that somehow she was to blame for the molestation.

Jane 1 graduated from high school but she had a daughter right before graduation from high school, and another daughter years later. The oldest daughter was 15 years old and the youngest was five years old. Her two girls were staying with her mother while Jane 1 was incarcerated. She did not know how her children were adjusting to living with their grandmother because Jane 1's mother never visited her in prison to provide updates on the children.

The instance of Jane 1's first drug arrest occurred, one night when she was out riding with her then boyfriend in her car. They stopped by a convenience store to buy snacks. The boyfriend paid with a counterfeit $100 bill and the store clerk without their knowledge called the police. Two policemen in a car arrived at the store as Jane 1 and her boyfriend were about to enter their car. They asked for her license and registration, which she provided. They asked if they could search her car, and Jane 1 gave them permission to do so. Unbeknownst to her, the boyfriend had a half a gram of methamphetamine in the glove compartment of her car. One of the police officer pulled it out of the glove compartment. "Whose is this?" the police officer asked. "It's not mine," replied both Jane and her boyfriend simultaneously. "I'm sorry but I have to put you both under arrest," replied the police officer, "since neither of you would admit to being the owner of the Schedule II drug." He read them their rights and handcuffed them, as another police car pulled up to the store. As they were being handcuffed Jane 1's boyfriend whispered to her, "Would you take the rap for possession of the methamphetamine for me?" "I would think about it," whispered Jane 1. They were put into two different police cars and Jane 1 was taken to the county jail.

This was not Jane 1's first criminal offence. She had had numerous offences in the past ranging from DUI at the age of 18 to numerous minor assault charges, for which she had spent time in Jail. Bail for the methamphetamine possession charge was set at $94,000 and since she did not have the 10% of the bail required for bond, she had to stay in jail to await court proceedings.

According to Jane 1, she was in jail for almost a month before she had the opportunity to speak with a public defender. "My public defender was not interested in knowing if I was guilty or not," stated Jane 1 during the interview. He was just interested in our reaching a plea agreement with the prosecutor as soon as possible. So, she pled guilty as part of the plea bargain to a charge of possession and intent to sell one half gram of a Schedule II drug. She was sentenced to probation in lieu of six at 30 (i.e. six years with the possibility of being paroled after serving 30% of her sentence). She accepted the conditions of the plea bargain, because she was desperate to get out of jail. Under the terms of her probation she was expected to report to her probation officer weekly and to be available for drug testing whenever required by her probation officer. Jane violated her probation in less than three months. Her violation was because she tested positive for drugs in her urine. Her probation officer issued a warrant for her arrest and she was arrested. Because she had violated her probation, when she went before the court again the judge sent her to prison to serve out her sentence, and discounted her street time. (i.e. the three months time she had spent on probation). So she had to serve at least 30 percent of her time before she would be eligible for parole.

Jane 1 was asked why she kept using drugs when she was on probation, especially since she knew it was going to cause her to violate the terms of her probation. She responded, "I did not care about the consequences of my actions at that particular point in time." She elaborated by explaining that she believed then that nobody cared for her and so she did not care. Jane 1 had been treated in the past for bi-polar disorder.

Since being at the Tennessee Prison for Women, she had continued with her medication for bi-polar disorder, and she joined Therapeutic Counseling (TC, where she had undergone drug rehabilitation and behavior modification classes). Prison in her view, was an interesting experience, and somewhat rehabilitative. She knew for a fact, that she never wants to come back to prison again.

When asked what she would do upon release to make sure that she did not reoffend and become re-incarcerated, Jane 1 said that she would enter a halfway house once released. She would also make sure that she attended Narcotics Anonymous regularly upon release. Most importantly she would endeavor to stay away from her former friends and acquaintances as well as try to enroll in college classes.

Jane 8

Jane 8 was a 50-year-old Caucasian. She grew up in a two parent working class household. Her mother was a homemaker; Jane 8 never specified her father's occupation. She was one of three children. According to Jane 8, a younger brother was a doctor at Stanford University Medical Center. Her older sister got married at 14 and moved out of the house. Jane 8 noted that her father started sexually molesting her when she was six-and-a-half years old. Jane 8 specified that her mother knew about it but did not say or do anything to stop the molestation. Her father eventually stopped molesting her when she was 11 years old. He stopped the molestation, simply because she became a ward of the State of California. Her father eventually committed suicide when she was 14 years old.

She got emancipated at 15, and she somehow managed to earn two years of college, prior to dropping out of college because, "she was bored."

She got married in her late teens and gave birth to five children. Four of the children were hers and the 5th child was a surrogate baby she had for a friend of hers. While married and living in California, her husband introduced her to methamphetamine, and she eventually got involved with manufacturing it. She eventually moved down to Clarksville, Tennessee and set up a methamphetamine manufacturing laboratory, as well as counterfeiting and forgery operation in her house.

One cold day in April 2002,[3] a few police officers showed up at Jane 8's house in Clarksville with an arrest warrant. She was arrested and taken to jail. Her house was cordoned off. The methamphetamine lab in her house blew up while the policemen were watching over the house. The police men called the fire service, but before they could get to the house, it burnt to the ground. The flames of the fire burnt up evidence of her counterfeiting, forgery and methamphetamine manufacture and production.

She got a public defender because she did not have any more money to hire an attorney. She had 26 indictments against her. According to Jane 8, the prosecutor wanted her to plead guilty and get sentenced to a total of 85 years for all the 26 indictments against her. Her public defender finally managed to get her a plea bargain where by all her indictments would total up to seven years sentence. Jane 8 said that she was not totally impressed with her public defender, despite the fact that he was able to point out to the prosecutor, that the majority of evidence against her was destroyed in the fire. In October 2002, while still at Montgomery county jail, she was allowed out to attend a synergy program and she never reported back to jail. She eventually somehow managed to get to the airport and book a flight back to California. She flew to California and was in the state until April 2006. According to Jane 8, her surrogate daughter wanted to meet her. So they arranged a meeting. She ended up bonding with her, but that made the mother envious. The mother thus called the police department in California and reported Jane 8 as a convict on the run. She was extradited to Tennessee to complete her sentence at the TPFW. In October 2006, she met with the parole board, and they told her that she would be released in six months. She was released April 2007 on parole. As a condition of her parole she was supposed to report regularly to her parole officer. But Jane 8 said that her parole officer was not strict about the reporting, and thus never really expected her to check in frequently. So Jane 8 felt that her parole officer would not notice if she left for California. So Jane 8 left for California, to be near her surrogate daughter. When the "mother" found out that Jane 8 was back in California, she once again called the authorities to report Jane 8. Jane 8 was arrested and taken back to Tennessee. Her parole was revoked in September 2007. She had since been

3. Jane 8 believed an informant must have had something to do with the police showing up at her house with an arrest warrant.

at the Tennessee Prison for Women. It was important to note that throughout the interview process Jane 8 was very verbose, sometimes incoherently verbose. She said that she had been diagnosed amongst other disorders with schizophrenia and bi-polar disorder.

She vehemently stated during the course of the interview that there was no "Justice" within our Criminal Justice system, when a woman like Cindy McCain can steal drugs from her charity and still manage to be the wife of a presidential contender,[4] while she, Jane 8 was incarcerated for a similar offence. When asked if prison had been rehabilitative, she responded, with a question, "What is rehabilitation?" She followed up by explaining that Tennessee Prison for Women was not set up to rehabilitate women. She pointed out, that there were women in wheelchairs that were old and feeble at the prison. Sometimes these old and feeble inmates were sent to isolation for "acting out." "Is that rehabilitation," asked Jane 8? "One thing I know for sure is that I do not want to come back to prison once my time here is done."

When asked what steps she would take to ensure that she did not get rearrested, Jane 8 responded that she had to take time to figure herself out. She was thinking about going back to school to study theology and she would definitely keep away from her surrogate daughter. She did not want anything more to do with her surrogate daughter. In her opinion, "children are the bane of womanhood and the downfall of women."

Jane 10

Jane 10 was a 45-year-old African American woman that grew up with 12 siblings. Her mother had 13 children. She grew up in a two-parent family. Her mother was a homemaker. Her father worked at the nuclear plant after having served in the USA marines. Jane 10's father died when she was six years old, and her mother remarried about a year later.

Her stepfather started molesting Jane 10 when she was about seven and a half years. He would have her perform oral sex on him and he would also penetrate her vaginally, depending on how he was feeling. The molestation continued till she was 14 years old, when Jane 10 decided, she had had enough. So she dropped out of high school and moved in with her older sister. After moving in with her older sister, Jane 10 became very promiscuous, and started sleeping around with boys. She ended up getting pregnant at 17 years old. During her pregnancy, she decided to stay with her mother for a while. One afternoon, she was lying down in bed, while her mother was out. Her stepfather came into the room whence she was lying down, and tried to pin her down to have sex with her. She managed to get off from under him. She then ran into the kitchen where

4. Cindy McCain is the wife of John McCain, who was the Republican nominee for the Presidency of United States of America. She had admitted publicly, her former addiction to prescription medication.

she picked up an axe and chased him out of the house with it. Jane 10 said she had meant to kill him, because she was so tired of feeling violated. She was stopped by some utility workers that were outside her house fixing a telephone line. She reiterated that had it not been for the utility men working outside her house that day, she would have axed her stepfather to death. When her mother came back, Jane 10 told her what had happened, but her mother did not believe her. So Jane 10 packed up her things and moved back in with her sister. She had the baby, and it turned out to be a baby girl. Shortly after the birth of her baby, Jane 10 was diagnosed with cervical cancer[5] at the age of 19. She had to undergo surgery and radiation therapy. During that period, Jane 10 started using marijuana, cocaine and alcohol.

Sometime after turning 20 years old, Jane 8 began to dupe men and take their money. She would bring men home to supposedly sleep with them, and then surreptitiously slip Thorazine[6] into their drinks, which would cause them to pass out. She would then take their wallet, money and any other valuables. With the help of her then current boyfriend, they would put her victims back in their cars, and drive them while passed out to an isolated location. Jane 10 would drive the victim's car and her boyfriend would follow behind. Once there, they would prop the particular victim in the driver's seat of their car, such that it would look like the victim drove to the location while in a drunken stupor. Jane 10 would then get into her boyfriend's car, and he would drive her home leaving the victim propped up in his car in an isolated location. She always played the wide eyed innocent when the men would wake up without their wallets. They would drive back to her house or call her to find out what had happened and how they got to be in an isolated part of town. She would always tell them that after they had sex, they drove away and maybe in their drunken state they passed out and while they were passed out their wallets were then probably stolen. She would use this ruse on every single man she conned. It worked everytime. She said she never really had sex with the men she duped this way, because prior to actually having sex with them, the Thorazine would kick in. She supported her lifestyle this way for some years.

Shortly after turning 23 years old, Jane 10 met a married man, and started dating him. When she got pregnant, the married man broke off with her, so she quickly found a boyfriend and deceived him into thinking that the pregnancy was his. The boyfriend turned out to be very abusive. He knocked out two of

---

5. Cervical cancer is when malignant abnormal cancer cells begin to grow at the cervix. The cervix is the narrow portion of the woman's uterus or womb. Some of the risk factors include: Starting sexual intercourse at an early age. Note Jane: 10 started intercourse at the age of and when her stepfather started molesting her. Another major risk factor is having multiple sexual partners.

6. Jane 10 said Thorazine is the colloquial name of a drug/product that will render an adult unconscious. It must be noted that archival and web search of the word Thorazine did not yield any results.

her teeth one day, when he was punching her for a supposed infraction on her part. One of the teeth was reattached at the hospital. Jane 10 recalled that the reattachment of the tooth was very painful. One day sometime in her second trimester of pregnancy, he beat her so badly that she started bleeding. When she eventually went to the pregnancy clinic she found out that she was having a miscarriage. She had a complete miscarriage of the baby. Jane 10, stated that she had called the police a few times and filed charges against him, but according to her the judge would always let him go. Her boyfriend would not allow her to work anywhere that was more than five miles outside their apartment radius. He would not allow her to drive and he would always pick her up from work. She finally managed to escape from him in 2004.

She started selling drugs after her escape from her abusive boyfriend. When asked why she reverted back to selling drugs, Jane 10 responded that she did not have any job, thus did not have any money and could not afford to buy "stuff" for the unborn baby of her 15-year-old daughter. One day her sack of drugs was stolen from her, so she asked her acquaintance Amy to help her steal a check. Amy told her she would get a stolen check for her on the condition that Jane 10 would give her a specific amount of drugs. Jane 10 agreed. Amy got her a stolen check, and Jane 10 wrote a forged check, cashed the money and used it to buy more drugs to sell to make up for her stolen cache of drugs. She did not give Amy the agreed amount of drugs for procuring the check for her. So Amy reported her to the authorities because Jane 10 had reneged on their agreement, and would not give her the specific amount of drugs she had demanded for stealing the check. "You do crazy things when you do drugs," Jane 10 offered by way of explanation. "Your thinking is not clear." Unbeknownst to her, she also sold crack twice to an undercover agent and twice to an undisclosed informant.

Toward the later part of 2005, (inmate was not clear as to the particular dates), she got a knock on her door. When she opened the door, there were two police officers with warrant for her arrest, for sale and delivery of drugs. She was taken to downtown jail. Jane 10 did not see nor speak to a public defender, till about a month after she had been arrested. Thus she was in jail for a month prior to speaking with a public defender. Jane 10 could not make bail because it was set at $64,000 for the four counts of sale and possession, and $1,000 for check forgery; therefore she had to stay in jail till her court date.

Jane 10 was not happy with the representation of her public defender, because according to her, he did not file for discovery for the two unknown informant charges. Her public defender tried to work out a plea bargain for her. The initial offer was six at 30 if she served a year in jail, but she wanted better. The prosecutor in aggravation increased the sentence for the plea to eight at 30 and informed them that she and her attorney could take it or go through trial. Her public defender advised her to take it. He informed her that at that particular point she was not going to get a better offer, since her family was well noted in McMinn County as law breakers. According to her attorney if she went through trial and lost the case, she would probably be sentenced to many more years in prison, but if she accepted the offer, he could probably get her to serve the sentence as probation in lieu of prison time. So she accepted the offer and around March 2006 was put on 8 years probation (minus the approximately seven months she had spent in jail prior to the final adjudication of her case), in lieu of prison.

She missed an appointment with her probation officer towards the mid part of 2007, and her probation officer violated her. She was arrested July 31, 2007, and placed in county jail till she was brought to the Tennessee Prison for Women on October 29, 2007. She would be eligible for parole on December 1, 2008.

Jane 10 said that being incarcerated in prison had been a learning and rehabilitative experience. But at the same time the experience was a nightmare that she would never want to repeat.[7] She had never been diagnosed with a mental illness. She stated that she regretted all the things that she had done. She would like to "Do right" such that she would not have to come back to prison.

When asked the steps she would take to make sure she would not re-offend, Jane 10 responded, that upon release, she intended to attend regular drug meetings to help her stay off drugs. She also intended to work in drug volunteer programs and hopefully get a job.

Jane 11

Jane 11 was a 38-year-old Caucasian woman that was adopted when she was 3½ months old. Her adoptive parents were married for 11½ years prior to adopting her. She was raised in a working class two parent Christian home. Her father worked as maintenance man and her mother worked as a homemaker. She was the only child of her parents. Her childhood was conventional and uneventful. Jane 11 did not finish high school. She got pregnant at 16 years old, and married the father of her unborn baby. Shortly after the wedding she dropped out of high school and moved with her new husband into a trailer home right next to her parent's home. Her husband was very abusive. He would beat her regularly for the smallest infraction. One day, while she was still pregnant, they got into an argument and he beat her so much that she started bleeding. Her husband eventually took her to the hospital where she had a miscarriage and lost the baby. She subsequently had another miscarriage a few months later. This too, was caused by the severe beating she had received from her husband. When beating her up,

---

7. Jane 10 indicated that some of the incidents that occurred in prison are horrible. For instance she said that if you got into trouble, e.g. fight, you will be put on segregation as punishment. In segregation you are locked up for 23 hours a day, and you are only allowed out for one hour a day, and for that hour the inmate spends it in a big metal cage. She said that they also have routine urine drug tests and a few months ago, one test in a unit came back positive and the whole unit was searched, drug tested and each inmate strip searched. Prison officials found the marijuana and four women were identified to be the culprits in bringing the drug to prison. They were put in segregation.

he would hit her anywhere, on her face, stomach, head and back. After, her second miscarriage, she turned to smoking weed and drinking. She eventually managed to carry a baby full term despite her abusive husband's beatings. When Jane 11 was 18 she gave birth to a baby girl. Despite the fact that she had just given birth to a baby, her husband still continued with the relentless physical abuse. Jane 11 then decided it was time to leave him. So she left him and filed for divorce. Her divorce was finalized when she was 19 years old. Jane 11 said she went "wild" after her divorce, sleeping around, drinking, taking pills and smoking pot. She then met second husband to be and moved in with him. They co-habited for three and a half years before she ended up getting married to him. He also was very physically abusive. She had her second child, a boy in December 1996.

When her son was 15 months old, Jane 11 got addicted to methamphetamine. Her husband introduced her to it. She continued to use methamphetamine even after she got pregnant with her third child. After the birth of her third child in 2001, she started shooting up methamphetamine with her husband and their friends. She made an effort during the interview, to point out that her children were never there when she did drugs. They usually were next door at her parents when she was using drugs. She had been getting high on methamphetamine with husband since 1997.[8] Then her husband got arrested for selling and delivery of marijuana. He was put on probation but since he was still addicted to methamphetamine, he never met with his probation officer. He violated probation a total of about six times. He finally had to serve an extended period of time in prison. Prior to serving time in prison, he was diagnosed with lymphoma.[9] He was prescribed a lot of medical narcotics to help manage his pain and discomfort from lymphoma. When he was transferred to men's prison, to start serving his prison term, Jane 11 capitalized on that fact by continuing to have his medical narcotics prescriptions filled out. Her father would drive her to the hometown pharmacy to get the prescriptions filled.

One afternoon, sometime in July 2004, she went to the neighborhood pharmacy to pick up more of her husband's prescription for narcotics. She invariably noticed that the pharmacist had been taking too long to fill the prescription. She did not know that they had called the police. Since it was taking so long to fill the prescription, Jane 11 started getting edgy, she finally got the filled prescriptions and turned around to leave, but noticed a police cruiser pull into the parking lot. The police officer asked her to go with him to the police station, such that they could talk and she complied. She was not read her Miranda rights. She

---

8. Jane 11 had been using methamphetamine with husband for about eight years, from 1997 to 2004.

9. Lymphoma is a type of cancer that attacks the immunity producing cells of the body. There are no iron clad prevention for lymphoma, but risk factors include sharing needles, razor blades and personal items with individuals that might be contaminated with blood or secretions infective with the HIV, EBV (Epstein-Barr virus) or the hepatic B or C virus. Thus drug addicts especially drug addicts that share needles can be considered at higher risk.

was tested in jail for drugs in her system, and was charged with two counts of prescription fraud,[10] and two counts of narcotics for sale. She told the police officers that she was not guilty and they told her that if she did not sign a confession statement, they would arrest her father,[11] since he was the one that drove her to the pharmacy. She thus signed a confessionary statement. When she had the opportunity to meet with a public defender, her public defender informed her that it was all right that she had signed the statement. He worked out a plea bargain, whereby she would serve four years probation in lieu of jail time. That was July of 2004.

Sometime, in January of 2005, Jane 11 failed to meet with her probation officer, thus violating her probation. She was rearrested. Her public defender never showed up in court after she violated her probation. So she was transported from jail to court on her court date. She did not have any public defender with her in court that day. Jane 11, said that when she stood before the judge, he looked at her and said "TPFW."[12] She did not even have the opportunity to ask for drug court. She was serving out the terms of her combined consecutive four-year sentence for the drug offences, and one year for forgery of check, for a total of five at 30. She had been incarcerated for almost four years and she said it seemed that she would have to serve out the total five years instead of five at 30.

The check forgery occurred while she was on probation. Jane 11 recalled forging the check of $4,000 to use to pay her court costs. She was not happy with representation of her initial public defender. She was satisfied with another public defender, which defended her in 2002 on charges of conspiracy to manufacture methamphetamine and felony drug paraphernalia possession. She indicated that in that particular case her husband's friend had his drug paraphernalia (everything but one ingredient required to make methamphetamine) at her house. There was an altercation at her house, and someone must have called the police. When the police arrived they saw the drug paraphernalia. This particular public defender from a different county got her two years community corrections. She noted that the drug paraphernalia charge originated from a different county from her prescription fraud and narcotics for sale charges. [13]

Jane 11 noted that she quit methamphetamine cold turkey while in jail waiting for her court date. She stated that she did not have significant withdrawal symptoms. She also mentioned that she had once graduated from outpatient drug rehabilitation. She indicated that the program was not very effective. According to her they watched movies on how to make drugs, use it, shoot it up, and smoke it. She said that the program particulars were not conducive to help-

10. Jane 11 had two filled bottles of Valium and Hydrocodone/Loritab.

11. Note, according to Jane 11 her father was not aware of the fact that she was forging prescriptions. She would usually ask him to drive her down so that she could buy pain relievers for female cramps.

12. Tennessee Prison for Women

13. Jane 11 noted that the county line was right down the middle of her house. Thus there were two different counties on either side of her house.

ing a drug addict quit. She was being treated for depression and she was on Prozac medication.

When asked about her prison experience Jane 11 responded that prison was a life saving experience for her. She had found God, while in prison. She had since found a "purpose" to her incarceration. Her stated purpose was to make people more aware of the dangers of methamphetamine. She believed her time in prison would be helpful and rehabilitative for her, but she did not want to ever come back to prison. Jane 11 said that upon release she would attend narcotics anonymous, which would hopefully help her not to re-offend. She would also like to work with programs, volunteer or otherwise, that help make individuals aware of the dangers of drugs and how addictive they could be. Jane 11 said she would definitely avoid her former friends, and make sure she stayed away from them in the future.

Jane 13

Jane 13 was a twenty nine-year-old Caucasian American from a working class two parent household. She grew up with sister and four half siblings. None of her siblings had ever been in trouble with the law. Her father was a plumber and an electrician but he was on disability. He had kidney failure. Her mother was a factory worker, but she died when Jane 13 was only 15 years old. After her mother's death Jane 13 started acting out. In her own words, "She got Wild," but still managed to graduate from high school at the age of 16.

Upon graduation, she moved to New York City, got a studio apartment and a job at MacDonald's. She took the job at MacDonald because they were willing to hire her despite the fact that she was only 16 years old. When she turned 18 years, she became eligible to work in the field of diet and personal care. So she applied for and got a job as a personal care attendant.[14] She was working very hard in her new job and after a while she got tired of all the hard work. She thought it would be so much easier to sell marijuana instead. Thus she started selling marijuana. She sold marijuana for some years. One afternoon while only 21 years old, she inadvertently sold marijuana to an undercover drug agent. She was subsequently indicted, arrested and sentenced to 16 months in county jail in New York, in addition to three years probation. The jail time and the probation were to be served concurrently. Jane 13 described being in New York City jail as being very laid back. She indicated that it was so laid back that visitors could easily bring in marijuana without being detected. She noted that visitors to the jail were never searched; the jail officers only used metal detector wands on

14. A personal care attendant is paid to help individual with disability in functions of their daily living. That makes it possible for the disabled person to still remain in their home as opposed to moving to a group home etc. The personal care attendant is usually hired by the person with disability, who also decided the functions they need the personal care attendant to help them with.

incoming visitors to jail. There was no strip-searching of inmates after they had had contact with visitors. After her stint in jail, she was allowed to serve the rest of her sentence on probation.

When she was almost 23 years old she failed her routine drug test that was part of her probation requirements. Therefore her probation was violated, so she had to serve six months in prison and subsequent one and half year probation. She was released early from her probation and she decided to go back to Nashville. She moved back to Nashville in 2003 when she was about 25 years old. She secured three jobs and had different shifts. She worked at Sonic from 6 a.m. to 2 p.m., and at Scepters lumber company from 3:30 p.m. to 11:30 p.m. Then on weekends she worked at Cadillac Range. She was doing so well financially with the three jobs, that she was able to buy a house and afford a nice car.

A few months after settling in, she met an older woman, Doris that eventually became her lover. Doris was a "pill head" meaning she was addicted to prescription pills. They were together for almost four years. Jane 13 kept her Sonic job, but resigned from her two other jobs in order to spend more time with Doris. Doris did not have a job, and since the money she was making at Sonic was not enough to help pay her expenses, she went back to selling weed in order to supplement her income. She eventually evolved to selling cocaine. Doris introduced her to using cocaine, prescription pills, crack and methamphetamine. They would both use copious amount of the above mentioned drugs, in addition to marijuana. It was a very expensive addiction and Jane 13's fast food Sonic job could not cover the increased expenses. Thus she really had to sell more quantity so as to be able to cover her drastically increased expenses. Somewhere in between her drug sales she got arrested for driving without a license. She was put on probation.

In 2007, Jane 13 sold cocaine to an informant, and on May 2, 2007; her house was raided by about 20 police officers with a warrant. They tore out the walls and ceilings of her house while searching for drugs, but they did not find anything except for an ounce of marijuana. She was arrested for marijuana possession. She was able to get out on a $5,000 bail. She posted bond of $500. A week after getting out on bail she received a letter from Tennessee drug task force stating that her house was going to be seized because her house had been raided three times by the drug task force. So she lost her home, and was told by her probation officer that she had violated her probation as a result of the raid on her house. But in lieu of having her arrested, her probation officer offered her the opportunity of attending a six-month rehabilitation program. Jane 13 agreed to the offer proffered by the probation officer. She stayed for a while at Doris's house, and got a good job working at Shionke Wick. She managed to pass her drug tests that were required as a condition of her continued probation.

In December of 2007, she went to court for the marijuana possession charge,[15] and found that she had 13 indictments. Seven of the indictments were

15. This refers to the marijuana that was found at her house during the police raid.

for marijuana possession and the other seven indictments were for cocaine possession and sale. Her public defender worked to get the charges dropped down to two counts of Schedule II (cocaine) sale and one count of Schedule VI (marijuana) sale. The prosecutor offered six years each for each cocaine charge and two years for the marijuana charge, to be served concurrently. She spoke to her probation officer and he suggested that she should have her time flattened to six years such that she could serve an even six years at 30. Her public defender suggested that they make a plea for eight years at 30 but Jane 13 said that she would prefer to go with six years at 30. Her public defender put forward the offer and the prosecutor agreed to the plea bargain. She was sentenced to six at 30 in January of 2008 and sent to jail to await transportation to Tennessee Prison for Women. Jane 13 mentioned that she was not happy with the representation of her public defender. According to her, the public defender never returned her calls, and the only time she would speak to the public defender would be when they met in court. He never saw her prior to court to discuss her case.

She arrived at TPFW on April 8th 2008. She said prison life was quite an experience. She had been taking the opportunity to find herself; she was attending Narcotics Anonymous, and had signed up for substance abuse program. She also attended church regularly in prison. She did not want the drug life anymore. Jane 13 noted that she would go up for parole in November of 2009, if she does not make parole then, she would probably go up for parole again about six months later.

She stated that when she gets out of prison upon completion of her sentence, she intended not to re-offend. She would stay close to her family as well as try to keep away from her former drug friends and from drugs and the drug culture. Hopefully these changes would help her stay out of trouble. She refrained from saying if she had ever been diagnosed with a mental health problem.

Jane 18

Jane 18 was a 30-year-old Caucasian American that was raised in a fractured home environment. Her mother had five children and all five children were by different fathers. Her mother got married a total of nine times. Jane 18 was the youngest of the five children of her mother. When Jane 18 was 18 months old, her mother married her 9th husband and he adopted Jane 18. Jane 18 grew up thinking her stepfather was her father. Her mother worked as a nurse and her stepfather worked as a diesel mechanic. Her mother moved with Jane 18 and her oldest brother to her new husband's house. A few months later she brought two of her other sons home with her, from their fathers' homes to live with them. A fourth son decided to stay on with his father. So Jane 18 was raised with three of her brothers, by her mother and stepfather. It was rocky in their household with the new stepfather. He got into furious arguments with Jane 18's oldest brother, Jake who had a problem with smoking weed. The arguments got so bad, that the stepfather finally told Jake to either straighten out or move out of the house. Jake decided to move out. That was very hard on Jane 18 who was in her preteens when he moved out. She was very close to Jake. Then a few years later, the middle brother got arrested. Jane 18 did not provide the details of the arrest. Thus Jane 18 and the youngest brother were the only ones still living at home. A few years later the youngest brother as a teen held up a woman at gunpoint and took her wallet, he then went home and stole his stepfather's money ($1,500), from his wallet. He was arrested and sentenced to prison. From then on Jane 18 was the only child living with her mother and stepfather.

Things were fairly calm and nice at home but Jane 18 missed her brothers very sorely. Then her mother and stepfather got divorced when Jane 18 was 12 years old. After the divorce her mother bought a house and some land and she and Jane 18 moved onto the property. One evening Jane 18 got into an argument with her mother, because she kept asking her mother why she decided to leave her stepfather. In a fit of anger at her stepfather, Jane 18's mother told her that her stepfather was not her biological father, but instead was only her adoptive father. Jane 18 took the news badly. She accused her mother of lying to her. She told her mother that she did not believe what she was saying. Her mother replied, "I will show you who is lying." Her mother then took her to see her biological father. Jane recalled that made her very angry, confused and sad. She could not believe that the father she had looked up to all those years was not actually her father. She went wild then, and at the young age of 12 she started partying hard. She started smoking marijuana, drinking alcohol and sleeping around. She got pregnant at the age of 14 years old when she was still in high school. She continued attending school, till she was five months pregnant. About five months into her pregnancy, she started having pregnancy related fainting spells. It got so bad that she had to stop attending school. Therefore, she was pretty much home bound till she had the baby girl at the age of 15 years, and then she got a job as a carhop.[16] She got so many citations for truancy, because she was not attending schools so she had to go to juvenile court for hearings on the citations. The court decided that she was to be sent to a group home and she ran away as a 16 year old, rather than be sent to a group home.

She stayed with a brother of hers, and while there got a job at Family Dollar. While working at Family Dollar she got into heavy drugs. Her older coworkers introduced the drugs to her. She was using methamphetamine, marijuana, acid,[17] cocaine and prescription pills. When the drug culture got too much for her young mind she decided to go back home and meet with the probation officer for her truancy charges. She met her probation officer and informed her that she had been using all those aforementioned drugs. She was tested for

16. A car hop usually denotes a waitress who brings food orders to people in their car.
17. Lysergic acid diethylamide, is usually known as acid. It is synthesized from naturally occurring compounds. Acid is used to acquire a mind transcending high, since it acts on the central nervous system especially the brain to produce visual and mental changes in perception. Wikipedia LSD http://en.wikipedia.org/wiki/LSD (accessed March 23, 2009).

drug consumption and she tested positive. Her probation officer got her processed to attend an inpatient 60-day rehabilitation program. Upon completion of the rehabilitation program, she was then sent to an all girls group home. She stayed at the group home for seven and a half months, after which she was allowed to go home. She was then about 17 years old. For a year after leaving the group home she tried valiantly to stay off drugs, while working at odd jobs. She also started dating her long time male friend, Bill Watts. A few months after they started dating he was arrested for burglary. While he was still in prison he proposed to Jane 18. She accepted his proposal and they managed to get married while he was still in prison and she was only 18 years old. She had a serious car accident later on that year.

She worked odd jobs while her husband was serving his prison time. Sometimes she worked double shifts. One day after working two shifts, she was driving home from work around 3 a.m. and she fell asleep at the wheel. Her truck rolled off a bluff, and smashed into the bottom of the bluff. Her ankle was almost severed. It had to be pinned back and stitched. She actually walked into the research interview with a limp. Her doctor put her on prescription for OxyContin to help her manage the pain of injured ankle. She developed dependence to the OxyContin. Bill Watts was finally released from prison about 30 months after her accident. Jane 18 was only 21 years old, when he was released and he moved in with her. He was very physically abusive. They would fight constantly and she would usually call the police. Upon arriving at their home, the police officers would usually arrest both of them and book them for minor assaults. Her husband started using OxyContin with her. She and Bill both found solace in the OxyContin pills prescribed by her Doctor. Once, Bill beat her up so much that he cracked her eye bone. She had to be taken to the hospital to receive medical attention. He always apologized after each abusive incident. Meanwhile Jane 18 delved deeper and deeper into her addiction to OxyContin. She found every excuse imaginable to have her prescription constantly renewed by the doctor. She also bought some from friends. At about the time her doctor decided that maybe she should taper off on her prescriptions, when she informed her husband of what the doctor had said he decided he would go with her to her next doctor's visit. On the subsequent appointment with her doctor, her husband stole prescription pads from the clinic, while Jane 18 was consulting with the doctor. After that medical visit, Jane 18 started writing prescriptions for OxyContin pills with the stolen prescription pads.

One morning, she filled out a prescription for OxyContin, and she drove with Bill Watts to the drug store to have it filled. Unbeknownst to them the pharmacist had called the police officers. The police came to the drug store whilst both of them were still at the counter waiting for their prescription to be filled. They were arrested for prescription fraud and Jane 18 got a sentence of four years probation for the prescription fraud charge. Jane 18 got into a fight with her husband about the arrest and subsequent probation. He grabbed her by the hand and jerked her. Her hand was sprained and while she was screaming at him in agony, he walked out of the house leaving her alone with her sprained hand. She had to drive herself to the hospital. She never informed them at the hospital that she got the sprained hand from her husband. She got a cast on her hand and went home. According to Jane 18, her probation was violated, because the police said she made a false statement. The false statement supposedly occurred when a few days after she got her arm cast, the police came over to her house looking for her husband. They knocked on her door and she opened the door. There was a policeman at the door; he said they were looking for Bill. Jane 18 replied, “Bill who?” The policeman told her she was making a false statement and told her she was under arrest. “Excuse me officer, could I get dressed?” asked Jane. The police officer responded, “Make it quick!” Jane changed into her workout pants. She popped some pills into her mouth and then wrapped a few pills in plastic and pushed them down into her cast, while the police officer was by the door waiting for her. “I'm ready,” said Jane as she walked back into the front room. The police officer took her downtown to be processed and placed in jail. By the time she was processed and then placed in her jail cell, she was beginning to feel the effects of the pills she had popped, wearing off. So she decided she needed to pop some more pills. Jane poked her fingers down the inside of her cast as she desperately tried to retrieve the pills from her cast. Finally she her fingers touched the edge of the plastic wrapping of the pills and she was able to pull on the plastic wrapping containing the pills. As she pulled the wrapping, up out of the cast with her fingers, it tore in the process and the pills spilled out of her cast and onto the jail floor. Jane 18 immediately started grabbing them from the floor. In her desperation and drug induced haze, she knocked on the glass partition of her cell to implore the guard to help her hide the pills. Of course the guard sounded the alarm and Jane was strip searched. The jail officers found the remaining pills still stuck to her cast. For that incident she was charged with introducing drugs into a penal facility.

Jane 18 was appointed a public defender. When she got to court for her court hearing, her public defender informed her that her Bill Watts had signed a statement implicating her for various forged prescriptions. The judge sentenced her to 60 days in jail for all the charges and enhanced probation for the remainder of her four-year probation.

Jane got out of jail after serving the 60 days jail time, and was on enhanced probation. With enhanced probation there is more focused supervision on the offender. One Saturday, Jane 18 went to visit her friend Ann and they got into an argument. A fight subsequently broke out between Jane 18 and Ann. Ann called the police and told them that Jane had assaulted her with Ann's gun. Ann claimed that Jane 18 pointed the gun between her eyes. Jane was arrested. That arrest violated the terms of her enhanced probation. She was charged with felony reckless endangerment. There was no finger printing of the said gun, recalled Jane 18. Her public defender was able to work out a deal of two years prison time for the charge. Jane 18 indicated that she guessed her public defender was okay with regards to his defense of her.

Jane 18 was diagnosed as bi-polar and maniac depressive. She had also been diagnosed with osteoporosis. Jane said she had this inbuilt anger and racing thoughts. In her own words, prison had been rehabilitative, in that being in prison had taught her that she could make it through life without the pain medications. Some days the residual pain from the accident still haunted her, but overall she said she had learnt to live with the pain, so as to not be dependent on pills anymore. She did not want to come back to prison for any other offence. Thus she would do everything within her power, to stay away from drugs.

When she "flat-lines,"[18] and is released she would endeavor not to take pain pills even when she would feel the residual pain from the accident. She "now knows" that she can make the decision not to take prescription pills for pain. It was up to her. She would receive disability when she is eventually released and she would try to focus on her daughter. She hoped that by keeping away from prescription pills, she could live life and be happy without worrying about the law anymore.

Jane 19

Jane 19 was a 30-year-old Caucasian American that was raised in a two parent middle class family. Her parents had been married for 36 years. Her father was the Vice President of his company, an electrical wholesales company. Her mother was a homemaker, though she went back to college and graduated from college in 1996, the same year Jane 19 graduated from high school. Her mother was on disability, though, because she hurt her back in a car crash. Jane 19 grew up with two brothers in the city of Mason, Tennessee. None of her siblings had ever been in trouble with the law. One of her brothers was an electrician and another brother was a mechanic in Norfolk, Virginia.

Jane 19 had a good childhood. When she was in her last year of high school she met an older handsome college graduate, Scott, and fell in love with him. He was about six years older than her. She dated him from high school till she was about 20 years old. One day she got a call early in the morning from Scott's mother informing her that Scott was in the hospital, and that she needed to get to the hospital. She immediately got dressed and drove to the hospital to see him. When she walked into his room he looked very alert. She hugged and kissed him and they started talking. Jane 19 said that Scott was talking to her and suddenly, she noticed that he had started turning blue. It seemed to her that he was struggling to breathe, and moments later, it looked like he could not breathe anymore. She screamed for the nurses to come but before they could get to Scott, he had expired. Jane 19 explained that Scot was overweight. And she learnt after his death that an artery in his heart had burst and he had died from internal bleeding. Jane was devastated by his death. She could not handle the thought of his death.

18. Flat lines is the colloquial term that the inmates used to describe the completion of their prison time.

She "totally flipped out." She started using drugs especially cocaine. Over the course of two years, she incurred a lot of petty misdemeanors. Some of the misdemeanors included driving under the influence; driving with a suspended license; marijuana and drug paraphernalia possession, and shoplifting. She got tired of racking up the misdemeanors and the subsequent arrests so she decided to stop using drugs. She ended up weaning herself off of cocaine at the age of 22. During the two years that she was "flipped out," she never had a job. When she finally weaned herself from cocaine, she got a job at M&M factory in Cleveland Tennessee. She worked at M&M till she was 24 years old, when she was then terminated because the factory was scaling down. In an effort to find another job, she signed on with a temporary agency and they found a job for her to work in a Duracell factory, on a contract basis. When her six-month contract expired, she left the job. She could not find another job easily after leaving the Duracell factory, because of her criminal record. Jane 19 said she went "nuts" after she stopped working at Duracell. She was then diagnosed as being bi-polar. She was able to get on disability due to her bi-polar diagnosis. She reverted back to her old habit of using marijuana.

One night, Jane 19 was driving back from a friend's house and as she drove toward the junction leading to her block, she noticed that there was a police roadblock in front. When she drove up to the road block, her car was stopped. A police officer walked to her car to ask for her license and as he asked for her license, he shone the flashlight on the inside of her car. There in plain view was a marijuana butt (according to the court affidavit)[19] in her ashtray. She was arrested and taken to jail. Her bail was set at $1,000. She posted $100 bond and was released to await her court date. She failed to appear for her court date. When the police came over to her apartment with a warrant for her arrest for missing the court date, they saw some marijuana on her coffee table. She was indicted for the marijuana. She pled guilty to two counts of marijuana charges. She was released on her own recognizance. When her case was adjudicated, she had $250 fine for the first marijuana charge, $500 fine for the second charge and court costs of $150, for a total of $900. She had the option of paying off the total $900 in lieu of probation or being on probation for 11 months 29 days while she paid off the court cost. If she chose not to pay off the $900 immediately, not only would she be on probation, but she would also have to meet with the probation officer monthly as well as do community services every weekend at the recycling place plus get a job. In essence she was either going to buy off her probation or serve probation if she did not have money to pay the $900. If she violated her probation she would serve out nine months i.e. 75% of her 11 months 29 days sentence. She paid the $900.

A few months later she was arrested for a drug paraphernalia charge and driving on a suspended license. She was put on probation again, without the option of buying out of the probation. She failed to perform the community ser-

19. Jane 19 said it was a tobacco butt.

vices. She was arrested in April as a result of that and the judge said she had to serve four months in jail. She was taken from court to jail to start serving her jail sentence. She was supposed to have been released on the 5th of August. But prior to that date, sometime on June 18th she jumped down from her bunk bed and cut her foot on the bed. She received 18 stitches at the medical clinic for the cut, and was told that her stitches would be removed in 15 days. Jane 19 said that after 15 days her stitches were not removed. She filled out a jail medical form for the stitches to be removed but they would not take her stitches out. Thus while she was with 15 other inmates for checkup at the jail medical clinic, she stole tweezers from the suture kit, while the nurse was busy with other inmates. She hid the tweezers in her hair and when she got back to jail she laid it on her bed. She un-wrapped her bandages in preparation for taking out the stitches from the sutures on her leg, by herself. Unbeknownst to Jane 19 another inmate Shirley was having intercourse with a jail officer. Somehow during the course of Shirley's rendezvous with the guard, Shirley had managed to steal some keys from the officer. The officer discovered that the keys were missing around the time Jane 19 was getting ready to remove her stitches. The alarm sounded. Officers were dispatched to the cells with metal detectors. They found Jane 19's tweezers. She was put on lockdown, till she was released on August the 5th.

She did not know that there were charges pending against her, from that incident. A few months later, when she was about 26 years old, one of her friends got into trouble with the law, and Jane 19, stopped by the jail to bail her out. A police office recognized her and told her that there was a warrant for her arrest for theft under $500 and introduction of a weapon to a penal facility. She was arrested. She got a public defender. Jane 19 did not like the defense provided by her public defender. Jane said that he kept postponing her court date. He eventually got promoted to Assistant District Attorney, according to Jane 19 without ever addressing her case in court. She got a new public defender. Jane 19 recounted that this new public defender failed to provide her with information pertaining to her required presence at her court date. Jane 19 said that this public defender never appeared to be interested in knowing the details of her case. Interestingly Jane 19 said that this particular public defender was now a judge. Jane 19 stated that she did not know that she was supposed to stay in court until after her case had gone before the judge. Accordingly she was in court early in the morning, when the court had a short recess, she left and went home thinking that they were finished with her for that day. According to Jane 19, all her public defender needed to do was explain to her that court was in recess and that Jane needed to hang around till the case was heard. So, she was not there after recess when her case was called. She received another charge of failure to appear in court. For that she was held in the county jail for 78 days. Her "preoccupied" public defender finally came to Jane 19 with three options; (1) Go to trial, which would have been seven months from that day. Jane 19 would stay in jail till trial since she already had a failure to appear she was not eligible for bail; (2) She could plead guilty and get three years probation; or (3) Jane could serve her 11 months and 29 days.

Jane 19 decided to take option two. She reiterated that neither of the two public defenders appeared committed to defending her. She pled guilty and was sentenced to serve three years intensive probation, and her 11 months 29 days sentence was suspended. Jane 19 failed the drug test in less than a couple of months after she got on probation. She said, she was on diet pills and marijuana, which caused her to fail the drug test. She was arrested for failing the drug test, which was a violation of her probation. She served nine months in jail for that violation and was put on intensive probation again. She did fine for about six months, but then decided to try and lose weight again. She was prescribed amphetamine, which is a stimulant that is popularly used to reduce weight, amongst other uses. After going in for her periodic drug test, her probation officer called to tell her that she had failed the drug test and that she needed to turn herself in. Jane 19 refused. She immediately packed her belongings and moved. She was on the run for a few months. Sometime, in early June of 2007, Jane 19 was driving to the grocery store and she was not wearing her seat belt. A police officer pulled her over for seat belt violation and when he checked her driver's license he found out that there was a warrant out for her arrest. She was arrested and the following day she was taken to Tennessee prison for women to serve out her sentence. She would flatten out her sentence late 2008.

Jane 19 said that prison had been a learning experience, both good and bad. She proffered the opinion that a lot of the women in prison had no home life prior to their incarceration. She surmised that about 60% of the women at the prison are doing life for murder,[20] killing their babies, robbery or teachers having sex with their young students. (She elaborated that some of the students they had sex with were as young as 11 years old). Jane 19 thought that it was sad and bad that, the sentences for drug offenders were as long as and sometimes longer than the sentences for "murderers or baby killers." Her time in prison had also helped her come to that point in her life whereby she now wanted to do something positive with her life. Thus in that sense, incarceration had been positive for her but not necessarily rehabilitative. She did take a class that focused on "thinking for a change" but according to her the class was not really informative. She knew for a fact that she did not want to come back ever again to prison.

When she gets out she would do everything in her power to make sure that she is never re-arrested. She would not use marijuana anymore except in her house. She also wanted to further her education and join the Eastern Star.[21] That would give her something positive to do, and help her work towards being a

---

20. According to the Tennessee Department of Corrections, about 27 percent of the women in prison are there for murder.

21. The Eastern Star is the largest fraternal organization in the world that also allows both men and women to join. It is an organization that has alliances with the Masons, although the masons is entirely just for men.

productive member of society. She also would like to try ibogaine[22] and Iboga. Iboga is a hallucinogenic compound that is derived from perennial African rain-forest shrub; anecdotal evidence suggests it might be used to cure opiate addictions. Jane 19 noted that she would like to try those two treatments and hopefully they would help her with all her past addictions to marijuana, amphetamines, cocaine and Xanax.

Jane 20

Jane 20 was a 42-year-old Caucasian woman that grew up in a working class family. Her parents were married and raised Jane 20 in addition to her two brothers and a sister. Her parents were functioning drunks. Her father worked at a coal plant prior to transferring to work in zinc mine. He was still working at the zinc mine. Her mother worked in a sewing factory and then left a few years after getting married to become a stay at home mother. None of Jane 20's brothers had ever been in trouble with the law. One of her brother's was a district manager at MacDonald's, and another brother was on disability. Her sister was diagnosed with mild mental retardation, and had mental problems. Her sister had been in trouble with the law for different petty offences, including forgery. Her sister was recently charged with abetting of statutory rape because she allowed her 11-year-old daughter to have sex with a 30-year-old man. Someone saw her walk with her young daughter and two men into a hotel room and called Department of Children's services. When a staff member from the Department of Children's services got to the hotel room, he knocked on the door and when the sister opened the door, the staff member saw her daughter in bed with an adult 30-year-old man. Apparently her sister had been facilitating sexual intercourse between her 11-year-old daughter and different men for money. She was arrested and charged. She was yet to appear in court in connection with the charge.

Jane 20's childhood was fairly non memorable apart from the fights that usually erupted between her parents when they were drunk. After her 10th birthday, her life changed. She was coming back from school one afternoon and as she walked past some bushes on her way back to her house from the bus stop, her father's brother stopped her. He told her that he wanted her to lie down beside him in the bushes. Jane said she was too scared to resist. He commenced to touch her breasts and her vagina. Finally according to Jane 20, he put his penis into her vagina. Jane 20 stated that it hurt so badly when he inserted his penis into her vagina, and she started whimpering. Her uncle stifled her whimpering, by placing his hand over her mouth. He kept thrusting into her, and with every

22. According to Wikipedia, Ibogaine is a naturally-occurring psychoactive compound found in a number of plants, principally in a member of the dogbane family known as iboga (Tabernanthe iboga). It has anti addictive properties. http://en.wikipedia.org/wiki/Ibogaine, (accessed 22nd August 2008).

thrust Jane 20 would grimace in pain. He then grunted and fell on top of her. After the forced intercourse with Jane 20, her uncle left her laying there amongst the bushes. She painfully got up and slowly walked home. Upon getting home, she and went into the bathroom and scrubbed and scrubbed herself, in an effort to wash away the feel of him upon her. After that incident, her uncle would occasionally stop her, on her way back from the school bus or when she would visit her Grandma. He invariably would force himself upon her on those occasions and have sex with her. He always made sure to stop her at her grandma's or at the bushes, when nobody was around. Jane 20 never told anybody, because she was afraid of what her uncle would do if she told. As a result of the sexual abuse Jane 20 started doing poorly in school. It also affected her behavior around other people.

At 14 years, she started drinking and using marijuana, to "mask the pain," she said. She was in 8th grade. Her school grades suffered. Her father eventually pulled her out of school because she was doing so poorly in school. He signed the school release forms stating that he was going to withdraw her from school.

After dropping out of school, she hung around at home, and then she met their landlord's son Ryan whom at that time was only 16 years old. They dated for about a year and she married him upon turning 16 years old. He was 17 years old at the time of their marriage. Ryan got a job as a factory worker to support them since they were now married. He worked as a factory worker for three years, and then decided that he wanted to be a farmer. So he quit his factory job. Henceforth he became a farmer and Jane 20 became a farmer's wife. She delivered her first baby, a girl at the age of 16, and subsequently had another baby at the age of 30 years, after which she had her tubes tied.

Jane 20 started mental health counseling at the age of 19, in order to deal with residual issues stemming from her past sexual abuse and molestation. She was then diagnosed as schizophrenic[23] and bi-polar.[24] She was doing well with counseling but at the same time she would use marijuana and get drunk occasionally. Jane 20 stopped attending her counseling sessions sometime after her 21st birthday. She felt that counseling was no longer helping her mental state of mind. She was able to finally stop using marijuana and alcohol by the time she turned 24 years old.

About a year after the birth of her second child, she got a job at a TV parts factory. From that period till she was 34 years old, she devoted herself to her children, her job and to having a happy married life. One day she went to work

---

23. According to Schenkel et al, It is important to note that childhood experiences of trauma or abuse have been implicated in later diagnosis of schizophrenia. Schenkel LS; Spaulding WD, Dilillo D, Silverstein SM 2005. Histories of childhood maltreatment in schizophrenia: Relationships with premorbid functioning, symptomatology, and cognitive deficits". *Schizophrenia Research* 76 (2-3): 273–286.

24. Bi-Polar disorder is characterized by intense high mood or mania and intense depression. Thus a person with bi-polar disorder can swing or vacillate from mania to depressive state.

as usual at the TV parts factory in Tennessee where she worked. While pulling the half finished back cover of a TV out of the machine that molded them, she noticed that one of the parts was at an awkward angle. She walked over to the machine to pull it out and as the machine doors started to close, she hurriedly pulled her hands out and fell hard on the ground on her tail bone. She was put on painkillers as a result of the injury. Because of her injury and the fact that she had been diagnosed with mental health issues, she got onto disability, and stopped working.

Once again, she became a full time homemaker. She stayed at home, took care of the children and visited friends. On one such visit to her friends, she saw them smoking crack. Her friend asked her if she wanted to try. Jane 20 said yes. She tried crack cocaine for the very first time at the age of 34 and she shortly became addicted to it. Jane 20 said that crack cocaine addiction was a mind thing. According to her, it was an addiction of the mind to the high one gets the first time a person tries crack cocaine. In her stated opinion, "Your mind remembers the feeling or high gotten the very first time you tried crack and so you use more and more of the crack cocaine to try to get that initial feeling (or the high) that you got the very first time that you tried crack cocaine."

She was now a crack addict, and had been using crack cocaine for years, and her addition was progressively getting more expensive, but she did not really have the money to fund her addiction. That was the justification she gave for stealing a woman's wallet. When asked what transpired during that particular criminal incident, Jane 20 responded that she had approached the lady, while the lady was in her car in a parking lot of a shopping area. She asked the lady politely if she had any extra money to give her for gas. She told the lady that her car had run out of gas but that she did not have any money with her to put gas in her car. The lady responded, "Oh dear, here is $2 for gas." Jane 20 said that she politely gave the $2 back to the lady and informed her that $2 was not enough for gas. The lady said, "Oh well, I tried to help you." Then she started her car. Jane 20 reached inside the window of the car and grabbed the lady's billfold, took $20 from the billfold and then dropped the billfold on the ground and walked away towards her car. For that offence she was later arrested and charged with theft of property. She was 38 years old. The court provided her with a public defender. She told her public defender that she wanted treatment for her drug addiction. Thus the public defender plea-bargained for 30 days rehabilitation and one-year probation for her. She successfully completed her probation. But about a year after her probation; she was in a car with a friend of hers. Unbeknownst to Jane 20 the car was a stolen car. So when the police pulled the car over, she was arrested along with her friend. Her public defender got her two years probation for that arrest. Towards the end of the two-year probation, her former crack friend dropped by her home, and she offered some of her crack to Jane 20. Jane 20, tried it again and lapsed back into crack cocaine addiction. She worked out a schema, whereby she would go to her doctor, and get a prescription for Loritab[25] for the residual pain she was still experiencing. She would then have the prescriptions filled and sell them for money to support her crack habit. She happened to sell 20 pills of Loritab to an informant and as a result she was arrested. This time her public defender was only able to work out a plea of four years at 30%. She could serve the time on probation in lieu of prison time. She chose to go with probation, and its attendant restrictions and requirements. Shortly thereafter she violated probation because her neighbor had called the police, and reported that Jane 20 was drunk and being loud outside. When the police arrived she was arrested. Her public defender got her released on continuing probation.

Her marriage had begun to deteriorate at this point. A few months after she was released on probation for her drunken charge, she got into an argument with her husband. In a fit of anger she threw "scrimshaw" at her husband, he dodged and the scrimshaw hit the window and broke the glass. The neighbor called the police and she was arrested for vandalism. That was also a violation of her probation. On August 2007, she went back to court for her court date. The judge sentenced her to serve out her time in prison in lieu of probation since she was so prone to violating her probation. She was moved to Smith county jail and five months later on December 3, 2007, she was moved to the Tennessee Prison for Women. She had been at the prison since then. Jane 20 thought that her public defender was "ok enough" with regards to her defense.

Since she had been in prison, Jane 20 had taken several classes. She noted that if an inmate got to the prison with latent problems, the Tennessee Women's Prison had programs and classes that would help such inmates. Prison in her view had been rehabilitative, especially with regards to the fact that being in prison had forced her to address her addiction. She knew that she definitely did not want to be re-incarcerated once she was released. To that end, when she is released, she would work part time and also attend Narcotics and Alcohol anonymous. She would also be very involved with church. Hopefully these efforts would help her stay off drugs, and prevent subsequent arrest and incarceration.

Jane B

Jane B was a 25-year-old African American woman that grew up initially in a two-parent working class family. She grew up with two sisters and two brothers. Her sisters wewe both nurse technicians. One of her brothers committed suicide when he was 21 years old; the other brother grew up to become a drug dealer. Her father was a mechanic and her mother was a nurse technician. Then when Jane B was 11 years old her father died of a massive heart attack. Her mother

---

25. Loritab or Loretab, is a narcotic pain reliever that can only be bought with a prescription legally. It is in the same opiod family , just like Vicodin heroin, morphine etc.

then raised all five children by herself. Jane took the death of her father hard. She started drinking, using marijuana and cocaine shortly thereafter the death of her father. She was only in her early teens when she started abusing the drugs. She was only about 14 years old when her drug abuse commenced. It got so bad that her grades began to drop. She eventually ended up dropping out of high school when she was 17 years old. She then got a job at McDonalds. While working at MacDonald's, her sister persuaded her to earn her nurse's technician's license, which she earned within the year. Upon earning her license she, resigned from MacDonald's and got a job as a nurse's technician at a nursing home.

When Jane B was about 18 years old she met a man that offered to pay her $500 if she would drive a package for him from Tennessee to Atlanta, Georgia. She agreed to the transaction. She had just bought a new car, using benefits paid out to her when she turned 18 from her father's death benefits. She needed money for the maintenance and upkeep of the car. Thus she drove the package to Atlanta for the man, while he followed behind her in his car to make sure that she delivered the package safely to Atlanta. When she got to Atlanta he took the package from her and paid her the agreed upon $500. Jane B realized that she could make fast money that way. When she got back to Tennessee she talked to her friend about the possibility of selling crack cocaine. They decided they needed to build up their clientele. So she and her friend would drive around the neighborhood. They would endeavor to talk to people that looked like possible clientele. According to Jane B they talked or made contact with individuals or "people that looked like crack heads." They would give them their cell phone numbers and tell them to call if they needed any crack or drugs. They established their clientele that way and when they felt that they had built a clientele base sufficient enough for them, they stopped canvassing the neighborhood. They would instead wait for their clients to call them up for drugs. Jane B was still living at her mother's house. Sometimes she would buy drugs from her drug dealer brother, for resale. She had brisk sales of marijuana, cocaine and crack cocaine for about two years. The she got pregnant when she was about 20 years old. She then moved out of her mother's house and moved in with her boyfriend John who had gotten her pregnant. Upon moving in with him, she started selling in partnership with him, though she tried to slow down a bit in deference to her pregnancy. Shortly thereafter her boyfriend was arrested for assault. He spent about four to five months in jail, and while he was in prison Jane B took up his clientele. She also had the baby while he was still in jail. She increased her selling activity during this time. When John got out of jail, they both kept up with their sale of drugs. A few weeks after John was released from, Jane B got a call from a customer. He wanted her to deliver some cocaine to him. John decided to go with Jane B to make the delivery to the customer. So John and Jane B drove in the car with the baby to make the sale. When they got to the venue for the sale they noticed that their customer had a friend with him, but regardless they made the sale. Unbeknownst to them the "friend" was an informant. She and John were arrested for that sale in April of 2004. She gave birth to a second baby sometime in January of 2005. John's charges were dropped and Jane B hired a lawyer to defend her. At the adjudication of her case in April of 2005, her lawyer managed to get 3 years diversion for her. Thus if she was trouble free for 3 years all the charges against her would be dismissed.

Despite the fact that Jane B was on diversion, she went back to selling drugs soon after the adjudication of her case. She had gotten a job as a nurse's technician after her arrest and subsequent release. When her employer found out after about two and a half weeks of her working there that she had been arrested for drug charges, she was fired from her job. She got a letter from her attorney explaining that she was on diversion and that the charges against her were going to be dismissed after three years. They rehired her. But while still working as a nurse's assistant she was also selling drugs on the side. When asked why. She responded that she had to make a living; she was barely making a living as a nurse's technician to take care of her two children. She sold from 2005 up until 2007.

One day on January 9, 2007, Jane B received a call form a regular client of hers. He wanted 7 gm of cocaine and half an ounce of marijuana. Jane B did not have either but she told the customer that she was going to check around to see if she could supply the order for him. She told him that it would cost him $365. He said okay, he just needed her to quickly fulfill the order. He called her just about every 30 minutes thereafter to see if she had managed to supply the order, such that he would come by and pick them up. Jane B said she had a somewhat "wiggling sensation" at the back of her neck at his determined insistence in calling her back every so often to check on the drug order. Nonetheless, she called every supplier she knew, in her quest to find the particular amount of cocaine and marijuana that he had ordered. She finally was able to buy both from one of her long forgotten suppliers. When the customer called again to see if she had filled his order, she responded in the affirmative and they agreed to meet at the Wal-Mart parking lot. Jane B confessed during the research interview, that she shortened his order of cocaine by one gram on the off chance that her customer would not notice that he was shortened on his order. She asked her friend Kim to ride with her to Wal-Mart to make the delivery. When they got to Wal-Mart, she gave him his order, but he only paid her $300 in lieu of the $365 they had both agreed upon. Jane B did not argue with him about the $65 difference because she knew she had shortened his cocaine order by one gram. After selling to him, she parked her car in the Wal-Mart parking lot. She gave Kim the one gram of cocaine she had skimmed off of her customer, and told Kim to hold it for her while she went to Wal-Mart to pick up something from the store. As she walked into Wal-Mart, just as she passed through the automatic doors she heard a voice that said, "Excuse me ma'am." She looked up and saw a man wearing a badge. He said, "Ma'am you are under arrest please put these handcuffs on."

Jane B responded, "Sir you don't understand." He repeated, "Put the handcuffs on." Jane B repeated, "Please sir you don't understand." He said, " I would advise you to put the handcuffs on." So she let him put the handcuffs on her, and as they walked back towards her car she noticed that there were police officers by her car. He took her to her car and her car was searched. They found crack cocaine rocks in her car including the one gram of cocaine that she had skimmed from her customer.[26] She was taken to jail and she posted bail. According to her, her probation officer did not know that she was arrested. When asked how that was possible and how did she manage to pass drug testing. Jane B responded that she was tested only once soon after she got on probation but after that first initial drug testing, her probation officer did not require further testing of her.

In September 2007, she got into a particularly nasty argument with John. John in a fit of anger called her probation officer and informed the probation officer that Jane B had been arrested for sale of illegal drugs. Jane B's probation officer looked up the criminal record and when she found it was true, she violated Jane B. She called Jane B and told her to get herself together and then turn herself in. Jane B took a few days and then turned herself in for the violation of her three-year diversionary program, which was in Davidson County. Her arrest for the sale of cocaine and marijuana at the Wal-Mart parking lot was in Rutherford County. When Jane B went to court in Davidson County for violation of her three year diversionary program, the judge ordered her to attend a 45 day inpatient intensive drug program and he said upon successful completion of the program, he could possibly grant a suspended sentence. Jane B completed the intensive drug program and went to Rutherford County to see if the judge there would allow her to go on probation for her charges there. The judge there sentenced her to eight years at 30% but he also informed her that she needed to serve at least six more months in prison before he would consider suspending her sentence. The judge in Davidson County refused to suspend Jane B's sentence for her charges in Davidson County since she still had to serve time for her Rutherford charges, but he did say that her sentence would be served concurrently with her sentence in Rutherford County. So Jane B was sent to prison to serve at least six months, and she would go back before the Rutherford County judge in September of 2008 to see if he would suspend her sentence. If the judge suspends her sentence then, that would mean that she would be on probation for the remainder of the eight year sentence. If the sentence was not suspended, she would then have to try and shorten her sentence through parole. Jane B was satisfied with the legal services provided by her attorney. She had never been diagnosed with any mental illness.

Prison had been rehabilitative for her, said Jane B. In her opinion, prison was much better than jail. Prison was a deterrent for her because she hates it there and would not want to come back. It was like she was missing out on her life by being in prison. Jane B said that, "When you are in prison, you lose part of your life on the outside and it is a setback on your life." She stated that the pre-release classes offered in prison were okay though not really educational nor

26. It turned out that her customer had turned informant. He was actually an addict that was arrested for possession and since he wanted minimal to no penalty, he agreed to be an informant.

rehabilitative. She said she already knew all that they taught in the classes. She was cognizant of what not to do and what to do. All she had to do was to keep away from drugs. Drugs were the root causes of her incarceration. She had used cocaine, marijuana and ecstasy pills, though she inferred that she did not use drugs like a crack head. When asked if she ever felt remorse about having sold to the crack heads. Jane B responded that she never thought about how crack was affecting the families of the individuals she sold to, till she took drug rehabilitation classes. She attended "New Avenues" 45-day intensive drug program. When asked if she was ever afraid a drug deal would go bad, she responded that she had had a situation whereby a drug deal almost went bad. She remembered meeting a client by an alley and he wanted her to drive down the alley to give him the drugs. After giving him the drugs through her window she asked him for payment of $25. Jane B said that it seemed like he was about to rob her at that particular moment. She elaborated by saying that, he made a movement that looked like he was about to pull out a gun, so she gunned her car and drove off without collecting her payment. That did not deter her though from carrying on with her drug sales, because the money she made from drug sales was very good.

Jane B said that when she gets out, she would focus on taking care of her children, and would go back to design school. She would also move back in with her mother in Nashville and try to stay out of trouble. She was going to try and keep away from drugs. Hopefully these efforts would help keep her from re-offending.

Jane E

Jane E was a Caucasian that said she grew up within a dysfunctional family. She did not know who her father was. Her mother was a homemaker. When she was three years old her mother moved her and her five brothers to the James Casey Housing projects in Nashville, Tennessee. Jane E grew up in the projects with her five brothers. Three of her brothers had been incarcerated for criminal offences; only two of her brothers are without criminal records. Of those two brothers, one was a car salesman and the other worked for Custom Disability, a private company that provides customized equipment and services for individuals with disability. When Jane E was about eight years old her mother married her stepfather who was African American. Her step-father, whom was an alcoholic, had five children that he brought into the marriage with him. Thus there were a total of 11 children in the house when Jane E was growing up.

Jane E's stepfather began to sexually molest her when she was about nine years old. She recalled being jolted awake form her sleep. She woke up to find that her stepfather had his penis inside her vagina. She pushed him off and ran from her bedroom to her mother's bedroom to complain to her mother that her stepfather had forced his penis into her vagina. Jane E said that instead of her mother being angry with her stepfather, she told Jane that she was going to call her sister Ellen to come and pick up Jane E and keep her for a while. Jane E remembered being so hurt and angry at her mother's reaction to the violation that she yelled angrily, "Call Ellen now and have her pick me up now." So her mother called her sister immediately that night. Her mother's sister Ellen came over and picked up Jane E to live with her in Joelton. Ellen was a housewife, and she had four young girls with her husband Joe who was a construction worker. Jane E was more comfortable at their house but she had one major problem with living there. Ellen's husband did not want Jane E attending church services. The following Sunday after she had arrived at their house, Jane E asked Joe if it was possible for him to take her to church. Joe reprimanded her saying that his family did not attend church and that she was never again to mention the desire to attend church while living with them. Subsequently, each time Jane E mentioned the desire to attend church services; her aunt's husband would beat her up. Apart from the church attendance issue with Joe, she rather enjoyed staying with Ellen's family. She stayed there for a few months and then returned back home. Ellen called children's services to report that Jane E's stepfather was abusing her. The Department of Children's services sent a social worker to talk to the family. According to Jane E, her stepfather was put on notice that if he ever abused her again like that he would be prosecuted. Jane E shuttled between her house and Ellen's house.

When Jane E got to her teens she began to date and have sex. At the age of 13 she started dating a 21-year-old man. She got pregnant twice but she miscarried both times. She got pregnant a third time, at the age of 16 and she successfully carried the pregnancy to term and delivered a baby girl at the age of 17 years. Her boyfriend, who was the father of the baby girl, was 22 at the time of the birth of the baby and was already incarcerated for selling drugs. So she broke off with him. Shortly after the baby's birth Jane E got introduced to injecting cocaine. She said that the introduction occurred when she walked in on her youngest brother injecting himself with the drug and she asked him if she could try it. She said she loved the feeling she got after injecting herself and it made her forget everything that was going on in her life. After that experience she started using cocaine regularly. She said she lived for the feeling she got after shooting up. She gave her baby girl to her mother and her stepfather to raise, while she lived the life of an addict. Some friends she met at the local drug place introduced her to prostitution. They informed her that she could make lots of money on Dickerson Road in Nashville Tennessee. Thus at the young age of 17 years she started working as a prostitute on Dickerson road. She was still addicted to intravenous cocaine but then she also started using crack cocaine. One day after she had left a customer, she stopped at a phone booth on Dickerson road to call her brother. While she was on the phone speaking to him, she shot 60 mg of cocaine into herself. She recalled feeling herself going under. She told her brother that she was feeling funny and then passed out. Her brother luckily managed to find the phone booth where she was at and took her to Vanderbilt hospital. Jane E said she was in a coma for about 60 days at Vanderbilt.

After that episode she went through the Vanderbilt rehabilitation program known as VITA (Vanderbilt Institute for the Treatment of Addiction). She was in the outpatient program for two years and she noted that was a wonderful addiction treatment program. Jane E said by the age of 18 she had been diagnosed with heart failure, endocarditis,[27] (which she thought was caused by her regular injection of cocaine) and she had overdosed so many times.

One day, shortly after she had completed the two-year VITA program at Vanderbilt, she was walking into a hotel on Dickerson road about to relapse. She was on her way to score some drugs, so she knew she was about to relapse. As she walked towards the hotel entrance she passed by an African American man that was about to get into his car. He called out to her, "Miss you are too pretty to be working as a prostitute." Jane E turned around and asked him if he was addressing her and he said yes. They struck up a conversation, and he asked her, if it was alright for them to go get some food to eat. Jane E, replied that she would love some food, so he took her out to eat. After dinner he took her back to her family's house and he met her daughter. They started dating. Jane E got arrested a few months after they started to date. She had an outstanding warrant for receiving concealed and stolen goods.[28] She was sentenced to nine months in Coffee County jail. Her new boyfriend James visited her every single visitation day. He was there to pick her up, the day she was released from jail. They made love that night and she got pregnant that night with his baby. When James found out that she was pregnant he proposed and they got married. About a month into her pregnancy she relapsed. She had gone to visit a friend of hers and when she walked into her house she saw her friend injecting cocaine. She wanted some. Henceforth she would get high and not go home for days. Then she would go back home to her husband James' house. This was the pattern that she adhered to all through her pregnancy. She delivered her baby at 30 weeks old. It was a baby girl. The baby weighed in at 1½ pounds and was very sick. When the baby was just a day old, she somehow managed to get herself dressed and left the hospital and her baby to go and get high. She went back home a week later. Her husband James took care of her. That became their usual pattern.

She would go out for days on drug binges and then go home to be taken care of by her James. Occasionally while she was out on her drug binges she would prostitute herself to make money for her addiction. Her baby was about two months old when she got pregnant with the third child. She decided to get herself cleaned up, and she also started working at a restaurant. She somehow managed to stay relatively clean during her third pregnancy. She had the baby successfully. Money was tight because her husband now had to feed and take

---

27. Endocarditis occurs when the inner lining of the heart valve is infected. This infection is usually caused when bacteria from the other parts of the body for example the mouth travel through the blood stream to the heart. .

28. Jane E said she bought a gun and jewelry from an acquaintance she did not really know. Accordingly she was not aware that they were stolen. did not know that the gun and

care of three children (her first child was now living with them). So he started selling crack to make ends meet. He was arrested and sentenced to prison for seven years. Jane E was thus left with two babies and a child to take care of. His mother helped with taking care of the two babies. While her husband was in prison, Jane E met a guy that introduced her to Dilaudid, which is a pain reliever but produces similar effects to morphine. She began selling those. Jane E stated that she was making a nice amount of money selling those. At this time she was over the cocaine and crack addiction and was just totally focused on making money. According to her calculations, she was making about $5,000 to $10,000 a day.

When she was 31 years old she sold to an informant, and was later arrested for selling Dilaudid. She posted bail. While still awaiting her court date, she got arrested again in March of 2001, for again selling Dilaudid. Her bail was about $100,000. She posted bond and was out. According to Jane E, she laid low and desisted from selling any more drugs but she would run little side scams, for instance she would shoplift at Wal-Mart and sell the items on the side. She also gambled, played the numbers and bingo.

She went to court January 2002 and was sentenced to 10 years each for each charge. The charges were to run concurrently. She commenced her prison sentence January 4, 2002. She said it was horrible. She thought she was going to go crazy, since she felt so confined. But she diligently completed 32 months in prison and was released on parole on July 14, 2004. Her husband was released just prior to her release. She got a job at MacDonald's, and worked there for about a year and half. During that period she also had heel spurs surgery. Then she met a female crack dealer named Lily and she started an affair with her. Since she was usually around Lily, and Lily was a crack dealer, Jane E relapsed and started using crack cocaine again. One day, they were at Lily's home and Lily got a call to deliver some crack. She asked Jane E if she wanted to ride with her. Jane E said yes. They drove to the street corner where the client was waiting for his crack. It turned out the client was an informant, and after the drug sale, Lily and Jane E were arrested right there and then. When Jane E got to court with her public defender, the judge said that she had to go back to prison and serve out her sentence since she had violated the terms of her parole. She was brought to Tennessee Prison for Women and she had been at the prison since then. Thus far she had served about two and half years since being back at prison. She went up for parole again and was granted parole. She was slated to be released on September 15, 2008, with about one year of her original sentence left. So upon her release she would be on parole for a year. Jane E said her public defender did not do much for her defense.

Prison had been depressing for her, because of the fact that in prison she was shut off from her family and friends. But at the same time she had gotten to know herself better in prison, and had taken classes that helped her better deal emotionally and psychologically with what she went through her in her young years of life. She now "loves" herself. It took these last two years she spent in prison to sort of make peace with herself. Incarceration was a sad thing for her but at least on the bright side; she could say that she had learnt a lot from incarceration. She did not ever want to come back to prison. This was her second time in prison and according to her it would be her last time in prison. She found out in 2007, while in prison that she had colon cancer. She was treated for the cancer. She had learnt to be spiritual and she was also diagnosed as bi-polar and depressive. She had been taking medications for the two diagnosed conditions.

When she is eventually released from prison, she would endeavor to do all that she can to make sure that she does not re-offend again. She would be spending her time with her grandchildren, her husband and family. She would not associate with her old drug friends anymore.

Jane F

Jane F was a 33-year-old African American woman that grew up in a two parent working class family. She was born in New York City. Her parents had two children together, Jane F and her brother. Her brother was about 14 years older than Jane F. Her father had two other older children from a previous marriage, prior to marrying her mother. The father's other children are at least 20 years older than Jane F, so she was practically raised as an only child. Her brother was a felon; he was convicted of promotion of prostitution and white slavery. He served about 15 to 20 years in prison for those charges, but died in a car accident shortly after his release from prison. The accident occurred while he was involved in a high-speed chase with the police. He had picked up one of his prostitutes, from her street corner, but she informed him that she had not made any money that day. So he had dropped her off. Since her brother was addicted to drugs he needed money to buy drugs. Then he drove to K-Mart and snatched the purse of a woman at K-Mart, and drove off. Coincidentally there happened to be a police cruiser nearby. The policemen in the police cruiser saw the purse snatching occur, and they immediately activated the police car sirens and as they went after him, they radioed for him to stop. He refused to stop. A high-speed chase ensued. He crashed his car during the high speed chase and died instantly.

Jane F noted that all of her immediate family members had abused drugs. Her mother, father, and brother had all abused drugs, alcohol, and ecstasy. In fact her father[29] was a drug dealer and a hustler. Her father and mother split up when Jane F was about seven years old. Her mother then moved from New York to Tennessee after the divorce. Her mother stayed with Jane F's grandparents to help take care of the grandfather who was dying of cancer. So Jane F had to stay with her aunt and the aunt's five older children. Jane F said that she was abused when she was eight years old. One day after school, an older neighbor of

29. Note that father died about 12 years ago from throat cancer and diabetes, when Jane F was 21 years old.

hers who was 12 years old at that time asked her to perform oral sex on him. She did. The boy later on told her peers and they commenced to ridiculing her at school, because of the sexual act that she had performed. Her mother initially worked for a year at a little juke joint club that served alcohol, while taking care of her father (Jane F's grandfather) and visiting Jane F everyday. About a year later when Jane F was about eight years old, her mother got a place at the project and got a job also working as food supervisor at head-start for children. She kept the job for 26 long years, prior to retiring. Her mother shortly thereafter started dating Paul, and when Jane F was 10, her mother moved into Paul's house. Paul's house was located very close to the projects. Her mother thus far had been with Paul for 26 years and had been married to him for the last 12 years of the 26 years, that they have known each other.

When Jane F turned 11, she decided to start babysitting for pocket money. One night she was babysitting for one of the neighbors in the project and she woke up to find the children's uncle, with his face buried between her legs. When she sat up in alarm she noticed that her vagina and thighs were wet. When Jane F got home that day, she told her mother what had happened. Her mother walked her over to the uncle's house and asked him if it was true that he had his head between her daughter's legs. The uncle denied it, and her mother simply took Jane home without challenging the uncle.

When they got home, Jane F's mother told her that she was never to baby-sit anymore. Some months later, when she was about 12 years old, she was in the living room with her stepfather and Jane F said that he rubbed against her breast. She informed her mother of the incident. Her mother asked her stepfather if it was true. He denied it, and Jane F said that her mother believed the stepfather over her. By the time she turned 13, Jane F was very sexually active, and at the onset of her menstruation her mother took her to get birth control pills. Jane F stayed on birth control pills for about six years. She graduated from high school at the age of 18 and got a job working in a fast food restaurant. She then moved out and into a small apartment. All her friends had boyfriends that were drug dealers and they all appeared to Jane F to have a lavish and extravagant lifestyle with money to spare. Thus Jane F wanted to have a drug dealer boyfriend too. She eventually started dating a drug dealer named Mike at the age of 19 and got pregnant soon after they started dating. She delivered a baby daughter at the age of 20. A month after the birth of her baby daughter, Mike was sent to jail to serve a five month sentence. Jane F therefore quit her job at Wendy's to take over his drug business. Mike served his five months in jail and was released, but about a month later he was arrested and incarcerated again for 45 days, on another drug charge. After he came out of incarceration, he was re-arrested and served 10 months for violation of his parole. He was released after serving 10 months and a few years later in 1999 he was sentenced to seven and a half years for another drug charge.[30]

30. Note: While Mike was in and out of penitentiary, Jane F was involved in other relationships, and she delivered two other children by two other different drug dealers. Of the

While Mike was involved with his odyssey through the criminal justice system, Jane F was selling cocaine, crack, and weed while attending different technical institutes. Some of the programs she enrolled in at the technical institutions she attended, included pharmacy technician, bartending, real estate, hair and nail technical programs.

One day, which happened to fall on the 5th of July 2000, Jane F had been smoking marijuana, at home but then suddenly decided to go shopping to buy some underwear. She drove to the mall, and went into Sears. She picked out some underwear, and walked over to one of the counters to pay. According to Jane F, as she took her credit card out of her wallet to pay, it slipped out of her hands and fell to the ground. With the underwear and her purse clutched to her chest, she bent down to pick up the credit card. She was surrounded by Sears security who thought she was trying to stuff the underwear into her purse. They helped her up and took her purse and opened it. They saw about 12 grams of crack in her purse. They held her and called the police. Jane F was arrested and charged for possession of 12 grams of crack. She posted $3,000 bond and was released from jail to await trial. She got a public defender to defend her because she had no proof of income and thus was considered indigent.[31]

After her arrest and subsequent release on bond, Jane F started selling drugs in earnest to earn money to help defray the money spend on bond as well as to make money to help pay for a private lawyer. Though she had been caught once, she still thought she was untouchable. She delivered a baby boy in August, and in October, she decided to have a birthday party for her daughter. She invited one of her friends, namely Glenda, from New York to come down and help her with the birthday party preparations. Glenda came down with her boyfriend Peter. Upon arrival in Tennessee, Glenda told Jane F that she did not have any spending money. She was dependent on Peter for spending money and according to her Peter tended to be stingy with money. Jane F, told Glenda that she could sell drugs to her customers for money. Glenda did and was making enough money such that she did not need to ask Peter for any more. She actually started being assertive whereas in the past she was docile and demure towards him. Apparently the fact that she was making money, made her feel independent.

Some days after their arrival in Tennessee, Peter and Glenda got into an argument. Jane F joined the argument in Glenda's favor, and Peter got extremely angry. He brandished a gun at both of them and told them that he was going to kill them. Jane F ran out of the apartment to the neighbor's apartment. When she

---

two men, one got shot in the head and he is dead, and the other was currently incarcerated for drug offences. So all of the three men that fathered her three children were involved in drugs, with one dead and two incarcerated.

31. Indigent individuals are individuals that are considered too poor to afford an attorney. Because the United States Constitution provides citizens with the right to an attorney regardless of ability to afford one, the state will provide a public defender for a defendant that is too poor to pay for a private attorney.

got to the door of the neighbor, she knocked and when the neighbor Martha, a Caucasian woman came to the door, Jane F asked if she could make a call. Martha let her into the apartment, and according to Jane she suddenly felt the need to urinate, perhaps a delayed reaction from the threat posed by Peter. Martha directed her to the bathroom. Jane F had about five grams of cocaine (about $500 worth), in one of the pockets of her pants. Unbeknownst to her, when she pulled her pants down to urinate, it fell out without her knowledge After using the bathroom she made the call, thanked Martha and went back to her apartment.

There she noticed that the ball of cocaine was no longer in her pant pocket. She searched the apartment, and when she did not find it, she suspected that it must have fallen off while she was in the bathroom in Martha's apartment. She went back to Martha's apartment to look for it, but Martha and her husband had discovered it and had called the police. Evidently Martha had gone to the bathroom to clean it after Jane F had used it. That was when she had discovered the cocaine and told her husband and they had called the police. Jane F was not aware of all that when she went back to the neighbor's apartment and rang the doorbell. They opened the door, and Jane F saw Martha behind her husband holding the piece of cocaine in tissue. They thought Jane F was the police that they had called. Without a word to them, Jane F turned away to go back to her apartment and saw two police coming towards them. They probably recognized her from the description Martha and her husband had provided them, when they made the call. One of the police officers escorted her to the police car, while the other officer went to speak with Martha and her husband. Jane F, said when they got her inside the police car they said, "Are you going to be down on organized crime, or not."[32] Jane F said she was not going to be down on organized crime. She was arrested and taken to jail. She posted bond of $1,300 and was released to await trial.

Jane F once again felt that it was pertinent that she "boosted" sales of drugs such that she could make enough money for her defense. Sometime in 2002 Jane F was parked on the wrong side of the road near her apartment, smoking weed. A police car drove by and cited her for marijuana possession. Her public defender got the charge put on diversion. That meant that if Jane F did not incur any more marijuana charges, within the period of the diversion, her charges would be dismissed. That particular charge was dismissed after 90 days without any more marijuana charges. Towards the later part of 2002, she got pregnant and from then till she delivered her last child in 2003, she stayed clean for the sake of the unborn child in her womb.

Sometime in mid 2004, she appeared in court with her private attorney to defend the drug charges against her. She received 12 years at 30 for the two pending drug charges but her attorney managed to procure probation, outpatient

32. According to Jane F, that meant that the police were asking her if she was going to "snitch' or tell on her suppliers.

rehabilitation and drug court[33] for her in lieu of serving time. She said it was very intensive. For instance Jane F said that out of the 60 people that were in the program with her, only about five graduated. She did not graduate. She was supposed to have graduated from the program in a year, but she attended for about 13 to 15 months without graduating. But she always tested clean. She had to attend five drug classes a week, three or more Narcotics Anonymous meetings in a week and at the same time meet with a probation officer once a week. In addition she was also expected to participate in community service once a week as well as be subjected to three drug screens a week at a cost of $11 to $20 a week per test. Jane F said that from 9 a.m. to 9 p.m. she was away from her apartment fulfilling all the requirements of her drug court and probation, in addition to attending college/technical school while working two jobs. So she did not really see her children that much. She only managed to wake them up for school in the mornings prior to departing and then putting them to bed at night. She was on that grueling schedule for about 15 months. During that period her brother got killed in a police chase in 2004 and her uncle committed suicide that year by jumping off a bridge in Knoxville.

So she was stressed out, grieving while trying to make ends meet and working as well as selling drugs on the side. She was in a child custody dispute with one of her child's father, Alonzo. Shortly after her legal dispute with Alonzo, her drug court officer informed her that she had failed the drug screen.[34] So she went to meet her drug court officer, and she confessed to him that she was selling drugs to make ends meet. She was "violated." Thus on July 20, 2005, she received a four month jail sentence for violation of her probation. She was released December 9, 2005 to a halfway house.[35] She was at the halfway house for about three weeks and was then moved on December 29, 2005. Jane F said that she had complained about vicious racist behavior on the part of her two roommates towards her. Jane F stated that she could not stay any longer at the halfway house because of the rampant vicious racism that was inherent in the house. One of her fellow roommates informed her that she grew up in a racist household and Jane F said that was self evident from the way the roommate acted towards her. She was at the second halfway home from December 29, 2005 up until March 1, 2006. Jane F recounted that at the halfway house they were usually given four weekend passes a month after they had been there for 30 days. That averaged out to a weekend pass per week. She got a courtesy weekend

33. Refer to Chapter 9 which discusses drug courts, specifically the drug court program in Tennessee.

34. Jane said during the interview that she suspected that Alonzo or his mother had reported her to the drug court officer.

35. A half way house is usually a residential place that affords formerly incarcerated offenders a means of gradual integration into society. These offenders usually are serving time and they are released to a halfway house, where they receive counseling, monitoring, feeding and housing. Offenders that are released to halfway houses are expected to have a job while they complete out their sentence in the halfway house.

voucher, which she thought (since it said on the voucher, weekend voucher) meant a whole weekend pass in lieu of one day. So she was out for a two day weekend instead of one day weekend mandated by the house for each pass. Her two day weekend was a violation of the halfway house rules. Thus she was given a homeless paper to look for another house and kicked out of that particular half way house. On March 30, 2006, she was to go pick up her voucher for another halfway house, but she was also scheduled to appear in court that day. She chose to appear for her court date. Part of the proceedings involved her submitting her urine sample for drug testing. The urine sample she submitted in court that day tested positive for cocaine. She was sent to jail for about two months and during that period her urine was retested and came back negative for cocaine. She went back to court on May 18, 2008, to appear before the judge. Her attorney convinced the judge to allow her to go back to intensive street probation, and informed the judge that Jane F was going to live with her mother.[36]

Jane F said that her probation was very intensive. She stayed with her mother and met with her probation officer once a week. In addition they would send a police patrol car over to cruise her house on the weekends, usually after 10 or 11 p.m. Her mother did not appreciate the intrusion and unwanted attention generated by the police car cruising by her house every weekend. So Jane F went back to her probation officer and asked the officer to let her go back to jail to do time such that when she got out she would be put on regular probation in lieu of intensive probation. Her probation officer told her she would consider it. During that week she was supposed to pick up her daughter by 12 noon but her daughter's father John was not there, and she had to wait till he came back with her daughter, which was around 4 p.m., she was supposed to be back home for her probation by 6 p.m. She got into a furious argument with John. She was so mad that when she got home, she somehow managed to get into another argument with her mother. Jane F called her probation officer to let her know that it was after 6 p.m. and that she was leaving the house because she had gotten into a furious argument with her mother. After the call to her probation officer, she stormed out, and then picked up a friend in her car. According to Jane F, she drove with her friend Mary to a gas station. She had about seven grams of crack or $700 worth. She got out to buy a phone card and bubble gum, and gave Mary the crack to hold for her while she went in to the gas station. As she was going back to her car she saw that Mary had left her car to go make a sale. She had sold 0.2gm, about $20 worth of crack to a buyer. Mary got into the car as Jane F was about to drive off, and they stopped at a stop sign. There, the car was surrounded by police. The person Mary had sold the crack cocaine to, while at the gas station had been an informant. Jane F stated that she was still mystified and

36. Street probation, is the slang used for probation, whereby the offender can stay in their home in lieu of jail or prison while being monitored by the probation officer to ensure that the offender abides by the condition or terms of their probation. The length of probation is usually equivalent to the amount of time the offender would have served behind bars.

could not imagine how Mary had managed to dispose of the almost seven grams of crack cocaine left in her possession, prior to the police getting to the car. So when the police searched the car and also searched both women incident to arrest, they did not find anything else. Nonetheless Mary was arrested for the sale and Jane F was arrested for facilitation/manufacturing, which was a class D felony.

She was looking at possibly two to 12 years on top of her prior sentence, but her public defender was able get the felony charge down to simple possession.[37] Since she did not want to fight the charge she agreed to the simple possession charge and got 11 months and 29 days, to be served concurrently with her other sentences. Thus she had been locked up since June 30th 2006, and would be released on parole July 30, 2008. At the time of the interview Jane F had about two weeks left to her parole release date. Upon her release she would have eight years of parole left.

Jane F said that prison had been a humbling experience. She was grateful and blessed, because on the day that she was arrested, she had been planning to buy $400 worth of drugs and then stay out all through the 4th of July weekend till she had made $4,000. She did not care if she lived or died as long as she made the $4,000 that she needed to put a deposit on an apartment as well as get furniture for the apartment, since there was no way she was going to continue living with her mother. So had she not been arrested maybe she would now be dead. She was happy with the representation of her public defender.

In her own words, prison had also been a life changing experience, and she said, "I can now say that the Tennessee Department of Corrections had corrected me." She had seen inmates that have died in prison while serving out their sentences and she definitely did not want to spend the rest of her days in prison. Jane F, indicated that when she used to sell drugs she felt bad about it, but she could not stop because she felt there was no other way for her to make money. Eventually, now, she felt like she was killing people or taking money from their children because they spent their money on drugs in lieu of spending the money on their children. Jane F stated that she did not ever want to be rearrested for drug offences and likewise did not want to ever come back to prison. She noted that upon release she was going to focus on taking care of her children, attending church and working. She really would like to work hard on turning away from the drug business. Upon release, she would probably work at Crystals and Goodwill to make ends meet, but she really would like to be a forensic scientist, or maybe a business owner. She would eventually want to own her own home.

Jane I

37. Note Jane F had nothing in her possession when she was arrested by the police in her car.

Jane I was a 25-year-old African American woman that was raised by her mother and stepfather. Her mother was a nurse and her stepfather was a commercial painter. They were not yet retired from their respective jobs at the time of the research interview. She grew up with a younger brother who was mildly autistic. He worked at odd jobs at places such as Burger king, Kroger etc. Her brother had never been in trouble with the law. Her mother left her biological father when Jane I was five years old, because he was very physically abusive. Her biological father died of cancer of the larynx when Jane I was six years old, but by then her mother was already living with the stepfather. Jane I said she had had a history of sexual abuse, by various different people. According to her, when she was around two or three years old she could remember being touched around her vaginal area by her older cousin, who was three-years older. When she was eight years old she smoked marijuana for the first time. Her family was visiting her uncle, aunt and cousins. Sometime during the visit, Jane I was alone with her older cousins and she joined them in smoking marijuana. She had been smoking marijuana on and off since then, depending on whenever she could get her hands on some. She stated that the older boy she was dating when she was nine years old would sometimes give her some.

At the age of nine years, two neighborhood boys climbed through her bedroom window at night and one of them sodomized her. Jane I said she did not tell her mother about the incident. Later that year at school some boys her age ganged up on her to feel her up and she swung at them with her school backpack. By the age of 11 years she was already sexually active with her boyfriend who was 15 years old.

When Jane I was 12 years old, she had a very good male friend that she used to "hang out" with. One day, he climbed through her bedroom window. Jane I said she woke up to find that he had penetrated her vaginally. She did not scream or yell, nor did she ask him to stop. When asked why she did not scream or yell, she responded that she felt guilty since she was no longer a virgin and perversely she was enjoying it. "It felt good." After the sexual act, Jane I got up from bed and went and knocked on the door of her mother's bedroom. When her mother opened the door, Jane I told her what had happened. When she finished recounting what had transpired, her mother said to her emotionlessly, "Go back to bed." She went back to the bedroom and went to sleep with the boy beside her in bed. The following day her mother drove the boy back home. She never said a word of admonition to the boy.

Jane I got pregnant at the age of 13 years. She delivered the baby at the young age of 14 years. She brought the baby home to her parents' house, but she felt that her mother was constantly telling her how to take care of her baby. She stated that she did not appreciate the fact that her mother usually took issue with the way Jane 1 was taking care of her baby. One day she got into an argument with her mother regarding the appropriateness of Jane I bottle feeding and cereal feeding her baby. The argument got pretty heated. Jane I told her mother that she did not need her telling her how to feed her baby, her mother retorted, "if you don't like it, you may leave my house." So Jane I did. She left the house at the age of 14 with a baby in tow. She moved in with her current boyfriend Dale, a construction worker who was then 18 years old. She got pregnant again at 15 years old, and delivered the baby at the age of 16. Thus by the age of 16 she had two young children in tow. In order to make ends meet Dale in conjunction with his father took on a job out of town in Virginia. He would send money occasionally, back to Jane I. Thus at the young age of 16, Jane I had two little children, was working at Taco bell, and private sitting Alzheimer's patients, while concurrently attending high school. Her school, Franklin High school, then had a free in school childcare program for high school students with babies. The program made it possible for such students, not to drop out of high school. The stress was too much, so she finally dropped out of high school at the age of 17 and took her GED instead.

Jane I said that her mother would not allow her to move to Virginia to be with Dale, because, her mother was afraid she would lose the social security benefits designated for her, if she moved out of town. Her mother was receiving social security benefits for Jane 1, because of the fact that Jane I's biological father was dead. Dale finally broke up with Jane I when it became apparent to him that she was not going to join him in Virginia. A few months later Jane I started dating a 29-year-old woman, Pheng who was enlisted in the U.S. Air Force. She was still 17 years old. She met Pheng, when she took her children to visit Dale's mother. Pheng was at the house of Dale's mother, visiting with her, when Jane 1 arrived with her two children. They struck up a friendship, which later turned into a sexual relationship. Jane I recalled walking into their bathroom one night and seeing Pheng bent over the sink snorting cocaine. She informed Pheng that she could not be with somebody that used cocaine in her home especially considering that her young children were living there too, so she asked Pheng to leave.

After Jane I broke up with Pheng, she started dating, Pheng's former girlfriend, Lisa. They subsequently moved in together. Jane I also walked in on Lisa, snorting cocaine, so she kicked her out too. Jane stated that she did not understand why her lovers would chose cocaine over her and their relationship. She had told them clearly prior to dating them that she was not going to be in a relationship with anybody that was abusing cocaine. She felt that the lure of cocaine must be powerful for them to choose cocaine over her. One night in a fit of curious anger and loneliness (since she was missing Lisa), she called the neighborhood dealer and bought some cocaine from him. She indicated that she wanted to find out for herself what exactly the lure of cocaine was for her former lovers. Lisa kept calling her asking her to forgive her, finally Jane I told Lisa she could come back. Lisa moved back to the apartment, but Jane I never informed Lisa that she was also now using cocaine. Lisa finally figured that fact out, after Jane I turned 18. Jane I had gone into the bathroom to snort cocaine and she came out with remnants of white powder on her nostrils. Instead of getting angry with Jane 1, Lisa[38] decided that they should start selling, to support their habits.

So they both started selling cocaine on the side. They sold for about two years without incident. Then sometime in June of 2002, when Jane I was about 20 years old, Lisa happened to sell cocaine twice to an informant.[39] Jane I was captured on tape during the drug sales. On one of the tapes she was talking about having her hair done, and in another tape she was talking about having birthday parties for her children, while Lisa was selling cocaine to the informant. According to Jane I, both tapes showed that she was not the one making the sales, but because she was there, there was a sealed indictment for her as well as for Lisa. She was arrested in February of 2003 about six months after Lisa had made the cocaine sales. She was charged with two counts of sale and delivery of 0.5 grams or more of cocaine. She was also charged with intent to resell.[40] She posted bail.

Jane I went to court and was sentenced to 8 years at 30. Jane said that despite the fact that the charges against her were thrown out, since she was coerced and was not read her Miranda rights,[41] the judge still decided that she should go on probation for 8 years. She had to go through intensive outpatient treatment at Cumberland Heights. She lost custody of her two daughters to Dale during this process. She and Lisa managed to stay clean for about two years. They each moved back home to stay with their respective parents, during that period. After about two years of staying with her parents, Jane I finally found an rental house and was in the process of moving in to the rental house, when she found out that her mother and stepfather were in the midst of a financial bind. Her mother was arrested for writing fraudulent checks. Her parent's house was foreclosed and they were given 12 days to move out of the house. During the sentencing hearing for her mother,[42] her stepfather had a heart attack right there in court. He was

---

38. Lisa in the meantime was still using cocaine but she had made every effort to keep that fact from Jane I till the day she discovered that Jane I was using. Once it was out in the open they both started using together.

39. Informants are usually drug addicts and or small time sellers that are arrested for buying or selling drug and in return for not being prosecuted or for leniency in prosecution will then serve as decoys in apprehending other drug users and sellers. They usually wear a microphone or mini-camera on their bodies when they make a buy from a drug dealer. The camera records the transaction between the drug dealer and the decoy or the informant. The videotape will be used later as evidence in the prosecution of the individuals so captured on tape.

40. Jane I said she was also charged with intent to resell because, in February of 2003, when the police came to her apartment to arrest her, they saw and seized marijuana scale, cocaine, marijuana and wads of cash.

41. She did not expound on why the necessity for her Miranda rights to be read to her during arrest. Usually Miranda right attaches, when a suspect is interrogated, i.e. questioned with regards to a crime for which that person is the main suspect. It must be noted that if a suspect is arrested by police and simply taken to jail, with no questioning whatsoever by the police, then there is no violation of Miranda rights.

42. Jane I's mother was facing the possibility of a 40 year federal charge.

rushed to the hospital and her mother was sent back to jail to await another sentence hearing. Jane I was in despair. Her stepfather was in hospital, her mother was in jail, she could not pay all the bills and her parent's house was lost to foreclosure. Jane I moved into her rental house. In order to make money to survive on, she then started strip dancing, and prostitution. In her own words, she was "fulfilling the sexual desires of clients, men, women, judges, doctors and lawyers." She also started using and selling drugs. She continued with that particular lifestyle for about six months. By then she was on ecstasy, mushrooms, cocaine and marijuana. She started dating her drug dealer, Rico. She then gave up prostitution, strip dancing etc and instead started selling with Rico at a drug house. Jane I described a drug house as a place where every interested drug dealer would pay a set rate, usually about $35 a day to set up shop, and sell to addicts in Nashville. In return the drug dealers got a safe place to set up shop. The drug house was barricaded, allowing the occupants enough time to discard their merchandise in the event that police was going to raid the drug house.

Jane I found out that she was pregnant after some months of dating Rico. Shortly after that discovery, Jane I and Rico were robbed at gunpoint and Rico got shot. The police arrived at the scene and Rico was arrested. Jane I's probation officer called her to inform her that she had violated probation, so Jane 1 went on the run. She travelled to Virginia to visit her two daughters. She then returned to Tennessee and moved to another county, with a lady named Clara. She had met Clara somehow during the period she was travelling to Virginia. She lived on the run with Clara till April 2005. One fine day in April, 2005, Jane I decided to drive into Nashville to visit her parents, buy more drugs and see Lisa. She knew that one of her car taillights was broken, but she had never gotten around to fixing the broken taillight. When she drove into Nashville she was stopped by a police car for the broken tail light. Jane I said that she knew it was over, when the police car turned on his sirens such that she would pull over. Before pulling over for the police car, she called her mother, to tell her that she was going in to prison. She then pulled her car over to side of the road. When the policeman checked her license and "ran" it through his car computer database, he saw that there was a warrant for her arrest. She was arrested, and taken to the Davidson county jail. She was there for a few days prior to going to court. On her charge for failure to appear in court, in Davidson County, her sentence was the time already served in Davidson Jail. She was then moved to Williamson County where she had a violation of probation charge. She spent four months in jail in Williamson County, and was then moved to Tennessee Prison for Women, where she served six months prior to being sent to Memphis prison for women.

She was at Memphis prison for a year and half before being moved back to Tennessee Prison for Women in Nashville. Jane I, said that she hated Memphis prison. In her opinion, the prison was run in a very "corrupt" manner. There was no respect or focus on the safety of the inmates. Jane I stated that she was raped while in Memphis prison. She never reported it. She preferred the Tennessee women's Prison in Nashville. She was transferred to Women's prison in Nashville, such that she could join Therapeutic Community (TC) program. Therapeutic Community program is a nine to 12 month program for inmates who have less than two years left of their sentences, or inmates that are going to be paroled out, in about a year or two. TC is targeted towards preparing inmates for life outside of prison. The program also helps guide the women through logical processes in decision making vis-à-vis life choice decisions. Jane I was serving the remainder of her sentence at the prison Annex.

The Annex is part of TPFW, but it is for women who have almost completed the requirements of their sentences and are getting ready to be released. Thus it is a low level security area of the Tennessee Prison for Women. The inmates are considered minimum trustees because they have shown that they do not need direct supervision and as such can actually go out and work on work release.

Jane I would go up for parole in September of 2008. If she failed to get paroled in September of 2008, she would be out in about 14 to 18 months when she must have served 30 percent of her eight year sentence. In 14 to 18 months she would have served about 39 months. She said that prison had not been educational at all for her, but her time in prison had been rehabilitative, simply by choice. Her incarceration coupled with going through TC had provided her the opportunity to learn a lot of stuff. It had also provided her the opportunity to reflect on her life and her past behavior. The process had also allowed her to accept accountability for pain caused to her children, to herself, to those directly or indirectly associated with her family and to society. Jane said that she also learnt while in prison and during participation in the TC program that "life is about choices, and it is about being able to make the right choice." She now had the knowledge that she was capable of asking for help if needed. She had become aware of personal boundaries. "I know now that I am a worthy individual". She did not think that she would reoffend again upon release, but the possibility is always there. Jane I indicated that it was also possible for her to die on the streets if she were to decide to continue with the "drug life" upon release. She felt empowered because she thought that there was a good possibility that she could make it upon release without reoffending, but at the same time she was frightened because she was aware that she could reoffend and thus be re-incarcerated. She had no set plans for what she would do to ensure that she did not get re-incarcerated. But she knew one thing for sure, and that was the fact that, "I do not want to come back to prison".

Sally 3

Sally 3 was a 39-year-old Caucasian woman that grew up in a fractured home environment. She was raised by her father, stepfather, mother and stepmother. Thus she did not have a stable home base, since she was moved around between her parents and step parents. Her family was very large and she had 15 siblings all from different mothers. She was the youngest girl of her family. She was first sexually molested by her stepfather when she was only eight years old. The molestation continued until she was 13 years old. She did not tell anyone about the molestation. The molestation ended when she got married at 13 years old. She only completed 10th grade education and dropped out of school after her tenth grade because since she was already married she did not think it was necessary for her to continue with her education. At the age of 24 years old she was diagnosed with bi-polar disorder. She was also diagnosed with being habitually suicidal, chemically off balance, and borderline schizophrenic with homicidal intentions.

Her first arrest was for grand larceny when she was about 17 years old. She had just moved with her husband to Bretteith County, Kentucky and four days after their move, they were stopped by the police for failure to stop at a stoplight. Unfortunately, her husband who was driving had no driver's license and the tags were not registered to the car they were driving. To compound matters, they did not have any car insurance. When the police officer asked if he could search their vehicle, they gave the police officer consent to do so. During the course of the search, the officer found a collection of gold coins valued at over $1,000 that her husband had stolen from her late father. After a series of questions, regarding the gold coins from the police, Sally 3 and her husband Jay were eventually transported to the county jail. They were later moved to a county jail in Lexington, Kentucky. Sally 3 noted that they were in Kentucky for two days where they waived extradition[43] and were thus transported to Sumner County jail in Tennessee.[44] She was at the Sumner County Jail for about four months. During that time her four-month-old son was taken into state custody. At the trial they were ordered to stay out of Sumner County for two years. She had a public defender for this trial and was satisfied with his performance.

During the two years they went back to Kentucky but she and her husband ended up separating for a year. Now that she was on her own her living conditions were bleak and she was living in a house with no electricity or plumbing. She had only one electrical extension cord, and that sole extension cord powered her refrigerator and two lights. Since she had also just gotten back custody of her son and had almost no income coming in, she made the decision to become a prostitute, in order to make enough money to take care of her son and herself.

---

43. Extradition is a criminal justice process whereby a criminal suspect that is in the custody of a county, state or federal government is given over to another county, state or government for trial. Extradition also connotes a process that be used when a criminal has already been convicted, in a county, state or governmental trial and is handed over to another county, state or government to serve out his or her imposed sentence.

44. It is important to mention that Sally 3 grew up in Tennessee so, the theft of the coins must have occurred in Tennessee where her Stepfather used to live. Sally 3 did not expound on the reason for the extradition.

For nine months she lived at that house, while working as a prostitute. She managed to get onto welfare and started receiving food stamps. She eventually moved into a trailer and three months after the move, Jay came back.

Sally 3 felt it would be a good idea to give their marriage another chance at working, so she accepted him back. She got pregnant about a month and half after her Jay came back to her. Unfortunately, her husband became addicted to seven to 14 different pills (opiates) and alcohol. He was also prone to being very abusive to her. The abuse was so bad that during one of his violent outbursts he broke her arm, stabbed her, and cracked her ribs. Sally 3 continued to live with him despite the injuries Jay had inflicted on her. This continued throughout her pregnancy. A few months after her son was born, she became pregnant again with her third child. Her abusive husband was not happy with her third pregnancy, so he kicked her in the stomach sending her into premature labor. She gave birth to a baby daughter. The baby daughter was so premature that she died four hours after she was born. Sally 3 did not press charges against him for the death of their daughter. Despite the fact that Sally 3 was dealing with the pain and grief at the loss of her baby daughter, Jay continued with his constant physical abuse.

Sally 3 finally left in 1989 with her children and went back to Tennessee. Within five months of leaving Jay, she became a very bad alcoholic and gave her parents temporary custody of her children. Shortly after giving her parents temporary custody of her children she had a nervous breakdown, and was institutionalized in a mental hospital for a while. She was only about 20 years old when she was institutionalized. She was at the mental institution for a little over nine months. During that period her husband gained permanent custody of the children. Once she was released from the mental institution she turned to alcohol, cocaine, marijuana, crack, and shooting cocaine. She recalled that shooting cocaine into her veins was hard for her to do herself because she couldn't bear the thought of sticking herself with a needle. So whenever she needed a cocaine fix or injection, she would have a friend or fellow drug addict inject her with the liquid cocaine while she looked away.

When she was about 21 years old she was charged with criminal impersonation, forgery, and assaulting three police officers. She was represented by a public defender for all three charges. The judge sentenced her to three years at 30% for all the three charges. In lieu of prison she was to serve three years of probation for all of the offenses. During the three year probation she went to a rehabilitation center and managed to wean herself off her cocaine addiction. Unfortunately, with two weeks left on her probation, she violated her probation by getting a DUI, assaulting a police officer, and possession of pills in a non-pill bottle. This resulted in her having to serve out all the remainder of her probation in a county jail.

Once her sentence was completed she was back on the streets but she did not stay out of jail for long. A week and a half after she was released from jail, she was sentenced to county jail for nine months on new charges of failure to pay child support. While she was in the county jail she noticed that there were more drugs in jail than on the streets. As such she got high practically every day she was in jail. She noted that she had continuous contact with drugs while in jail. According to her, the dealers were the men (13 of which were trustees) who would sneak marijuana and cigarettes to female prisoners. She claimed that while in jail, she learnt more about how to deal and use drugs instead of being rehabilitated. She also noted that the guards were having sex with female inmates. She stated that she was raped by a male guard while in county jail. After her jail term was over, she was released. She noted that she harbored a deep seated anger against men since she had also been raped by her husband's friends.

Two years after her release from jail she met a woman named Deb who was the first person who truly cared for her and treated her with respect. They spent a lot of time together and Deb was there for her in 1997 when Sally 3 was diagnosed with endometriosis[45] and had a complete hysterectomy. Shortly after her release from the hospital, her girlfriend Deb called Sally 3 to inform her that her two nieces and nephews had died in a horrific car wreck. Sally 3 took the news pretty hard, but Deb was there to comfort her. The two of them remained close friends. They were such good friends that Deb accepted responsibility for a charge of shoplifting, when Sally 3 was stopped at a store on shoplifting suspicion. They had both gone into the store. In reciprocation, when Deb was arrested for stealing a check in order to buy drugs and alcohol, Sally 3 accepted responsibility for the crime, she informed police that she was the one that stole the checks and not Deb. Sally 3 sometimes for safekeeping, would keep Deb's marijuana at her home. At another instance when Deb was charged with criminal impersonation and for shoplifting, Sally 3 confessed to being the culprit, for both charges.

Sally was arrested by police in Franklin, Kentucky for failure to stop at a police stop and for evading arrest. She served 15 days in jail and paid $2,000 in court costs and restitution. Since she also had all the other charges that she had confessed to when covering up for her girlfriend, she was sentenced to and spent two calendar years in Sumner county jail. A public defender represented her and she was satisfied with his performance because he had the sentence reduced to two years day-for-day instead of five years at 30%. While in the county jail her father died, she asked for and was given a four hour furlough to attend his funeral. After the funeral she was taken back to jail.

Once she had completed her jail sentence and gotten out of jail she started drinking and abusing prescription pills and marijuana. She claimed she was OCD[46] about mail fraud and felt compelled to do it whenever she was not taking

45. Endometriosis is a gynecological problem of women, that can occur during their childbearing years. It occurs when the tissue lining the uterus manages to grow outside the uterus. It is not usually a life threatening condition but it can be very painful.

46. Obsessive-compulsive disorder (OCD) is a type of anxiety disorder. It is a potentially disabling illness that traps people in endless cycles of repetitive thoughts and behaviors.

her prescription medication. Eventually she was caught and was charged with 14 counts of mail fraud but her public defender had these charges reduced down to 14 Class 'A' misdemeanors by claiming that her medication was not correctly titrated for her during the period that she had committed those crimes. She asked her public defender to also request for access to rehabilitation program for her, but the judge did not grant it. As a result of the 14 counts she was put on two years of probation. She managed to successfully complete the two years of probation.

Sometime in late 2007, around October 4, 2007 she was sharing a house with her then boyfriend and was on a big drinking binge, when she saw a 15-year-old boy hang himself from a tree a few yards from her window. She called 911 and cut the boy down from the tree. She performed CPR[47] on the boy, but the boy died. The haunting image of the witnessed suicide of the young boy led her to go on worse drinking binges and she started to take 15–20 valiums a day. Then, on October 31, 2007 her boyfriend's brother Gray came over to visit the house and asked her if he could buy ten valium pills for ten dollars. She agreed and sold him 10 valium pills for ten dollars. That night they had a party and a few of them were snorting hydros,[48] taking valium, and drinking liquor. The following morning, she got up and took five valiums washed them down with a beer. Then she went to wake up Gray such that he would take her to cash her disability check. To her surprise she discovered that Gray was cold to the touch. She shook him and when he did not move she realized that he was dead. She called and reported Gray's death to the police. When this was reported she and her boyfriend were taken to the Police Department and were questioned. During her interrogation they finally got her to confess that she had sold him ten dollars worth of Valium. It is important to note that Sally 3 did not recall being read her Miranda Rights. The police let her go without arresting her or charging her with anything. When the autopsy was completed on Gray's body, the coroner concluded that he had died of natural causes due to heart complications and no pills were found in his system; just alcohol.

A few months later she was charged with prescription resale. A warrant was issued for her arrest and she was arrested and taken to jail on March 14th 2008. Sally 3 stated that she was charged by a sealed grand jury indictment. Her case went to court. For her defense she also had a public defender. She indicated that she was satisfied with his performance. She accepted a plea bargain and was sentenced in May 15th, 2008 to four years at 35% because she was a class II offender. She stayed in Sumner County jail until June 20, 2008 when she was

---

Web MD http://www.webmd.com/anxiety-panic/guide/obsessive-compulsive-disorder on (accessed August 15, 2008).

47. Short for *cardiopulmonary resuscitation.* An emergency procedure in which the heart and lungs are made to work by manually compressing the chest overlying the heart and forcing air into the lungs. CPR is used to maintain circulation when the heart stops pumping, usually because of disease, drugs, or trauma. 2005. The American Heritage Science Dictionary. New York: Houghton Mifflin Company.

48. Hydros is the colloquial name for Hydrocodone

transported to the TPFW. In prison she was diagnosed as bi-polar and was on medications for high blood pressure.

The prison experience had been scary for her but she felt that while incarcerated she would be able to get the support and counseling necessary for her rehabilitation. Part of the rehabilitation would occur by virtue of her attendance and participation in some of the programs offered at TPFW. She noted that it was important for her to participate in programs that would help bring closure to a few of the "issues" she had experienced in her life. Prison therapy programs would be helpful in her opinion, specifically "Theo Therapy." Theo Therapy is an inmate program that helps inmates deal with and resolve past conflicts. She was planning on also participating in the educational program offered at the prison. Sally 3 was determined to work hard on earning her GED. She stated that she was very focused on making her stay at TPFW a positive experience although during the process of the research interview she was still in classification and thus was locked up 20 hours a day.

Upon completion of her sentence and subsequent release, she would try to restart her disability checks and would work on improving her relationship with her son. Part of her relationship building with her son would include mutual support on both sides especially with regards to going back to school and earning a degree or certification. Hopefully, when she had developed a satisfactory relationship with her son, it would help her seek an education and help both of them stay on the "right path'. She would like to work with handicapped patients even if only in a volunteer capacity. Sally 3 said she wanted an opportunity to show that she could be something positive to society instead of the outcast she felt she was made out to be. To keep herself away from future incarceration, she planned on rehabilitating herself from alcohol and drugs while in prison. When she rejoined the community she would stay away from past relationships and friendships in order to break the vicious cycle that had kept her getting re-incarcerated.

Her advice to people was that, "If you ever try dope[49] or use dope, just say "no" while you are young and still ahead." She would "hate to see anyone end up in prison and if I am able to help anyone with my story than my purpose would have been served."

Sally 6

Sally 6 was 36-year-old Caucasian female. She was the only child of her parents. She was initially raised in a two parent family, but when she was only eight years old her parents got divorced. After the divorce she had to live with her

49. Dope: an illicit, habit-forming, or narcotic drug; especially : marijuana. Merriam Webster's On Line Dictionary http://www.merriam-ebster.com/dictionary/dope (accessed September 3, 2008).

mother, because her mother had custody of her. But she visited her father during the weekends. Her mother remarried a few months after her divorce. At the young age of ten she was sexually abused by her step-father. The sexual abuse continued for about six more years until she was 16 years old. Sally 6 stated that she felt bad about the abuse. She was subsequently diagnosed with depression as a teenager. She felt that the sexual abuse had everything to do with her diagnosis of depression. A doctor later diagnosed her as being bi-polar and depressive when she was 20 years old. She had been taking depressants, Prozac and Welbutren.

Sally 6 managed to graduate from high school despite the abuse and her diagnosed depression. She had also taken several computing courses at a community college; and was certified to help with income tax preparation. While she was at the prison she filed for divorce. It was her second divorce. She had a 15-year-old, a 12-year-old, and a seven-year-old and all three were staying with her second husband.

Sally 6 had gotten married to her first husband in her twenties. She had three children during the course of her first marriage. Her progression to drug abuse started after the death of her father. She was so heartbroken at the death of her father that she had a nervous breakdown. During the period of her breakdown she started using methamphetamine. It was easy for her to obtain since her first husband George was a manufacturer of methamphetamine. Thus while she was going through the stress of her father's death she started using some of the methamphetamine that George was manufacturing. She ended up getting dependent on the drug and incidentally her first arrest occurred in 2003 for manufacturing methamphetamine.

The police had been suspicious of her husband's activities and had obtained a search warrant to search the house. Upon execution of the search warrant they discovered chemicals in the house that were essential to manufacturing methamphetamine. Sally 6 stated that she was unaware that her husband manufactured the methamphetamine in the house or that there was even a meth lab in the house however, she was arrested and charged for the manufacturing of drugs along with her husband.

Later on during the same year she was arrested again for the same charges. This time she was tried separately from her husband. Initially, she wanted to plead not-guilty but her public defender convinced her to take a plea deal. He informed her that the evidence against her would certainly bring a worse outcome for her if she chose to take it to trial. Sometime in 2004 she took a plea deal and received seven years total sentence; four years for the first charge; and three years for the second charge to be served consecutively at 30%. She was not satisfied with the defense provided by her public defender. She ended up spending two years in a county jail. She then graduated from a 35 day program as an in-patient in a rehabilitation center. For the next four to six months she was on intensified outpatient program. After the completion of the intense outpatient program, the judge released her on probation. Her husband Gray, received seven years as well yet he got out of jail much quicker on probation than she did.

They got divorced soon after he was released from jail and in 2005 she met another man, Bob. He was also serving probation for a drug offence. Prior to meeting Bob, Sally 6 had been doing really well with regards to the conditions of her probation. Shortly after meeting Bob, Sally 6 decided to move in with him. So they moved in together. Both of them were serving their individual probations for their individual drug offences. One day there was a probation check at the house they were living in and their house was searched. The officer found two items used for a methamphetamine lab in a water heater closet. Sally 6 noted during the research interview, that she was aware that Bob was "fooling around a bit with meth" but that she was not aware that he was actually manufacturing it inside the house. This led to her third arrest in March of 2007. The charge was once again for manufacturing meth. At this point Sally 6 emphasized the point that, of the three times she was arrested for manufacturing methamphetamine, she had never manufactured it. She did agree that she was hooked on methamphetamine during the three instances when she was arrested for manufacturing methamphetamine. Sally 6 was taken to county jail. She was provided a public defender but she was not satisfied with her public defender because in Sally 6's opinion, he did not make any effort to help her. She received a six year sentence to be served consecutively with the seven years she had previously. After her sentence was issued by the judge, she was sent from the county jail directly to TPFW.

She was in a drug program at the prison. She noted that the drug program had been very helpful to her. The program was helping her deal with the root of her problems and how to make change in her lifestyle. The drug program had a duration of nine months and at the time of the research interview she had only eight weeks left to complete the program. She indicated that, "prison programs can actually help rehabilitate a person, if the person takes the programs seriously." After serving her time, she planned on moving back with her mother because in her opinion it was a "safe environment." She would also try to get joint custody of her children. She would like to work as a counselor and help young women who had been victims of domestic violence. To keep her from relapsing she was going to get into a dual diagnosis program which would help deal with her mental illness and addiction problems simultaneously. She stated that county jail was not rehabilitative at all, because there was no effort to rehabilitate inmates there. That was because the jail was constantly on lock down and as such had no effective programs. She had learned more in prison than in county jail, so prison incarceration had been a more positive experience than jail incarceration. Upon her release from prison she also had plans to get a job in the office of her uncle's sawmill shop. Her prison incarceration had helped her in some ways. Sally 6 stated that, "the drug programs as well as the other therapeutic prison programs are what prisoners need."

Sally 8

Sally 8 was a 26-year-old Caucasian female. She was raised with an older brother and two younger brothers in single parent family by her mother who was a registered nurse. Her father was not around much because he was incarcerated for drugs. She noted that his absence in her life while she was growing up left a void. The oldest brother was married with two children; her middle brother was a truck driver with two children; and, her youngest brother was killed in a car wreck when he was only sixteen. None of her brothers had ever been arrested for any criminal or drug offence. She dropped out of high school to get married at the age of seventeen. Soon after her marriage she gave birth to a son and a year later gave birth to a daughter. Two years after the birth of her daughter she gave birth to another daughter. But prior to having her third child, she separated from her husband and moved in with her mother.

While still living at her mother's house she met John who was a friend to her brothers. She started dating him. In the meantime her friends introduced her to methamphetamine. She did not initially like the drug. Then one day John happened to be out driving with her 16 -year-old youngest brother, and they were involved in a car accident. The impact killed her youngest brother whom was a passenger in John's car. Her brother's death left Sally 8 very despondent and she turned to using methamphetamine heavily. Then she got pregnant with John's baby and subsequently gave birth to a baby girl. She had serious post partum depression after the birth of her baby girl. She used methamphetamine to try to ward off some of the effects of her post partum depression. She was still living with her mother because she had no job. Desperate for some cash to support herself and her children, she began to work as the "middle man" for methamphetamine deals. As a middle man she would take the order from buyers and fill it with dealers. She "worked" as a methamphetamine middle man for about a year.

One afternoon, she left the house of a drug dealer named Rick, with a delivery of 12 grams of meth. She was driving Rick's car. Unbeknownst to her, the Tennessee Bureau of Investigation (TBI) had Rick's house under surveillance. She had barely left the driveway, when Tennessee Bureau of Investigation agents pulled her car over. The police asked if they could search the car.[50] The police agents had a drug dog with them and they had the dog go twice around the car. The dog hit on the door, so she grudgingly showed the police the bag of meth. The police seized the meth along with some drug pipes and took her picture and a picture of her passenger and then they let her go. A year later she was indicted for that incident.

She still hung around with her boyfriend John. One memorable day the drug task force broke into his house when she happened to be there and discovered a

50. It is important to note that Sally 8 never clarified if she gave them the permission to search the car.

kilo of cocaine in a safe. When they were questioning her she discovered that the drug task force had a warrant out for her arrest for "criminal responsibility" for helping John sell meth. She was sent to Montgomery county jail. She was "bonded" out after a week by a friend of hers. A little while later the lady that paid the bond "wanted off the bond" because Sally 8 would not keep the lady updated on her status. The bond was revoked and she was sent back to jail in Perry County. While there the TBI served her an indictment and she made bond two weeks later.

About two months later, she returned to court for her "criminal responsibility" charges. Unfortunately, the friend who drove her there had some papers and pills in the car. This happened to be the day that there was a random search of cars in the parking lot and the drug dogs found the paraphernalia. The pipe, papers and some pills that they seized got her seven courthouse felonies for having paraphernalia on court grounds. However, she claimed that all the paraphernalia found in her friend's car were not hers and all the charges were eventually dropped except for two which were dropped to misdemeanors. For the misdemeanor charges she got a sentence that was to run concurrently with her other sentences.

Two months later she was at her friend's house with her boyfriend John and the U.S. Marshall arrived to arrest John. At the time they searched the house and also searched her purse. A piece of methamphetamine was found in her purse. This provided probable cause for her arrest and thus, she was arrested and taken to jail. Bond was initially placed at $30,000 but then dropped to $10,000 at which point, John who was now out on bond could afford to pay her bond and get her out. They continued smoking meth together until her court date.

Her court date was about five months after her arrest. Her public defender offered her a plea bargain for the possession of meth charge and intent to sell or deliver meth. She was satisfied with her public defender but she was unaware that she could decline the first offer and try for better terms. Ultimately, she was sentenced to 8 years at 30% for each of the two charges, though the sentences were to be served concurrently. Sally 8 was supposed to turn herself in, on the following Friday to serve 30 days in jail, which was to be followed by three months of rehab. During the course of the week, prior to turning herself in, she began to think and worry about how to deal with her withdrawal symptoms once she turned herself in to begin serving her jail sentence. She was very afraid of the possible effects of complete cold turkey withdrawal from meth, which she knew was going to be the case once she was in jail. She was aware of the fact that in jail she was not going to be gently weaned from her methamphetamine addiction. She was mulling on her two choices, which were, going on the run or turning herself in to begin serving her jail sentence. It took her about two weeks to finally come to the decision that she should turn herself in. Thus she ended up turning herself in a week later than the court stipulated time. Over the two weeks prior to turning herself in, she devised a plan to bring some meth with her to jail. She felt that if she brought some methamphetamine with her to jail, she could gradually titrate down the amount she was using till she finally weaned herself off the drug. Her plan was to wrap black plastic tape over a small amount of methamphetamine until it resembled a tampon, which she would then insert into her vagina. She carried out her plan and inserted the "tamponized" methamphetamine into her vagina. Then she turned herself in, to begin her 30 day jail sentence.

As part of the intake process at the jail she was searched but they did not find the methamphetamine. Her later boasting to someone in the jail got her caught and she was charged with introduction of an illegal substance. Her public defender worked out a deal whereby she would serve out her sentence in prison in lieu of probation if that introduction of illegal substance charge was dropped. She was sent to the prison September 13, 2007.

By July 2008 Sally 8 had graduated from the nine month Therapeutic Community (TC) offered by TPFW. Sally 8 stated that the TC program with its intense behavioral modification focus really did rehabilitate but that depended on whether the person participating in the program wanted to be rehabilitated or not. She felt that she was not addicted to meth anymore and she was eligible for parole in February of 2009. Her plans after being released from prison would include a job as a drug and alcohol counselor. She had earned her GED and she would love to continue with her education and hopefully study psychology in college. She had finally gotten divorced from her husband sometime towards the later part of 2004. She hoped she would be able to rebuild the relationship with her three children upon release from prison. At the time of the interview her children were seven, six and four years old.

Sally 11

Sally 11 was a 40-year-old Caucasian female that was raised in a dysfunctional family home in Texas. She was the only child of her parents. She stated that her parents were not good role models for her. Both her parents had been married and divorced four times each. Her mother and father were also addicts and alcoholics. Because of the dysfunctionality in her family, Sally 11 started using alcohol when she was only still in the kindergarten. It was easy for her to get to the alcohol since her parents were both alcoholics and they did not care that their drinks were usually within reach. She could still remember having her first hangover in kindergarten. It was not too long after that she started to smoke weed. She was only seven years old when she tried some of her parents' marijuana. By the time she was nine years old she was already trying speed. All these drugs were so easy for her to access since both of her parents were heavily using drugs and alcohol. She did not like her home life, she felt life would be better anywhere else than home. So when she was 13 years old she ran away from home with her older friend Alice.

She and Alice had decided to move to California. So they made their way to California, and worked as strippers to make extra cash for their journey. They got to California, but Sally 11's mother was able to track her down to California. Sally 11 had to go back to Texas with her mother. But she ran away from home again shortly after her mother had brought her back from California. But this time Sally 11 went to Dallas, Texas, because she figured her mother would never think to look for her in Texas. Once in Dallas she obtained a false birth certificate that indicated she was 21 years old when she was really 13 years old. She stated that she was able to get away with saying that she was 21 years old since she had always looked older than her age. With this new false birth certificate she was able to establish a bank account and get a valid ID under her alias. When she was 14 years old she met a man who was 28 years old and straight out of the federal penitentiary. They started dating and she moved in with him shortly thereafter. They eventually moved to Florida. After the move to Florida, he started "moving" kilos of coke. With easy access to drugs she started smoking cocaine. By the time she was 16 years old, she had acquired an addiction to cocaine. Sally 11 emphatically noted that cocaine addiction was more of a mental and psychological addiction as opposed to a physical one. Apparently she had tried all other drugs but was only addicted to cocaine. She noted that at one time she had sold acid for two months for her mother's boyfriend, when her mother was working as a cocktail waitress.

Through all the running away from home and dropping out of school coupled with her addiction, Sally 11 was still able to earn her GED. She noted that she managed to also earn a Bachelor's degree in political science and have two children; a boy who was 10 and a daughter who was 13 at the time of the research interview in 2008. She had worked selling insurance with a company in Nashville and was making $40-50,000 plus benefits before going to prison. Both of her children lived with Sally 11's mother while she was in prison. Apparently her mother was no longer an alcoholic but had been diagnosed as being bi-polar.

Sally 11 specifically pointed out that in her life she never broke the law unless she was high or trying to get money for drugs. She recounted the sequence of events that led to her incarceration at TPFW. Her first felony arrest and subsequent indictment was for four counts of felony forgery in 1995. Her public defender did not take the case to trial, but instead worked out a plea bargain for her. For this she received four years at 30% and spent 18 months in a prison until the parole board released her on parole. This first felony was entered using her alias. She pointed out that under her real name she only had misdemeanor offences. Only her mother knew about her alias.

She had become pregnant sometime in 1995 and this prompted her to enter into a drug treatment program in an effort to get clean. She also wanted to attend college and earn her degree. Therefore, after the birth of her daughter in 1995, she enrolled at Austin Peay State University for a few semesters and then transferred to Tennessee State University. She gave birth to a baby boy sometime in 1998. She worked on the weekends while her mother looked after her daughter and son. Since she was planning on going to law school she used her real name to apply to the universities since the felony was under an alias and few states would let you practice law with a felony charge. Upon graduating from Tennessee State University, she was locked in an acrimonious battle with her mother. The battle was over her trying to regain custody of her daughter. Her mother did not want Sally 11 to have custody of her daughter. After two years she was finally able to regain custody of her daughter. She moved to a new residence but made sure she did not inform her mother of her new home address. She did inform her aunt of her new home address. Her aunt invariably passed the information along to her mother. She then got an internship at the state capitol but her mother called her employers and told them, that they were employing a convicted felon with a warrant going back to 1988. Her mother also knew where Sally 11 was living, since she had gotten the information from the aunt. Thus the mother in spite, called the police to inform them that her daughter had violated probation and that Sally 11 also had pending warrants for her arrest. She gave them the entire alias that Sally 11 had used. So she was arrested and incarcerated in Clarksville under her real name. Then the Memphis police were notified about the alias, since she had pending warrants in Memphis based on her alias. It took her three weeks to get a bond hearing and for the police to come from Memphis to arrest her. Her bond sponsor kept her son. Her mother kept her daughter. She did not appear in court to answer to her charges.

Sally 11 stated that after she bonded out of jail, she kept a low profile and from then on till 2005 she was clean. But then she relapsed and got a felony charge for drug possession when she was pulled over while driving. The police stop was a routine one for expired tags but they also found she had a suspended license. They asked to search her car but she had carefully kept the eight ball of cocaine on her body and thus they found no drug evidence. Regardless, they still arrested her for a suspended license, an expired vehicle tag and a failure to appear in court. Once downtown they searched her and found the eight ball. So another indictment for introduction of contraband into a penal facility was added to her charges.

For her defense she had a public defender that never asked for a motion of discovery. She thought this was odd since she had informed him that the police had come to her house and began to search her house without asking and without consent. When the police were through searching her house they told her to sign a paper. However when she asked them what she had just signed they said it was "a consent" to search. She had exclaimed to the police that she did not give them consent, but they just snatched the paper away. Her public defender did not challenge this and she ended up being incarcerated for six months and in her own words, "the public defender was nowhere to be found." When he did finally show up at the jail he asked her if she wanted to go home that day. Sally 11 responded, "What do you have?" and he said eight years of community corrections.

She noted that she was cognizant of what community corrections was all about. In her opinion, community corrections, "is a pure set up." In her experience, community corrections means you have to report once a week to a corrections officer; take a drug test once a week; have a 7 p.m. curfew; a 40-hour a week job; do community service; and, have a landline telephone so they can call you at any time. In addition she stated that on community corrections, your home can be searched at any time. In addition you have to pay fees and fines while on community corrections. But she wanted out of jail desperately, so she agreed to the eight year community corrections. She said she agreed to pay a $4,500 fine, but when she went to court to make the first payment she discovered that her fees and fines had increased to about $20,000. Thus she was unable to pay and because of that, she lost her house and her children. In the end even though she took the eight year deal she ended up violating community corrections because she stopped reporting to the community corrections officer. Sally 11 said that her negligence in not reporting was due to "too much stuff." She also indicated that she knew there was a high chance of her not passing the drug screening, so in her opinion, "it made no sense to report to the community corrections officer."

So when she violated, (because she did not report to the probation officer), she refused to turn herself in. She was free and on the run for a year until she was pulled over again. She was arrested because there was a pending warrant for her arrest for violating community corrections. After appearing in court with her public defender, she was offered a plea deal whereby she would spend a year in county jail, day for day, after which her community corrections would be reinstated for another eight years. She once more informed her public defender that in her opinion community corrections was a set up, because it could enhance a sentence, such that a person could end up serving double their time. Sally 11 emphasized during the interview that this "fact" was stated in fine print.

So she chose to serve prison time in lieu of community corrections. She had been at TPFW since then. Sally 11 specifically noted that county jail was terrible since the inmates were not well fed, thus they stayed perpetually hungry. She indicated that the general consensus of inmates at county jail was that it was better to serve prison time rather than stay in county jail.

Sally 11 felt that incarceration had been rehabilitative as far as she was concerned. She noted that she had been rehabilitated for the first time in her life. She also stated that her incarceration was needed in order to help her get the drugs out of her system as well as get her sanity back. Prior to being incarcerated, she had been diagnosed with depression, but she thought she was doing better with her depression since being at TPFW. She was not planning to reoffend again. Upon completion of her sentence, she would get back in touch with her addiction sponsor. She would go back to attending rehabilitation drug meetings. Hopefully in the future she would start a catering business.

Sally 13

Sally 13 was a 41-year-old African American female who was not raised by her parents. She ended up being raised by both her maternal and paternal grandparents, because her parents were alcoholics and thus could not take care of her. She lived in Tennessee with her mother's parents when she was a baby. She lived with her maternal grandparents until she turned eight years old. When she turned eight she was sent to live with her paternal grandparents in Ohio. She lived in Ohio from age eight to 19 with her paternal grandparents. Sexually, she had suffered a lot of abuse from various family members. The sexual abuse started when she was eight years old. She was molested by a female cousin, and then when she was nine she was molested by a paternal uncle. The uncle sexually molested her till she was 10 years old. The uncle must have moved away, because his sexual molestation stopped by the time Sally 13 was 10 years old. She had a short reprieve from sexual molestation. But that reprieve ended when she was 12 years old and her paternal step-grandfather began to sexually molest her. He molested her from age 12 up until she was 15 years old. Her immediate family was just as bad with regards to abuse. She was abused mentally, sexually, and physically by her father who was an alcoholic.

When she was living in Tennessee with her maternal grandparents, they lived on a farm, but when she moved to Ohio, her paternal grandparents were living in a house on a city block. She attended Catholic school in Ohio and played sports and the piano. Her mother later gave birth to a male sibling to Sally 13. The brother was 36 years old at the time of the research interview and was serving a four year sentence for an arson charge.

Sally 13 had three children; a 17 year old daughter; and an 11 and 12 year old. While Sally 13 was in prison all three were living with the father of the youngest two. She and the father of the younger two had spent 15 years together and he was not a drug user. She had also earned her cosmetology license.

She had moved out of her grandparents' home when she turned 19. She got her own place and started dating. She got pregnant when she was about 23 years old. In 1991, when she was about six months pregnant with her first child, she started using cocaine and marijuana. Sally 13 stated that she turned to cocaine and marijuana when she found out that the father of her baby had gotten someone else pregnant as well. She "explored this outlet" since her best friend was already on cocaine and weed. Unfortunately, this lifestyle impacted her pregnancy, and her baby daughter was born two months prematurely, in addition the baby tested positive for cocaine after birth. She indicated that while pregnant she had sporadically used both drugs but she had used cocaine more frequently than marijuana. Since her baby had tested positive for cocaine the state would not allow her to take the baby home. When she understood that being an addict meant that the state would take her daughter away, she entered a rehabilitation program and stayed in rehabilitation long enough to get her daughter. After the state allowed her to bring her daughter home, she stopped attending the rehabilitation program. When her daughter was five months old Sally 13 left Ohio and moved back to Tennessee. She applied for state assistance and moved into a low income neighborhood where there happened to be a lot of drug users. As a result, she had a relapse with cocaine. Thus she reverted back to her cocaine addiction. Short of cash she tried working as a prostitute but got scared into quitting after she had an encounter with a serial killer who had killed four of her friends.

When her father found out that she had been prostituting herself to support her cocaine habit, he sent her to rehab for 30 days in another county. He also sent for the father of her baby. The baby's father came down to Tennessee, picked up his daughter and took her back with him to Ohio. After 30 days at the drug rehabilitation program, she joined a half way house program, but she took leave of the half way program long enough to travel to Ohio for Christmas. After spending Christmas with her daughter she then returned to the halfway house program, which was a one-year program. She stayed clean for 16 months and then had a relapse again. A week later she went back to the halfway house. During this period she met Kevin, who would later turn out to be the father of her last two children and she was still dating him, despite the fact that she was incarcerated.

Her first drug charge was in 1996 for four counts of resale and delivery of crack cocaine. Like many other drug dealers she had sold cocaine to a wired informant. A public defender worked out a plea deal for her for six years at 30%. But in lieu of prison time she was to be on probation for six years. She violated probation by "getting a shoplifting charge." As a result of the shoplifting, which was a violation of probation, she had to serve nine months in jail. Instead of going to prison, she went straight to community corrections after getting out of jail. Hoping to clean up from drugs, she applied to a halfway house and completed six months of community corrections. She then applied to an outpatient program for one year. The outpatient program was called "Sisters of the Rainbow." She completed the program successfully, got a job and stayed clean for two and a half years but then violated community corrections with a dirty drug screen. She was arrested and sentenced to serve time in prison. She went to prison in 2002 and stayed five months before getting paroled. She completed her parole. Upon completion of her parole she got a job at Wendy's restaurant.

Sometime in 2005-2006 she was arrested again. She had sold cocaine to a wired informant. Interestingly she had sold the cocaine to the informant and they had both gotten high on some of the cocaine. She was charged with resale and delivery. Her public defender was a former District Attorney. He informed her that it was in her best interest to plead guilty because he was told she was eligible for community corrections and a halfway house. But during her court appearance before the judge, her neighbor showed up in court to protest any sentencing leniency on the part of the judge. Sally 13 said as a result she got 15 years at 30%. She spent six months in a county jail and was then transferred to TPFW. She had been at TPFW for about 10 months prior to the research interview.

She had graduated from the Therapeutic Community (TC) program. She was enrolled in Theo Therapy and Celebrate Recovery. Sally 13 noted that the TC program was an awesome program. According to her, she now understood why her neighbor showed up in court to instigate for harsher sentence for her. She would be eligible for parole in January of 2009, but her red date[51] would not be until 2011. She stated that she would rather be in a county jail only because she would be closer to her children. Her family lived very far away so she was not visited very often.

She believed that she had been rehabilitated from cocaine. She noted that she had been clean for two years. She said that prison had been a serious wake-up call. She felt that while in the Criminal Justice system she was treated unfairly. She specified that if she would have paid for a lawyer she would not have been in jail. In 1997 she was diagnosed as HIV positive. Her plans upon release from prison would include going back to a halfway house. She would also like to wean herself back into her family. She hoped to start a beauty shop with her children and likewise get married. She did not want to re-offend again.

Sally 16

Sally 16 was a 26-year-old Caucasian female who came from a dysfunctional family. Her family life was totally fractured. Her parents got divorced when she was four. She had a brother and a sister, but they moved in with her father after the divorce. Her younger sister worked as a receptionist and her brother worked in landscaping.

Her mother was a heavy drug addict. At a very young age she had to take care of her mother whose main preoccupation was injecting enough cocaine to satisfy her cocaine addiction. She dropped out of school at a young age, because she barely had time to make it to school since she was always busy trying to take care of her mother or make ends meet. Sally 16 then lived off and on with her grandmother, in broken down houses, or in their car. Living in this environment exposed her to the sordid world of drug addiction and sales. She was practically taking care of herself by the time she turned nine years old. She learnt the details of how to sell crack and she started selling crack when she was just 12 years old. At this age she was not tempted to use crack, but she enjoyed spending the money she received from each drug sale. As a young teen of 15 years she became pregnant with a son who was now ten years old. By the time she gave birth to her son she already owned her own home and was also supporting her mother from the proceeds of her drug sales. When she was about 16 years old, she got involved with a boyfriend Alex. Alex was very abusive physically and emotionally. He would beat her up at the slightest issue. The abuse got so intense that by the time she turned 17, Sally 16 had started smoking marijuana to help her cope. Sally 16 was currently working towards her GED.

When she was 18 years, she moved into a new house with her son and Alex. Her mother stayed in their former house. After Sally 16 and her son had moved out of the house, her mother entered a drug rehabilitation program. Meanwhile

51. Her red date would be the day her sentence would be served in full.

Sally 16 and Alex both sold drugs together from their new house. Her son's father applied for custody of the son. Somehow it was determined that her home environment was unsafe and the court awarded custody of her son to his father due to the Sally 16's unsafe home environment. After six months of getting full custody, the father of her son, cut off all her access to her so. Thus the only way Sally 16 could see her child was by sneaking over to see him, when the father was not around. On one of the trips she discovered that her five-year-old son was being molested by another older child in the house. He had also lost weight. These events led her to feeling down and generally not caring about anything anymore. In her despondence she got together with some acquaintances and started snorting cocaine. Nine months later her mother returned rehabilitated. When Sally 16 informed her of the molestation of her son, her mother managed to get temporary custody of her son. The fact that her mother now had temporary custody of her son did not stop Sally 16 from her abuse of cocaine. She was by now heavily addicted to cocaine.

Sometime on February 14, 2004, Sally 16 was in a car with a fellow drug addict friend of hers. He was a known drug dealer. Perhaps because they were high on cocaine the driver was driving very slowly. A police car pulled their car over for driving too slow. After asking for the driver's license and registration, the police officer asked both of them to step out of the car. They did. Another police car pulled up. One of the police officers asked the driver if it was alright to search the car. The driver responded, "go ahead." Now that he had consent to search the car the police officer proceeded to search the car. There were no drugs found on the car but they found 28 grams of crack lying in her bag. Sally 16 was arrested and taken to jail. Her bail was set at $50,000. She was charged with attempt to resale over 14 grams. She was assigned a public defender. Her public defender advised her to plead guilty in return for a lesser sentence. She pled guilty and received nine years at 30%. She was at the county jail for one and a half years and was then released on probation. About two weeks after she had been released from jail, she ended up admitting to her probation officer that she was selling drugs. This violated her probation. She was arrested and placed her back in jail for 16 months. After the 16 month jail stint she was released to a drug rehabilitation program, for a 12 month stay. Sally 16 only stayed three months at the drug rehabilitation program prior to absconding. She was on the run for 13 months. Then she happened to have been pulled over in her car for a cracked passenger window. When the police officer affecting the stop checked her license he found out that there was a warrant for her arrest. She was arrested and was sent back to jail until July 28, 2007. She was transferred on July 28, 2007 to TPFW. She would be eligible for parole in November of 2009.

Since being incarcerated at TPFW she had been diagnosed with depression and bi-polar disorder. She was on Remeron[52] but she stopped taking it. She did

---

52. Remeron is a tetracyclic antidepressant. It affects chemicals in the brain that may become unbalanced and cause depression. It is thought to increase the activity of

not like the effects of the drug on her. She stated that incarceration at TPFW had helped with her rehabilitation. According to Sally 16, the programs available at the prison do work. She would like to continue her education either in cosmetology or in an area within the medical field. But she indicated that upon release, it would be of first and foremost importance to find better and legal means of supporting herself. She would exercise her talents and abilities towards that end of getting a job and continuing with her education.

Sally 18

Sally 18 was 47-year-old African American woman. She was raised by both parents in a Baptist home. Neither of her parents were alcoholics or drug users. She was raised with a younger sister. Her younger sister was now a preacher's wife. Her sister had never been in trouble with the law.

As a young girl of 12 years old, Sally 18 she was molested by seven different uncles. The worst sex offender was an uncle who lived next door to her house. He would sometimes break into her room at night, or he would stalk her on her way to and fro from school. It was easy for him to stalk her on school days since she would have to walk past his house to get to and from school. As much as she hated the molestation, she did not tell on him. Instead she would try to hide or fight him off. Sally 18 mentioned that this particular uncle was also raping another cousin and niece who lived in the neighborhood. She did not tell anyone about these incidents until she was 21 years old.

The abuse was affecting her as well as her grades. She finally dropped out of high school when she was in the eleventh grade. She eventually got married when she turned 19 years old. She had four children during the marriage and had six grandchildren. She divorced her husband in 2004.

Her first contact with drugs occurred when she was 32 years old. She had gone to a girlfriend's house such that their children could play together. She was then working as a preschool teacher. When she knocked and entered her friend's house, she saw that her friend and a few other people were smoking crack cocaine. They offered some to her and she tried it. She loved the feeling she got from smoking the crack cocaine, so whenever she had the opportunity she would buy some crack cocaine for her use. As she continued to use the drug she developed an addiction to the drug. She abused the drug so much that she lost 30 pounds during her first month of addiction. Since she was now so addicted to crack cocaine, that she was always totally focused on obtaining more crack. She started stealing to support her habit. Her strategy was to steal from unlocked cars and people she knew. During that period she was also arrested for petty theft off and on. Sometime in 1993 she had gone into a cousin's house and stolen some jewelry. She gave the jewelry to Doug, her boyfriend at that time to sell for her.

---

norepinephrine and serotonin which help elevate mood. Remeron. Drugs.com http://www.drugs.com/remeron.html (accessed September 6, 2008).

Doug sold the jewelry that she had stolen from her cousin's house to a pawn shop. Someone recognized the jeweler and notified her cousin Maude. Maude then went to the police station and reported Sally 18. She informed the police that she wanted to press charges against Sally 18. Thus Sally 18 was charged with theft of property and trespassing. She was assigned a public defender for her court hearing. She said she was satisfied with his defense of her, since he was able to reduce 21 charges of theft to seven theft charges. For the theft charges, she received a six-year sentence. She served two years of the sentence in a county jail and was then released on probation.

In 1996 while on probation, she stopped smoking and stealing. She also gave up her son for adoption. Despite the fact that she was on probation, she actively sold crack cocaine for the period spanning 1996 to 2002. One day, sometime in early to mid 2002, she was driving in her car with two young teenage Caucasian male passengers. They were on their way back from a drug deal. She was pulled over for a speeding violation. Sally 18 recalled that the police officers that had stopped her, walked over to her car and asked for her license and registration. She handed both to the officers. She and her passengers were then asked to step out of the car. As they got out of the car, one of her passengers, a 17-year-old boy, Randy bumped his hip by the side of the car door. He had a bag of cocaine in his pocket. The five gram bag of cocaine inadvertently fell out of his pocket. Upon seeing the dropped crack cocaine, the police officers then searched her car without asking for her permission or consent to do so. Likewise she noted that they did not inform her of the reason for the search of her car.[53] She was arrested and subsequently charged with possession of crack cocaine Schedule II. Her two young Caucasian teenage passengers were allowed to go without being arrested or cited. She was taken to the county jail but was able to make bond the same day. She said she ultimately hired two private attorneys, but that "they were both no good." In her opinion, she was tricked by her lawyers into taking a plea deal. They had informed her that she would only get charged with what she was guilty of. Invariably, she believed that they must have thought that she was guilty. Nonetheless she took their advice and pled guilty. She was sentenced to ten years and was sent to prison in 2004. She was incarcerated until 2006. She was up for parole in 2006 and her parole was granted. Sally 18 believed that the fact that she was diagnosed with breast cancer had a bearing on the parole decision.

Sally 18 violated her parole, when she allowed a male friend Jerry to borrow her truck. He had informed her that he needed to borrow her truck to go pick up some scrap metal that his neighbor had told him he could have. She informed him that she would allow him to borrow her truck on the condition that she rode with him. He agreed. He stopped by her home and they drove together

53. It is important to note that legally the police officers do not need her consent to search her car, when there is probable cause to believe that a crime is being or has been committed. In this instance the bag of cocaine that fell out of Randy's pocket warranted or justified a search of the car.

to his neighbor's yard to pick up the scrap metal that his neighbor had "agreed to let him pick up." However after loading the truck with the scrap metal, as they were leaving, the real owners showed up and claimed that they had not given permission to take the scrap metal. Somehow they got into an argument and the police were called, as Jerry drove away with the scrap metal. Sally 18 said the scrap metal was worth about $64 but the owners claimed that the metal was worth $800, which would make it a felony theft.[54]

The owners were able to get her car licensee number and based on that she was arrested in conjunction with Jerry. She was able to make bond and thus get out of jail. Since she did not let her parole officer know about this incident; he violated her parole when he found out about her arrest. She was arrested again and sent to TPFW in January 2008. She hired three lawyers to beat the violation charges and was awaiting the court date. When she finally goes to court she would then know if she was charged with a misdemeanor theft, or a felony theft charge. If the charge was a misdemeanor theft charge, then according to Sally 18 she would probably be able to avoid longer prison sentence.

Sally 18 noted that she was rehabilitated from crack cocaine. The rehabilitation occurred the first two years she was incarcerated at TPFW. Since then she had been clean for 15 years. She was also a cancer survivor. Both her breasts were removed as part of treatment for her breast cancer. She noted that her breast cancer experience had provided her the opportunity and ability to counsel both inmates and officers with cancer within the prison system. "I am a mother figure here," she said. She would make cards, sing, and minister to women in prison as part of her prison routine. Upon release from prison, she would pursue a pending case in claims court. She had a pending suit against a police captain for running her off the road and damaging her back in Franklin County.

Most importantly she would like to open up a community center for cancer patients. She emphatically declared that her arrests in Franklin County were due to racial profiling. Accordingly, the prison sentences at TPFW indicate that, "blacks get more time than the whites." She stated that in her town people still carry the rebel flag.[55] She was violated for theft of property a day before her claim was to be heard in court against the captain. She was told to turn herself in. Sally 18 believed that she was being incarcerated at TPFW such that she would not get her money from the pending court case. She noted that the police captain, the District Attorney and the judge are all close friends. Sally 18 stated that she did not want to ever be re-incarcerated again and as such she would endeavor to steer clear of breaking the law.

---

54. Under Tennessee law theft of property that is valued at over $500 but less than $1000 is a class E Felony that is punishable by one to six years in prison. On the other hand theft of property that is valued at $500 or less is considered a class A misdemeanor and it is punishable by jail sentence of no more than 11 months and 29 days.

55. The Confederate battle flag, called the "Southern Cross" or the cross of St. Andrew, has been described variously as a proud emblem of Southern heritage and as a shameful reminder of slavery and segregation. http://www.infoplease.com/spot/confederate1.html (accessed September 6, 2008).

Sally 22

Sally 22 was 67-year-old Caucasian that was raised in a two parent household. Her parents were married but they are now deceased. She was raised with a younger sister. She also had a twin sister, but her twin sister died three days after birth. Her father was not addicted to drugs or alcohol. He worked on a railroad and had a generally abusive nature. Her mother was a homemaker but also worked in a factory. Both her parents had worked in factories. When she was five years old, she was raped by her father. He continuously abused her sexually until she was about eight years old. When she was about eight years old, she finally informed her mother that her father was abusing her. After she told her mother about what the father was doing to her, he stopped molesting her. Instead he started molesting her younger sister. He raped and abused her sister. The mother did not divorce the father despite the fact that she was aware that the father had been molesting them.

Sally 22 eventually dropped out of high school, though she later on took some adult education classes and earned her GED. She got married soon after she dropped out of high school, because she wanted to get away from home. She had been married a total of five times. She was married for the fifth time in March of 2007 and was still married. She had three children; a son who was 48 years old and was a minister; another son who was 44 years old, and worked in a factory; and, a daughter who was 50, and was a stay at home mother. She had also held several different jobs. Some of the jobs would include, driving tractor-trailers, working in restaurants and nursing homes.

Her first two arrests for drugs were in 2003 for prescription fraud in Knox and Sevier Counties. She had lived for a while with a friend Lucy in Sevier County. Lucy had stolen a prescription pad, and she had also served time previously for prescription fraud. Lucy made out the prescriptions in Sally 22's name since Sally 22 had Medicaid and Medicare. When Sally 22 took the prescription to the pharmacy to get them filled, the pharmacist had gotten suspicious and had called the police unbeknownst to her. The police arrived and Sally 22 was arrested. She was subsequently charged with prescription fraud. Sally 22 stated that she committed prescription fraud because she was going to sell the pills to make enough money for rent and for food. The court released her on her own recognizance. She was scheduled to appear at a later date to court.

In Knox County she had done the exact same thing with Lucy. Lucy had forged prescriptions for her and she had filled them at a pharmacy in Knox County. She was able to successfully fill three fraudulent prescriptions on three separate occasions before getting caught on her fourth attempt to have some more fraudulent prescriptions filled. She noted that once she obtained the prescriptions her friend Lucy would sell them and then give her some of the money to help pay for rent. She was arrested for that and indicted. She was assigned a public defender. She claimed that her public defender was a liar, because he had informed the court that Sally 22 had never contacted him, with regards to her case, prior to the court appearance. She accepted a plea deal of four years at 30% to be served on probation. This same public defender also never notified her as to who was going to be her probation officer or where she could find him. She had to find that information out on her own.

Her sentence was to run concurrently with her charges in Knox County. Since her plea deal indicated that she would be on probation, Sally 22, as a condition of her probation had to report to her probation officer regularly. But she stated that she had violated her probation for failure to report. She reiterated her claim that her lawyer did not provide her any details regarding her probation, but she believed that she had met with her probation officer as required. Thus in her opinion the probation violation of failure to report must have been a computer error. Nonetheless, she was arrested and sent to TPFW. Sally 22 arrived at TPFW on April 24, 2008.

Sally 22 clarified that she had never been addicted to nor had she ever tried drugs, alcohol, or prescription drugs. She had never been diagnosed with any mental illness, but she was diagnosed with depression in Knox County but had never taken any medication for depression. She had also been diagnosed with hypertension and thyroid condition. She was on medications for high blood pressure and the thyroid condition. She noted that prison had been a positive experience, in that the programs available at TPFW were very helpful. In her opinion the rehabilitative programs and classes could possibly help with an inmate's rehabilitation process.

Her plans after completing her sentence would include finding gainful employment. She would also hopefully stay with her fifth husband and live off of his pension. That would negate the need for her to illegally try to make money.

Chapter 5

Voice from the Inside: The Lure of Big Money

"Since I dropped out of high school at age 17 I have been selling drugs full time to support myself. I grossed between $4,200 to $7,000 a day." Jane D

"'Crack heads'[1] would do anything for crack. I once saw a man who had no more money to buy crack. So the drug dealer told him that if he put his mouth on the exhaust pipe of their car and they started the car, he would give him free crack. The crack addict put his mouth on the exhaust of the car. When the car was turned on, the exhaust pipe of the car blew him backwards with a blast of smoky hot fumes into his mouth." Jane 6

These following interviews depict a range of sustenance and monetary desires or wants that formed the basis for sale of drugs. These run the gamut from the need to have enough cash to survive on, to wanting an extravagant lifestyle with nice cars, to being able to afford expensive illicit drugs. In all of the following cases these inmates had turned to selling drugs in the belief that it was the easiest or only possible way to make the money they needed. Once this flow of cash became established it was hard for the sellers to leave the business until they were arrested and subsequently incarcerated. According to United States Drug Enforcement Agency (DEA) in 2007, the retail selling price for small amounts of pure cocaine was up to $167 per gram and the mid-level wholesale price was $70.[2] The opportunity to make substantial sales and profits seemed to certainly overshadow the risk for many of these respondents. This was especially true when the socioeconomic conditions of the respondents are concerned. Apart from lack of education, the respondents have yet to perfect the finesse that was required when seeking a professional position. Hopefully some of TPFW programs directed at inmate re-entry, such as Exodus, will work on helping eligible respondents develop their life and job seeking skills.

The majority of the respondents have no university or college degrees and some of them have not even received their GED. As such, very few legal employment opportunities will provide them with similar or even comparative amount of "income" they garner from sale of drugs. Usually, attractive and well compensated employment opportunities are few and far between for inner city

---

1. Crack Heads is the street name that connotes individuals that are addicted to crack.
2. U.S. Drug Enforcement Agency, Cocaine Price/Purity Analysis of STRIDE Data http://www.usdoj.gov/dea/concern/cocaine_prices_purity.html (accessed April 9, 2009)

residents, and especially for those without a high school education. Most well paid jobs require some sort of college education, and since the majority of the respondents do not have such education, they do not have optimal options for securing viable legal income options. According to Bruce Jacobs and Richard Wright,

> the lack of legal income options speaks to larger societal patterns in which major changes in the U.S. economy have reduced the number of available good-paying jobs and created an economic underclass with unprecedented levels of unemployment and few options beyond income-generating crime-to exercise.[3]

The following narrations outline the circumstances leading to incarceration of such inmate respondents.

Jane 2

Jane 2 was a 30-year-old African American that was raised in a single parent household. She was raised with her three other brothers by her mother. Her mother worked as a nurse. Jane 2 described her father as a deadbeat father. She noted that she hardly had much contact with him. Jane 2's mother died when she was 11 years old, and she and her three brothers were shuttled in and out of group homes, because her mother's sister who was a drug addict could not take care of all of them. Her maternal grandmother was blind from diabetes and likewise could not keep Jane 2 and her siblings full time. Despite being shuttled from group home to group home, Jane 2 managed to graduate from high school, though she started using marijuana when she was 15 years old. Jane 2 never had a regular job; she depended on selling drugs for personal income. She started with selling marijuana and then her boyfriend introduced her to the use of cocaine and to subsequently selling cocaine. Her boyfriend smoked marijuana regularly and also abused ecstasy pills.

Jane 2 was living in Brentwood (a suburb of Nashville), Tennessee with her boyfriend and was supporting herself by selling drugs. One evening, a potential customer drove up to Jane 2 to buy 36 grams of cocaine. Just as Jane was in the process of handing him the drug, FBI agents surrounded them. It turned out that Jane 2's customer had been under surveillance by the FBI. He was wanted on suspicion for committing federal crimes. The FBI handed Jane 2 over to Tennessee State police. She was able to make bail and she hired a private attorney to defend her. Jane 2 thought her private attorney did a good enough job of representing her in court. They decided on a plea bargain of six years at 35% but in lieu of serving time Jane would go on probation, for six years. Jane 2 was also required to attend a 28-day outpatient drug program, which she completed. After

3. Jacobs, B., R. Wright, Stick-up, street culture, and offender motivation, *Criminology*, 37, 149-174.

completion of her drug treatment program, she reverted back to using marijuana and thus violated the terms of her probation by failing her routine drug test. She therefore had to serve out her six years in prison. After three years in prison, she was granted parole. She was released on parole for the remainder of her three years.

Jane 2 was apparently doing well on parole. She did not fail any of her required drug tests and she was meeting the conditions of her parole. But she would occasionally stop at the house of her boyfriend's father to pick up money that she would put on the "book"[4] for her boyfriend who was incarcerated on drug charges. This was in violation of her parole conditions because her boyfriend's father, Alfred was a drug dealer who also had weapons at the house. Her parole conditions specifically prohibited her from being around guns or drugs. One day Jane 2 stopped by Alfred's house, as usual to pick up some money for her boyfriend, but unknown to her Alfred was being investigated by Tennessee Bureau of Investigation ("TBI") for his part in their current prolonged drug investigation. As Jane 2 was getting ready to open the front door to leave, it was burst open by TBI swat team. She along with Alfred was arrested. The arrest and the fact that she was in a house where there were guns and drugs violated the terms of her parole. She had been out on parole for about two and half years prior to the TBI arrest. Thus she had only about six months left on her parole. Her parole was revoked and during her appearance in court the judge ordered that she serve out the rest of her time in prison. Therefore she was sent to Tennessee Prison for Women.

At TPFW, she was diagnosed as being bi-polar. She had been on medication for bi-polar disorder since then. Jane 2 was due to serve out her sentence at the end of 2008.

Jane 2 described her time in prison as being mostly rehabilitative but also depressing. She valued the structure that was inherent in her prison life. While in prison she was attending prelease classes as well as attending therapeutic counseling classes. She hoped that the insight gleaned from these classes would serve her well upon release. According to Jane 2, prison was depressing because there was no individual freedom to come and go as one pleased. The implication being that an inmate was always at the whim of prison staff.

When asked what steps she would take to ensure that there would be no recidivism on her part once she was released from prison, Jane 2 replied that she would first of all break off with her boyfriend who had been a negative impact on her life (he was a regular and consistent marijuana and ecstasy pill user), she had dated him for about 10 years. She would then hopefully find a job and focus on taking care of her blind grandmother. She also intended to register in a drug

---

4. Putting money on the" book" meant that she would visit her boyfriend in prison and deposit some money at the commissary in his name. Her boyfriend would then use the deposited money in his name to buy things like TV or cigarettes or anything else he wanted from the prison commissary while in prison.

outpatient program, and would try not to associate with her former friends and acquaintances that were still part of the drug culture.

Jane 6

Jane 6 was a 28-year-old African American from a single parent household. She was raised with three other siblings in Nashville. Her mother was a nurse at a mental health institution. She was the middle child of four children. Her older sister graduated from a two-year college and of her two younger brothers; one was 20 years old and he had dropped out of high school. The youngest brother was 16 years old, and he was still attending high school. Jane 6 dropped out of high school at the age of 15, though she later on earned her GED. She elaborated on the reasons for her dropping out of high school. She had borrowed books from her high school. According to her the books were usually shared amongst the students in her class, thus the books made the rounds from student to student. When it was a student's turn to have the books the student would have the opportunity to take the books home. When it got to her turn to borrow the books she took the books and read them in class. At the end of the school day, she decided not to take the books home with her because she did not think that she would need them at home. So she left them in her school locker. The following day when she went back to school the books were gone. She asked her classmates whether they had taken the books, but nobody owned up to having taken the books. Thus she reported the books missing. Her high school informed her that she was not to come back to school till the books were found. So she never went back to school. When asked, what her mother had said about that occurrence, Jane 6 replied that her mother seemed to have given up on discipline after her older sister got pregnant, when Jane 6 was about 13 years old. Since then her mother never seemed to care about enforcing discipline.

Soon after dropping out of high school, Jane 6 left Nashville and stayed with her grandmother in Columbia, Tennessee, for a while. Then in 1997, when she was 17 years old, she moved back to Nashville and started working at United Parcel Service. She worked there for about five months then quit and started working at Captain D's. She worked at Captain D's for about a year, then left the job and ended up getting another job at the stadium. According to her, the jobs never paid her much and she had to live with her mother because she could not afford her own place. In 1999, when she was 19 years old she decided to move back to Columbia where her grandmother lived. There was nothing really for her to do in Columbia Tennessee, there were no jobs, and eventually she gravitated to selling drugs. The lifestyle of drug dealers appealed to her, and all the drug dealers she knew seemed to be doing well. She noted that she was so tired of not having anything. So around early 2000, she started selling crack cocaine. One day, around October 2002, a male customer of hers stopped by her house. He wanted to buy crack cocaine from her. She eventually sold him point four grams (0.4 gm) of crack cocaine for $40, about a month later he stopped by her house again and bought another $40 worth.[5]

On January 4, 2003, she had a knock on her door. It was the police and they had an arrest warrant for her.[6] They knocked and announced themselves, but Jane 6 did not open the door, she was busy flushing down her stack of cocaine in the toilet. The police finally managed to break the door down as she flushed the last of her crack cocaine stack down the toilets. It was not clear if the arrest warrant included a warrant to search her house, but the police officers nonetheless searched her house and one of the police officers said that they found an eight ball[7] floating in her toilet. She was arrested and subsequently indicted.

She had three count indictments against her; two counts for the sale of less than a half a milligram of crack cocaine that she had sold earlier to the informants; and, one count for the eight ball she said was supposedly found in her toilet. Her bail was set at $12,000 and she posted $2,500 bond and was released, while waiting for her court date.

Sometime in June of 2003, while she was still out on bail, she got a call from one of her regular buyers. He wanted her to bring over $200 worth of crack cocaine. He wanted her to meet her at a corner block near downtown. She agreed. So she drove out to the meeting place to sell him the cocaine. When she got there he said he only had $50, so she took his $50 and gave him $50 worth of crack. As she drove away in her car, she turned the music on high; suddenly she heard shouting in the midst of her listening to music. She looked up and saw police officers, coming towards her from the bushes near the road; she also noticed that a police vice car was behind her. She heard one of the police officers yell out, "Get out, get out!" She got out and asked the police officer, why they had stopped her. He told her that she was stopped for music violation. Jane 6 emphatically pointed out during the interview that her windows were up. The police officer then told her that they were going to only issue a ticket for the violation provided they did not find anything in her car. While one of the police officers was writing the ticket, they had the police dog sniff around her car, but the dog did not seem to find anything. She was then informed by the police officers that they had probable cause to search her and the car because they could smell marijuana on her breath. They radioed for a female officer. When the female police officer arrived, she instructed Jane 6 to lean against her car and spread both her legs and arms. The female police officer conducted a thorough pat down search and then had her squat. While she was squatting the female officer felt around her vaginal area and probed deep into her vaginal area through her clothes. The officer felt a substance on her vaginal area, through her clothes. It was crack cocaine. Jane 6 had buried two point five grams of crack

---

5. Unknown to her, this prior customer had turned police informant. He was caught in drug transaction and in order to avoid prosecution he decided to become an informant.

6. There was a secret indictment against her, based on the information provided by the informant she had sold crack cocaine to.

7. An eight ball is the street name for three grams of crack cocaine. One gram has a value of about a $100.

cocaine inside her vagina.[8] She was arrested and she posted bond and was out while awaiting the adjudication of her case.

On December 8, 2003 she was at a party and a fight broke out. The police were called and when they came, they thought she was another African American lady named Kathy, who had an outstanding warrant, thus they arrested her, despite her protestations. When they got to jail and Jane 6 gave them her social security number, they saw that they had made a mistake but then the Sheriff told her that she had an outstanding warrant. At her first appearance in court for that arrest the judge set her bail at $200,000. She was able to post bond.

She hired a private attorney. In court, as part of her plea bargain, she pled guilty to five counts, namely, two counts of possession of three grams of crack cocaine,[9] and three counts of sale of less than a half a gram of crack cocaine.[10] She got sentenced to a total of 14 years for the five different counts, but in lieu of prison time, since she had pled guilty; her attorney had worked out a plea deal with the prosecutor, whereby Jane 6 would serve a year in jail and 14 years probation. So she served a year in Jail from December 2003 to December 2004.

Upon her release from jail, she decided to move back to Nashville to try to find a legitimate job. Jane 6 said she tried so diligently to get a job but she could not find a job because of her felony record. So she moved back to Columbia in January 2005, while still on probation. She went back to selling drugs and from January 2005 through February 2006 she did very well financially. According to her, for the first time in her life she did not have to worry about money. Sometime during the later part of February 2006, she drove with a friend to her cousin's house to visit. When they got there, she ran inside to invite her cousin out for dinner with them. Her phone rang while she was inside the house and it was her friend outside in the car that had called to let her know that the police were outside the house. The police kicked in the door. They had her lay down spread eagled on one of the beds in the house. The police searched the bed where she was spread eagled and found a stash of drugs. In a panic her cousin denied that they were his, he said the stash of drugs were hers and that she had been trying to sell him the guns he had in his pants pockets.[11] This situation violated the terms of her probation and she was sent straight to county jail for 6 months and was then transferred to Tennessee prison for women in October of 2006.

In January 2007, she appeared in court for her alleged possession of the drugs (two grams of crack cocaine) that were found at her cousin's house. Her

---

8. Jane 6 had tucked the two point five grams of crack cocaine into her vagina, prior to driving away, from the meeting with her customer.

9. For each possession charge Jane 6 received an eight year sentence, to be served concurrently.

10. She received three years each for the three counts, two of the counts were to be served concurrently and the third count was to be served consecutively.

11. Just by being there at her cousin's house, Jane 6 had violated the terms of her probation, which prohibited her from being in and around drugs and guns.

attorney tried to negotiate a plea with the prosecutor. The first deal was that she would plead guilty and get a 12 year consecutive sentence. She said no. The prosecutor then indicated that for a guilty plea she would get only eight years consecutive sentence, Jane 6 said no. Then her lawyer came back one final time and told her that the prosecutor would not go for a sentence that was less than six years at 35%. He advised her that it was in her best interest to accept the deal, because if she went to trial and lost she would be looking at 30 years. So she agreed to the plea bargain and pled guilty to the alleged possession of two grams of crack cocaine. Jane 6 was serving a total of 20 years combined for all her indictments, including the initial indictments whereby she was sent on probation. She had been in prison for about two years and she recently went before the parole board but she was turned down. She would go before the board again, possibly sometime in September 2009. She said she thought that her attorney did a somewhat manageable job of representing her.

She noted that she had never been diagnosed with a mental condition. When asked about prison, she indicated that prison had opened her eyes, in that it had been a learning experience. The majority of time in prison, she devoted to thinking, since she had a lot of time on her hands while in prison. She indicated that being incarcerated was a process that can, "make or break a person." She also specified that she was tired of hustling and selling drugs. She would like to do better for herself.

When asked what she would do, upon release after completion of her sentence, to ensure that she would not become a recidivism statistic, Jane 6 noted that she would go back to school. She would like to be a radiologist or X-ray technician if that would still be possible, since she would now have a felony record. She stated that she used to go to work with her mother after she had dropped out of high school. While her mother would be working she would head to the radiologist section. As a child it had always been a marvel for her, to see all the pictures of the human body. She was fascinated with the radiological pictures and she would dearly love the opportunity to work in that field, as an X-ray technician. Jane 6 said that hopefully her time and experience in prison would preclude her from going back to her old life. She noted that since being incarcerated, she had begun to feel bad about the people that were addicted to drugs, but when she used to sell drugs, she did not feel anything for them. She said that crack heads (individuals addicted to crack) would do anything for crack. According to her she once saw a man who had no more money to buy crack. The crack addict approached the crack dealer and his friends to beg for free crack. So the drug dealer told him that if he put his mouth on an exhaust pipe and they started the car, he would give him free crack. The crack addict put his mouth on the exhaust of the car. When the car was turned on, the exhaust pipe of the car blew him backwards with a blast of smoky hot fumes into his mouth. She also recollected seeing a woman agree to squat over a fourth of July fireworks rocket, while it was ignited under her vagina, so as to cop free crack. Crack was not pretty, it was a disease, Jane 6 emphasized. If possible she would not want to go back to that life.

Jane 9

Jane 9 was a 48-year-old African American woman that grew up in a working class Christian family. Her parents were married. Her father was a truck driver and her mother stayed at home as a homemaker. She grew up with four other brothers. A brother died from a car accident and the remaining three brothers had never been in trouble with the law. One brother was a preacher, another was a deacon and the third brother had emphysema and was thus on disability. Jane 9 met her husband when she was 15 years old and in high school. She got pregnant shortly afterwards and dropped out of high school. [12] She soon after married the man that had gotten her pregnant. She gave birth to a baby boy, and a short year later she gave birth to a second child, a baby girl. Her husband did not have a regular stable job, he worked odd jobs. He also used and sold illicit drugs on the side. He introduced Jane 9 to the use and sale of drugs. Thus she had been using and selling crack cocaine on and off for quite a number of years. Her first contact with the criminal justice system occurred when she was arrested for possession and resale of crack cocaine. By the time of this arrest she had been separated from her husband for a while.

According to Jane 9, she got a call from one of her regular customers. She was unaware that her customer had turned state informant to escape prosecution on drug charges. The informant had called her from his cell phone. Unbeknownst to Jane 9 he had made the call while he was with a vice police officer. After the informant had placed the call, he handed the phone over to the vice police officer. So she took the call thinking she was speaking to her customer while in actuality she was speaking to a police officer. The voice on the phone said he wanted a 40, which translated to about 0.5 mg of crack cocaine and cost about $40. Jane 9 told the supposed customer that she was on break getting high and thus was not inclined to make a delivery, but that if the customer wanted he could come over to her house to pick up the 40. A few minutes later she received a knock on her door, she opened the door and her regular customer was standing there. He gave her $40 and she gave him the crack cocaine wrapped in plastic. He took off the plastic and kept the crack in his hand. He said to her, "Mama please throw this in the commode for me." [13] She took the plastic cocaine wrapping from him, turned back and went into her bathroom and flushed down the wrapping. She then went back to her living room door where he was standing and let him out. She locked her door and went to her car. She had just sat down on the driver's seat of the car when she looked up and saw about four

---

12. Jane 9 ended up having two children with her then husband. The children were 31 and 30 years old respectively and they were doing well. They had never been in trouble with the law. The son, the older child, was a restaurant owner and the younger child a daughter worked at Vanderbilt Medical Center.

13. In hindsight Jane 9 believed that he had asked her to throw away the plastic wrapping of the cocaine, so as to buy time for the police officers to get there.

police officers in front of her. They demanded she put her hands in the air and then they forced her to the ground. They searched her car and patted her down but they did not find any drugs.

One of the police officers radioed for a policewoman to come over, and when the policewoman got there, Jane 9, was taken back into her house. The policewoman had her undress and when she did an eight ball fell from her panties. The policewoman utilized the Scott[14] test on a tiny piece of the eight ball right there and it turned blue, indicating that it was indeed crack. [15] The police officers then ran a check on her license to see if there were any outstanding warrants for her. There was none, so she was taken to the justice center, fingerprinted and taken to jail. She was in jail for a total of three months, since she could not make bail. She first went to court sometime in January of 2006, after three weeks of being locked in jail. It was at this junction of the criminal justice process that she first had the opportunity to speak to a public defender. The public defender worked out a plea bargain that day in court of five years at 30 but she told the defender to go back and get six at 30 for her. She explained that in Nashville, if a convicted person received a sentence of five years or less, the person would have to stay at the county jail and serve out their sentence there. But if a person received a sentence of six years or more, they would be eligible to serve out their sentence at Tennessee Prison for Women (TPFW). Thus most female offenders would prefer to receive a sentence of six years or more so as to serve their time at TPFW. County jail was horrible you see, Jane 9 explained. But with a sentence of six years or more, she would get transferred to Tennessee Prison for Women, if she had to serve her sentence, which would be so much better than staying at county jail. She had to stay a total of three months in jail though, so as to finish her paper work, since she could not make bail. Her attorney managed to work out probation for six years for her in lieu of prison time. When she was released from jail, she went on probation in 2006. She somehow managed to keep to the conditions of her probation. By all intents, she was fulfilling the conditions of probation with regards to abstaining from drugs. Jane 9 stated that she went back to crack soon after her release from jail, but she was able to avoid detection because her probation officer never asked for random drug testing. Her probation officer had specific days set for Jane 9 to come in for her drug testing. Jane 9 made sure. She utilized Rediclean[16] to get the drugs out of her system a day prior to her specified scheduled drug test dates.

---

14. Cocaine and its derivatives have customarily been detected by contact with cobalt thiocyanate solution. This solution turns blue when in contact with cocaine. Scott's thiocyanate reagent test is a three-step procedure in which first of all Colbalt thiocyanate solution is added to a small sample of the suspect substance, if it turns blue, hydrochloric acid can then be added which causes the blue precipitating color to disappear and when chloroform is added to the mixture the blue color reappears.

15. Note the validity of the Scott test for field operations have been questioned.

16. Jane 9 said she bought this product from a local store in her neighborhood and utilized it without fail a day or two prior to her scheduled drug test, and she always did fine on her drug test.

But one evening, prior to her scheduled drug test she drove over to the store to buy the Rediclean and the store was closed.[17] She figured she might be able to buy it early the following day, prior to the appointment for the drug test. Early morning the following day she stopped by the store, prior to going in for her drug testing, but the store was still closed. Since she knew she was going to fail her drug test, she moved to a different apartment that day and failed to report to her probation officer. Thus she was aware of the fact that there was probably a warrant for her arrest since she had failed to show up for her scheduled meeting with her probation officer. While at her new residence she reverted back to selling illicit drugs.

One night Jane 9, got a call to deliver a $50 (about a gram) worth of crack. Since Jane 9 knew that there was probably a warrant out for her arrest, she was cognizant of the fact that she had to be extremely careful such that she would not be stopped for a traffic violation. She drove carefully and delivered the crack, on her way home she noticed a police cruiser behind her car so she turned off into a McDonald's Hamburger drive through and acted like she was ordering a burger. When the police cruiser passed, she got back on the road, but a little while later, she noticed the same police cruiser, so she made a beeline for the nearest gas station. She got out of her car and went toward the gas pump as if to pump gas. She noticed that the police cruiser had also pulled into the gas station. The police officer had already "run her car tags." The police officer parked his car, and walked towards Jane 9. He asked her if she had a warrant out for her arrest and Jane 9 replied "No sir." The police officer said to her "Ma'am, would you mind stepping to my car." She entered the back of the police cruiser and saw her picture on the screen in the police car. The police officer said, "Ma'am is that you?" "Looks like me," replied Jane 9. He said "Okay, let me check and make sure it is you." He took her license and called her name in to the police station, such that they could check her name against the list they had for individuals with a pending warrant. It was confirmed that there was a warrant out for her arrest. She was arrested. About two or three weeks later when she went before the judge with her public defender, the judge said she would be allowed to serve out the rest of her sentence at home but with a leg monitor. Do you have anything to say asked the judge? Jane 9 mumbled, "Put my sentence in effect." The judge continued, saying that Jane 9 would also be required to attend a 45-day treatment program. To which Jane 9 interjected "Put my sentence in effect." Are you sure asked the judge? "Yes" replied Jane 9, "Put my sentence in effect." So the Judge put her sentence in effect, and she was sent to Tennessee Prison for Women.[18]

17. She had a specific store where she usually bought her Rediclean prior to her drug testing.

18. When asked why she wanted her sentence in effect in lieu of going home and wearing a leg monitor, Jane 9 responded that, her mind was so messed up by drugs that she did not understand what the judge meant. Did your attorney not say anything to you while

Overall Jane 9 was satisfied with the representation she received from her public defender. She was enrolled in the TC program in prison. She was satisfied enough with prison especially because she was no longer on drugs. She also stated that she appreciated having some structure in her life. She did mention that she was ready to go home. She also stated that she did not ever want to be rearrested again.

When asked what steps she would take to make sure that she did not re-offend in the future. Jane 9 stated that she would go to a halfway house upon release. She would likewise get a job, probably in the restaurant industry. She mentioned that she had left the husband that introduced her to drugs a long time ago, but upon release, she would make sure the separation was official by divorcing him.

She noted that she had never been diagnosed with a mental illness and did not have a problem quitting cold turkey during the time she was in jail. "Drug addiction is a mental thing," stated Jane 9. She did not have chills, cramps or any of the other withdrawal symptoms of quitting cold turkey when she quit in jail. But she indicated that she did not want to ever go back to drugs because she was tired of that life.

Jane D

Jane D was a 30-year-old African American woman that grew up in a two parent household though her parents were not married. They simply lived together. Her mother was a manager at Levis Jean factory and her father was a chef at a restaurant but was also a big time drug dealer. Jane D grew up with two other siblings. Her sister worked for the county government and her brother was a construction worker. None of her siblings had ever been in trouble with the law. Jane D's father used to keep his stash of marijuana at the bottom compartment of their home deep freezer. Jane discovered her father's marijuana stash at the age of 12. She said that one day she was digging at the bottom of the freezer looking for freezer pops. She saw the stash hidden there. She specified that she knew what it was because; she had seen Jackie the 18 year old lady she baby-sat for smoking it. She noted that her father usually locked the freezer but it happened that the day she discovered the stash he had inadvertently forgotten to lock it. She took a handful of the marijuana stash and hid it in her room. She started selling it to Jackie. She would sell her a handful for only $10. One day Jackie's sister came over to the house while she was babysitting. She asked Jane D if she had any for sale and Jane responded that she would get her some. Jackie's sister wanted to know how much Jane D was selling the marijuana for. Jane D told her that she was selling each bag for $10. The sister was shocked. She informed Jane D that $10 per bag was too cheap and that Jane D should

---

you were making the statement she was asked during the research interview? Nope she replied.

charge at least $50 a bag. She became one of Jane D's customers. Then Jane D also started selling to her classmates. When asked if she had introduced marijuana to the school children, she had replied that "all the white children I knew at the school smoked marijuana." Soon after Jane discovered the stash of marijuana, her mother and father had a big fight and her father moved out of the house. Jane D began acting out after her father moved out, and finally in desperation her mother sent her to live with her father. While living with her father, Jane D continued to sell marijuana to the children at her school and she eventually ended up finding a supplier. It was easy for her to find a supplier because her father's involvement in the drug scene around her neighborhood was well known. So the drug suppliers within her neighborhood trusted her enough to supply to her. Her father died suddenly of a heart attack when Jane D was only 13 years old. That was hard on Jane D. She struggled through school while at the same time keeping up with her marijuana sales. She eventually dropped out of high school when she was 17 years old.

After dropping out of high school, she branched out into selling cocaine as well. She indicated that she never smoked or abused any drugs till she dropped out of high school. After dropping out of high school, she started smoking marijuana. She also clarified that she had never worked a regular job in her life, apart from a summer job she once had. She had worked one summer at the YMCA center. Since she dropped out of high school at age 17, she had been selling drugs full time to support herself. She noted that she grossed from $4,200 to $7,000 daily. She got married to her boyfriend at the age of 20. Coincidentally her husband was also a drug dealer.

One day she got a call from one of her clients. He wanted to stop by and purchase 14 grams of cocaine. She agreed to allow him to stop by. He picked up the 14 grams of cocaine and paid her. Unbeknownst to her he had turned informant for the state. She was arrested and charged with sale of 14 grams of cocaine. She was 25 years old. She hired a private attorney and he negotiated four years probation for her. She went on probation and about four years later when her probationary period was almost expired, she failed her urine drug test. It tested positive for marijuana. Prior to being arrested for failing the urine drug test she had gotten into an argument with her boyfriend, and he had called her probation officer. He informed her probation officer that Jane D had illicit drugs on her. The probation officer dispatched the police and they stopped her car en route back to her home. They found 62 pills of Xanax, three ecstasy pills, and 40 pills of hydrocodone. She was arrested and she hired a private attorney to defend her. Her attorney told her that he could work out a plea whereby she would go to rehabilitation for about 18 months plus five extra years of probation. Jane D refused. She told her attorney that would be about 11 years total probation and rehabilitation.[19] She explained to him that she would rather serve her time

19. Jane D explained that the almost four years of probation that she had served. Prior to violating probation, plus the five more years of probation and 18 months of rehabilitation

rather than have extended probation plus rehabilitation. So the judge sentenced her to six years at 35%. She divorced her husband just prior to being sent to prison. She stated that she had caught her husband cheating with another woman. She got to Tennessee Prison for Women in February 2008. She would be eligible for parole August of 2008. Jane D noted that by August of 2008 she would have served a total of about two years, with the time she spent at the county jail included. She had never been diagnosed with any mental disease. She indicated that her attorney did an "OK" job with regards to his representation of her.

According to Jane D, prison had not really been rehabilitative; but could possibly be considered educational. She said that while in prison she had earned her GED. She had also taken drug and substance abuse classes. She appreciated the structure of prison life. She categorically stated that at this point in her life she felt she needed the structure. It would hopefully provide her the opportunity to get herself together as well as get her away from the drug scene. Jane D stated that, "selling drugs is in and of itself an addiction." To paraphrase her, there was an inherent addiction to the fast and albeit dangerous world of drug sales. In her opinion, prison was not a place for people that sell drugs. She expounded by saying, "I think drug sellers will be better served if they were provided rehabilitation and job or work skills." She went on further to clarify that it was important for drug sellers to know that, "they can make money legally and that they have the skills to work at a job that can pay them enough to survive on." She looked forward to getting out of prison and would really like to not re-offend. She did not want to be rearrested, but Jane D noted that she was doubtful that upon release, she would make it out of prison and stay out without re-offending.

She stated that upon release, she would be inundated with attention or calls from her former sellers. They would want to know if she was still interested in sale of illicit drugs. She hoped that she would be able to resist.

Sally 5

Sally 5 was a 26-year-old Caucasian female that was raised in a two parent dysfunctional family. Her mother was an alcoholic and she did not have a good relationship with her father. She was raised with two other siblings. She was the youngest of her siblings. She had one brother and one sister. None of her siblings had ever been in trouble with the law. Her brother was an electrician and her sister was a legal assistant. Sally 5 managed to graduate from high school despite the fact that she left home at the age of 13 years, because her mother was an alcoholic and Sally 5 was not "on good terms" with her father.

---

suggested by her attorney would translate into about 11 years of rehabilitation and probation.

After she left home she lived for a while with a friend of hers. The friend she lived with initially introduced her to selling crack although she did not try using crack when she first started selling it. She started using cocaine when she was 16 years old and had tried Loretabs,[20] marijuana, and had snorted cocaine since then.

Sally 5 met a man and eventually married him. She was married for seven years before the marriage disintegrated. She then separated from her husband for two years. Her marriage produced two children, a seven-year-old boy and a five-year-old daughter who was a special needs child. Her first arrest was sometime in early 2006 for selling drugs, specifically for selling 38 grams of cocaine, seven grams of crack and five pounds of marijuana. She had sold seven grams of crack to an informant. Two days later she sold one ounce of cocaine to a DEA agent.[21] When she was arrested her house was searched and the officers had seized five pounds of marijuana. She stayed one year in jail without bail. Because she fit the indicia for seizure of assets under drug forfeiture, her house, six vehicles, and her home-based business were seized. Her mother in-law, took in her children when she was arrested. Her estranged husband could not take custody of her children because he also had warrants out for his arrest for the sale of marijuana. For nine months she was in jail before going to court. She could not make the high bail that was set for her case. She was assigned a public defender. She felt that the public defender did not defend her, but she agreed to the plea bargain he had suggested because she wanted desperately to avoid waiting longer behind bars. Thus as per the conditions of the plea bargain she received eight years at 35%, but in lieu of prison time she was to serve one year in jail, one year on house arrest, and seven years on probation.

Once Sally 5 got out of jail to start serving her one year of house arrest, she moved in with another man but still left her children with her mother-in-law. Three months after her release from jail, Sally 5 violated the terms of her house arrest by failing a drug test. She noted that she tried to flush the drugs out of her system prior to her test, but she was not successful in doing so. Therefore she failed the drug test. Because she had failed the drug test her house arrest officer had her sent to rehabilitation for 28 days. She completed the 28 days rehabilitation program and thus her house arrest was reinstated. Eight months later she failed another drug test. Upon failing this second drug test she was rearrested and taken to the county jail. She was at the county jail for eight months prior to being transferred to Tennessee Prison for Women. During the research interview, she had just been at TPFW for only two weeks. She was scheduled to go

20. Loretabs are a narcotic drug in pill form. They are a mixture of the opiate hydrocodone and acetaminophen; acetaminophen is the same thing as Tylenol. Wiki Answers http://wiki.answers.com/Q/What_are_Loretabs (accessed August 29, 2008).

21. Drug Enforcement Administration (DEA) is a United States agency that is charged with enforcing the controlled substances laws and regulations of the United States. DEA website Drug Enforcement Administration (DEA) is to enforce the controlled substances laws and regulations of the United States (accessed September 2, 2008).

before the parole board sometime in September of 2008. She noted that she was diagnosed at the county jail for depression.

Sally 5 noted that in her opinion, TPFW offered the possibility of rehabilitation in contrast to county jail which did not offer any programs, degrees or education. Her plans upon release would include trying to find a job. She also stated that it was important for her to work on getting rehabilitated from her cocaine addiction. She felt that having a sustainable job and kicking her cocaine addiction would help reduce the possibility of her recidivism.

Sally 7

Sally 7 was a 34-year-old Caucasian female that was raised by her mother and stepfather. She grew up in the country away from the city. She was the only child of her mother. She never had the opportunity to meet her biological father. She was involved in rodeos. Her mother and stepfather worked a lot. Due to their busy work schedule, she was usually left alone by herself when she was growing up. When she was 17 years old she dropped out of high school but ended up earning her GED that same year. She got married when she was about 19 or 20 years old, but she had been divorced for ten years. She had only one child during the period of her marriage. The child, now a 14-year-old daughter had lived with her father since she was seven years old. Sally 7's ex-husband Rick, worked second and third shift at a plant.

Her first arrest was about 15 years ago for check fraud. She had somehow stolen a book of checks. She then filled them out and forged the signatures on the checks. She was caught when she tried to cash the check. For her defense she hired a private attorney. Her attorney was able to secure a plea deal of four years of community corrections for her. Sally 7 completed the four years of community corrections successfully. But she was depressed since her daughter was now living with Rick. Her depression was further exacerbated by her mother. Her mother kept harping to Sally 7 how unnatural it was that she let her young daughter live with Rick. In her mother's opinion a daughter ought to live with her mother. Eventually Sally 7 turned to drugs as a means of dealing with her depression and feelings of incompetence. Her drug of choice was crack. Although she had smoked marijuana in the past, when she was 15 years old, she never became addicted to marijuana, but after about eight months of smoking crack, she was seriously addicted to it. She recognized that she needed help especially after she lost her job due to her addiction. Therefore, she decided that she needed to get into a rehabilitation program. She called her friend who was a police officer. She informed him that she was a cocaine addict and needed to get into a rehabilitation program. She asked him if he could help her get into a rehabilitation program. He said he would. He checked around and found a rehabilitation center for her. He made the initial calls to the rehabilitation center and he took her to the rehabilitation center. She was in drug rehabilitation for a year.

Upon completion of rehabilitation she initially moved in with her mother while she looked for a job. She found another job, working at a factory.

Shortly after securing the factory job, she moved out of her mother's home, into her own place. She soon started selling drugs to support herself despite the fact that she also had a full time job at a factory. She initially started with selling marijuana, but after about three to four months of selling marijuana, she progressed to selling cocaine. At this point she was living alone, but she started visiting her former friends. These her former friends were the ones that had introduced her to marijuana and alcohol when she was a teenager. Once she started associating with them, all the restraints and tenets of drug rehabilitation were forgotten. She reverted back to smoking marijuana, using drugs and drinking with them again. She was still selling cocaine, but by now, she was also using cocaine. For three years she sold cocaine without incident. Then she invariably sold cocaine to her stepbrother on eight different occasions. She had even sold him cocaine once in a school zone.

Unbeknownst to her, the stepbrother was wearing a wire since he was an informant. He had turned informant to escape prosecution for his drug offences. Based on the wire recording from her stepbrother, she was indicted and arrested on drug charges. She was charged with manufacturing, selling, and possession of Schedule II cocaine and conspiracy. She hired a private attorney but felt that she would have been better off with a public defender. She noted that as soon as the private attorney was paid, he did not make any concerted effort to examine her case in detail. He advised her, that it would be in her best interest to accept a plea bargain. He informed her that if she opted to go through court trial in lieu of plea bargaining, she would be looking at the possibility of getting 30 years, if she was found guilty and convicted. So she took a plea bargain for six years at 30%. Since she had accepted a plea bargain, her attorney was able to get her probation instead of serving time.

Her first three years of probation passed without incident. But during her fourth year of probation, sometime in December of 2006, her doorbell rang. She opened the door to find a couple of police officers at her door. They had a search warrant, so Sally 7 let them into her home. They proceeded to execute the search warrant of her home. Sally 7 waited nervously by the living room as they checked out all the rooms. Finally one of the officers came out of the bathroom with five grams of cocaine in his hands. They seized the cocaine. Sally 7 said she was amazed that they did not arrest her on the spot. After the search of her home the police officers took the seized cocaine with them and left. She did not hear anything else from her probation officer or the police, with regards to the search of her home until June 2007. On that day, the police had come to her home to arrest her on an outstanding indictment and warrant. Prior to the search of her home, Sally 7 had not given her probation officer cause to "violate" her. But with the seizure of the cocaine from her home, she had violated the terms of her probation. She was taken to the county jail. She recalled spending eight months in Davidson county jail before her trial. On January 17, 2008 she was sentenced to serve out her sentence in prison. She was transferred from Davidson county jail to TPFW on January 24, 2008. She had never been officially diagnosed with any mental condition.

Sally 7 stated that prison was very structured. She noted that the structured time in prison had provided her the opportunity for an education. She had been participating in the prison programs. In her opinion, the programs offered at TPFW taught useful living skills that she felt would be beneficial for her when she was eventually released. Within that context prison had been rehabilitative. Upon release, she planned on going to cosmetology school and earning her cosmetology license. That way she could work and earn a respectable living as a cosmetologist. She also specified that her family had been very supportive since her incarceration. Her parents and boyfriend had been visiting her regularly. Likewise, her ex-husband Rick usually would bring her daughter to visit her. Sally 7 said, "I am completely rehabilitated from cocaine and I have no plans on ever going back to my old lifestyle or returning to prison once I am paroled."

Sally 20

Sally 20 was 26-year-old African American. She was raised in a single parent household by her mother. Her father intermittently "popped in and out of her life." Her parents were never married to each other. She was raised with an older sister. Her older sister worked for a collections agency and had two children. Her sister had never been in trouble with the law.

Sally 20 though never married had given birth to two children, a two-year-old daughter and a son who was 18 months old. She gave birth to the 18-month-old son while incarcerated at TPFW. Both of her children lived with her mother.

Sally 20 specified that her path to prison was because she had a money addiction. She was never addicted to the drugs. Though she did smoke marijuana she said that she was never addicted. She stated that, "If your addicted, you can't make money." Sally 20 was not into taking drugs and she indicated that she would do anything for money except sell her body. She dropped out of high school in her teens, because she wanted to get a job. She later on earned her GED. But a short while after dropping out of high school she got a job at Maytag factory. She worked for Maytag in a factory that manufactured car parts. Then around the time she was 18 years old she started dating a young man named Nick. Nick was a drug dealer and so he introduced her to selling drugs. Thus shortly after she had started dating Nick, she began to sell drugs. They sold drugs for a while without incident, but then Sally 20 unwittingly sold drugs to friend of Nick's who happened to be a wired informant. Based on the sale to a wired informant, sometime in 2000, narcotics officers with a warrant came to her home. They then searched the place and found drugs and guns. She and Nick were charged with sale of crack cocaine, and marijuana. They were also charged with possession of firearms.

They were both arrested. She paid her jail bond and was released to await trial. She hired a private attorney to represent both her and Nick. The attorney suggested going for a plea bargain in lieu of a trial. They both consented to a plea bargain. As part of her plea bargain, Sally 20 received six years at 30%. She served one year at the penitentiary and was then paroled after a year. Her parole was supposed to have been completed in 2007, but she ended up violating the conditions of her parole. The violation of her parole occurred, when she was stopped mid 2006, by a police officer for a moving car violation. The police officer walked over to her car and asked for her license and registration. She pulled out her sister's license and handed it over to the police officer. The license did not match the car registration; she eventually admitted to the police officer that she was using her sister's license as her own. The presentation of someone else's identification was known as criminal impersonation. She was invariably charged with "criminal impersonation." This new criminal charge violated the terms of her parole. So she was arrested. She was assigned a public defender to defend her on this new charge. She was visibly pregnant when she went before the judge. As a result of the criminal impersonation charge, she ended up with three more years added to her sentence, regardless of the fact that she was pregnant. She was transferred to TPFW on May 19, 2006. She delivered her baby boy while incarcerated at TPFW. Sally 20 noted that she was not unhappy with her defense by the public defender.

Prison had been rehabilitative in her opinion. She felt that she was now rehabilitated. She stated that the various prison programs were instrumental to her rehabilitation. The prison programs had helped her with learning how to think in a different way. She stated that, "I now understand that there are different alternatives to earning money." The time away from her children had also given her more opportunity to think about the welfare of her children.

She acknowledged that she still had an addiction to money, but she noted that upon completion of her sentence, she would work on getting a good manufacturing job. She would also like to have a second job such that she would be able to augment her income. That way she would not have to resort to illegal sale of drugs to make money for her livelihood. Sally 20 said that selling drugs was all about survival. It was a case where she, "simply felt she shouldn't have to do without." She was raised by a very hardworking mother and she just wanted to make enough money to be comfortable because she felt she deserved better. After her experience with incarceration, she was not planning on getting her income illegally anymore by selling drugs. She fervently hoped that she would not reoffend again, because she did not ever want to be incarcerated again.

Sally 21

Sally 21 was a 65-year-old Caucasian that was raised in a two parent dysfunctional household. She was raised by her mother and stepfather in Michigan. Her mother divorced her biological father after he got back from world war in 1943. Then when Sally 21 was about three years old her mother remarried. Sally 21 stated that she never saw nor had a relationship with her biological father. Her stepfather Paul was an alcoholic and very abusive to both her and her mother. Because of the constant physical abuse, by Paul, Sally 21 was very skittish and withdrawn. When she was about 13 years old, Paul's father gave her sufficient money for her to leave home. He wanted her to go to Tennessee and live with her biological father's parents. Paul's father felt that things would be much better for Sally 21 at her paternal grandparents' home, than living with her mother and stepfather. When she got to Tennessee she found out that her paternal grandparents were not too keen on keeping her. She ended up staying with an aunt, but felt that she wasn't wanted anywhere. A year after she arrived in Tennessee, when she was about 14 years old, her mother and stepfather came into town, to take her back to Michigan. Three or five months after she went back with her mother and step-father to Michigan, she left home again because her stepfather had become very abusive again. She left with a man named Jim whom she had met shortly after returning back to Michigan. He had a traveling yo-yo[22] show. He was very attentive and caring to Sally 21, so she was ready to leave town with him, despite the fact that he was older than she was. When she left this time, she never went back home again. Since she was moving from Michigan to Tennessee, she subsequently dropped out of school. She was working on her GED while incarcerated at TPFW.

Jim was a professional yo-yo exhibitor and Sally 21 said she left with him because he was the first person to really care for her. At the time she was about 15 years old and he was 21. They got a fake marriage license so that he could take her over state lines. She traveled with him when he did his shows but they settled in Florida. They lived together for about two years. She got pregnant just a few months after meeting him. When she gave birth to the baby, it turned out that the baby was stillborn. She was about 16 years old when she delivered the stillborn baby. After that tragedy, her relationship with Jim sort of spiraled downwards. She eventually left Jim after she met another man named Tom. Sally 21 moved in with Tom when she was about 17 years old. She explained that she could not stay in one place for too long. She married Tom. They ended up being married for a total of 12 years.

For a while after her marriage to Tom, she worked as a live in nanny for a family, and would go home on the weekends. During her marriage to Tom she gave birth to a son and later on had a baby daughter. Her son was 47 and worked on cargo ships. Her son was a habitual drinker and he had had several DUI charges. Her daughter was 45 and works odd jobs or "strike jobs" which meant that sometimes she worked out of state. Also during her marriage to Tom, she worked at different factories and plants. She then joined a Church of God,

---

22. The yo-yo is a toy consisting of two equally sized and weighted disks of plastic, wood, or metal, connected with an axle, with a string tied around it. Wikipedia Yo-yo http://en.wikipedia.org/wiki/Yo-yo (accessed on September 7, 2008).

whereby she started attending church services regularly. She eventually divorced Tom after 12 years of marriage. Three years later, she met another man Cory and married him. Three years later her marriage to Cory hit the rocks. So she got divorced again. She was about 36 years old at this point.

Sally 21 started drinking socially after her marriage to Cory ended, although she emphasized that she was not an alcoholic. At this point she also started smoking marijuana, but she would only smoke occasionally. She never used marijuana during the week because she had to work. Sometime in 1995 she got into a very bad car accident. She was seriously hurt and had to have ten surgeries on her leg. During this time she started taking painkillers and developed an addiction to her legitimate prescriptions for Loretabs and Xanax. She was able to financially maintain her addiction to Loretabs and Xanax, for more than 10 years. But, in 2006 she was going through some financial trouble and thus could not afford to maintain her addiction any more. Thus she started to sell drugs. Prior to 2006, she had never sold drugs and she had always worked "honestly" for her money.

She planned to earn some extra cash by selling a few pills to her cousin. She sold 10 pills to him. He came back on a second occasion and informed her that he needed to buy more pills from her. She sold eight more pills to him. The cousin, whom she found out later, was a confidential informant, had approached her while "wired" and claimed that he was on the same prescriptions as she was. He had told her that he needed some pills immediately while he waiting for his prescription. Based on what he had told her, she sold him some of her pills, since she needed the money. She was indicted, but she was not arrested because she had a heart attack a few days prior to being served with a warrant. Nonetheless she was charged with four felonies including TennCare fraud.

She was assigned a public defender. Her public defender encouraged her to accept a plea bargain. So Sally 21 accepted a plea deal. She was not happy with her public defender because she felt he could have done more to reduce her sentence. Nonetheless she took a plea deal and got three years probation in lieu of incarceration and a $4,500 fine however, one year later she violated probation, and was arrested.

Note; that at this point the inmate decided she did not want to continue with the interview and left. It was not possible to finish the interview with her.

Sally 23

Sally 23 was an African American woman in her early thirties. Sally 23 was not married and she did not have any children. Sally 23 was raised with a brother and a sister in a single parent household by her mother. She also had another brother but he was living with her father, by the time Sally 23 was a little girl. Her mother divorced her father when she was only 18 months old. So Sally 23 had no recollections of living with her father as a child. Her mother was an office assistant to the Kidney foundation at Vanderbilt for 20 years. Sally 23 noted that all of the women on her mother's side of the family work at Vanderbilt. Her mother remarried when Sally 23 was very young, but then divorced when Sally 23 was only eight years old. Her older brother was involved in a car accident when he was 12 years old. The accident was very bad and her brother was very seriously injured, he had hit his head during the accident which led to extensive brain damage. He was at the hospital for a long period of time. He eventually died as a result of the brain injury. Sally 23 started selling drugs around the period following her brother's accident. She noted that her mother was constantly away from the house, because she was usually at the hospital with her injured brother. During that period she was also exposed to marijuana and painkillers by her sister. Sally 23 said she tried both but never formed an addiction to either the painkillers or the marijuana. Her sister also taught her how to sell drugs and since then she had been living a double life of law abiding citizen and drug dealer. She graduated from high school when she was 16 years old and then moved to Florida to live with her father. Her father was a car salesperson. He had been in prison for ten years on an armed robbery charge. He had two brothers. One of his brothers was a preacher and the other worked for the CIA.[23]

After moving in with her father she soon discovered that he was a large scale drug dealer. He was moving large amounts of cocaine and marijuana from Jamaica to Florida. She was initially unaware of this at first. She originally thought that his income came exclusively from his job as a salesman since he was the top salesman in the company. She had decided after living with her father for a while to return to Tennessee to live with her mother and sister. It was during this period of time that she discovered (ultimately from her mother and sister) that her father was dealing in drugs on a large scale. Sally 23 also found out at this point that her sister was very heavily involved in drug trafficking as well. Her other brother lived in Florida as well and she likewise found out that

23. The CIA is an independent (government) agency responsible for providing national security intelligence to senior US policymakers. CIA Website https://www.cia.gov/about-cia/todays-cia/index.html (accessed September 7, 2008).

he helped her father traffic drugs. He had spent two months in a Jamaican jail on drug charges. Subsequently, after Sally 23's return to Tennessee, she met a man who was a drug dealer. They started dating and she began selling drugs with him. Her sister happened to be one of her clients. Her sister was very addicted to drugs. Her sister eventually committed suicide when she was only 26 years old. She had shot herself in the head. The tragedy of her sister's suicide when Sally 23 was 20 years old was a turning point in her life.

Sally 23 clarified that she had a money addiction. She noted during the interview that her addiction was never a drug addiction; instead it was a money addiction. Sale of cocaine turned out to be a very profitable enterprise for her. From cocaine sale proceeds, she bought two separate houses. One of the houses she lived in. It was located in a very wealthy neighborhood. The second house was in the projects. She utilized the house in the projects as a base for drug sales. As a matter of policy she was determined not to have drugs in her house that was located in the wealthy neighborhood. Her neighbors, who were attorneys and doctors, had no idea about her double life. She had two sets of friends in each neighborhood and each set was oblivious to the other. They were on two different sides of town.

Her first arrest occurred when she was 23 years old. She had picked up a friend Cindy who was a prostitute as well as a known drug user. Sally 23 said that her biggest mistake was taking Cindy to her normal home and not her drug home. She had just wanted to help her out and get her back on her feet. At this point her income was based solely on her drug sales as well as from sales from an escort service that she had acquired from a "madam." The "madam" was so indebted to Sally 23 that she had left her brothel to her, as repayment for the debt she owned Sally 23.

Sally 23 stated that Cindy "set her up." Cindy had introduced her to an "ex-boyfriend" who in reality was an undercover officer. Sally 23 ended up selling drugs twice to the ex-boyfriend. She was subsequently indicted, arrested and charged with two counts of possession for resale.

She was assigned a public defender. Her public defender encouraged her to accept a plea bargain. She was happy with the defense mounted by her public defender. She took a plea deal and received three years of community corrections. But she never reported to her community corrections officer and thus she was "violated" for not satisfying the conditions of her community corrections. When she went back to court regarding the violation of her probation, her community corrections sentence was doubled. She now had six years of community corrections and was sent to Johnson City to a work camp. Every day she worked at the work camp, would invariably deduct an additional day from her sentence. She finished her community corrections successfully by the time she was 30. She then worked for a real estate company which was a multi-million dollar company. She was still selling cocaine, "now and then." She noted that at that point most of her clients were wealthy. She also bred pure breed Rottweilers.

She then moved to Dixon County but soon after decided to move to Nashville. Thus she moved to Nashville a few months after moving to Dixon County.

She made a pact with herself after moving to Nashville. Her deal was that she would sell cocaine again and would stop once she reached her goal of $40,000. The day she reached her cocaine sale goal, she went to her bank and withdrew the money and took the money to her hotel room. That day she was set up by a friend. She had some cocaine left over but since she had reached her sale goal she was determined not to sell any more. So she decided to just give the remnant away. She had informed her friend that she was going to give her the rest of the cocaine. She drove to meet the friend to give her the rest of the cocaine.

The police were waiting for her and as soon as the transaction was completed she was arrested. The police seized 30 grams of cocaine, 20 grams of crack, $2,000 in cash, and a pistol from her. She was taken to jail. She hired a private attorney whom she said represented her well. He had previously helped her with a criminal charge she had of selling 14 grams of crack to a confidential informant. Some of her paperwork had "gotten lost" during that process so her attorney was able to get her eight years of probation instead of 12 years in prison. For this court date she was charged with possession of a weapon and manufacturing for wholesale. She was given 12 years to be served concurrently with her previous eight year sentence. At the time of the research interview, she had been in prison for two years but would be able to make parole around February of 2009. She indicated that everything she did prior to being incarcerated was for the money. Incarceration had made her realize that it was not worth it. She had never been diagnosed with any mental condition, and she was not on any medication at TPFW.

Her time in prison had been rehabilitative. She noted that TPFW had a lot of resources that could be applied towards rehabilitation of drug offenders. But she clarified that she thought that rehabilitation outcomes really depended on the age and mentality of an inmate. She stated that age and mentality of an inmate are relevant to whether an inmate can be rehabilitated successfully. She noted that she had a good support system at home. Her mother had provided her with a lot of resources. She stated that her mother had "pulled strings" in the past that were helpful in ensuring that Sally 23 did not receive harsher sentences for her crimes. The worst thing about prison was the fact that she was away from her family. Her plans after getting out of prison would include working for a drug treatment center and with animals. Animals were her passion. She would also start working as a volunteer for Humane Society and see whether she could work her way up from there. She would like to go back to college but she was uncertain as to what exactly she would like to study in college. She stated that she did not have any more intentions of selling drugs; likewise she would never want to be re incarcerated again after serving her current sentence.

Sally 24

Sally 24 was a 33-year-old African American female. She was a high school graduate and the oldest of three girls. When she was just one-year-old her father died. She was sent to live with her grandmother. So her grandmother raised her. But her mother kept her two younger sisters with her. Her mother lived in an apartment with the two youngest girls. Sally 24's grandmother died when she was 17 years old. Her grandmother had raised her in a religious household. They had attended a Church of Christ.

Sally 24 was not the only one from her family that had had an arrest for criminal drug charges. One of her younger sisters, who at 28 years was incarcerated at the Memphis prison for drug charges was her only sister that had been incarcerated on criminal drug charges. Her other sister, who at 18 years, was working and supporting a baby she had when she was only 16 years old, had never been in trouble with the law. Sally 24 had a daughter who was ten and a son who was two years old; both were living with their maternal grandmother.

The first time Sally 24 tried marijuana and alcohol, was when she was 18 years old. She was visiting some of her friends and they were drinking alcohol and smoking marijuana. She tried both on that visit. During the period that she was experimenting with alcohol and drugs, she was living with her mother. Her mother was an alcoholic but even when drunk she was not abusive to Sally 24 or her sisters. Her family was a low income cohesive family.

Sally 24 graduated from high school, after which she got a job at a factory. She smoked marijuana and drank constantly, during the time period she was working at the factory.

By the time she was 21 years old, she had started "holding drugs" for a friend for compensation. Then she happened to be downsized from her job at the factory. Incident to the loss of her job, she decided to start selling crack so as to be able to feed herself and pay the rent. She was not addicted to crack and neither did she use any crack.

She sold crack for a while, then in 1997 she had her first drug arrest. The arrest was as a result of her having sold crack cocaine to an informant. For the trial she hired a private attorney and ended up with a sentence of four years at 30%. But her attorney worked out a deal whereby she was supposed to spend 20 weekends in jail; one year in community corrections; and, five years of probation. She completed the 20 weekends in jail and the one year of community corrections, but she violated the terms of her probation. She had dropped by a friend's house who was a known drug dealer. As fate would have it, the day she visited her friend was the day her friend had gotten "busted" for drugs. She was arrested with her friend during the drug raid. Because of the violation she was sentenced to serve out the remainder of her original sentence in prison. Therefore she spent a year in prison and was paroled after serving about 13 months in prison.

Upon release from prison on parole, she found a job at a nursing home working in the kitchen but then quit from that job and moved to a job at an electronics factory. Now that she was working at a stable job, she was able to buy a car with "clean money'. At this point in her life she was working hard and she was not selling any drugs.

Unfortunately, she then met a man at a Krystal's restaurant. She had gone to Krystal's to eat, and the man had "chatted" her up. They eventually started dating. He was a drug dealer and within a short period of time she began selling drugs with him. This chance meeting also reintroduced her back into the wrong crowd. She started "hanging out" with his friends who happened to be "in the drug scene." About ten months after meeting her boyfriend, she violated parole. Sally 24 recalled that she had violated parole because she was "set up" by an informant during a drug deal. Her boyfriend who was with her during that incident accepted responsibility for the charge. Nonetheless she had to serve out the rest of her one-year of parole in county jail. Upon her release from county jail she kept away from her boyfriend and got a job working in a factory that manufactured car parts. She worked at the car parts manufacturing company for about five years, without incident. She did not sell or use drugs during that period. About five and half years after her release from county jail she ran into her former boyfriend. They got back together again, despite the fact that her boyfriend was addicted to drugs. She went back to selling drugs with him.

Sometime in December of 2004, Sally 24 recounted that she had sold drugs to an informant. As a result of that sale the police seized[24] the drugs along with her money, jewelry, and her cars but she was not arrested. They told her that they would serve her with the indictments later. She was indicted May of 2005 but she had decided to run away instead of facing the charges. She was on the run until April of 2006, when she was caught. She had gone back to her neighborhood and an officer had recognized her. She was arrested and taken to county jail.

She had a seven-count indictment including charges for the sale, delivery, and possession with intent to sell drugs. She was assigned a public defender but she recalled that at this time she was so tired of everything that she only wanted to take a plea deal and get it over with. She admitted that she was guilty but felt that she was not guilty enough to deserve the sentence she received. She had received a sentence of 14 years at 30%. The judge remanded her to county jail where she stayed for nine months and was then transferred to another county jail

---

24. Asset forfeiture is the civil part of a criminal issue. When a suspect is arrested, it's possible that their vehicle, boat, house, property, etc., be considered seizurable under the laws of the state. A criminal offense report is completed and also a Condemnation/Seizure Application is forwarded to the court for judgment by the court. If it is proven that the asset is used to sell/store/conceal/manufacture/transport illegal drugs it is considered for forfeiture action. If it can be proven that an asset was purchased through the illegal gains of drug related activities, the asset can be considered for forfeiture. Mirror of Justice http://www.mirrorofjustice.com/Real-Property-Law/52225.htm (accessed September 7, 2008).

in Hickman County. She was finally transferred to TPFW on October 26, 2006. Her parole review was slated for June of 2009.

She was originally diagnosed as having rheumatoid arthritis in 2004 prior to her incarceration at TPFW. But since being incarcerated at TPFW, she had been diagnosed with high blood pressure, high cholesterol and diabetes. The state was providing medications for all of those ailments. She said that prison had helped her to recognize the difference between what was right from wrong and she was determined not to focus on taking the easy way out any more. She believed that the one-on-one counseling programs at TPFW were much more effective than the group sessions they had. Overall she stated that prison did not have the "right focus" in their programs. While TPFW had programs that focused on nutrition and money management, Sally 24 proposed that the programs should be more focused on "reaching in and pulling out the problem."

She noted that she was trying to survive in prison, she also added that she was still hustling in prison because, "it's never what you need it's what you want." She said that in her opinion she was not completely rehabilitated but she hoped that by the time she was released, she would have been rehabilitated. She was still struggling with trying to address internal issues. At the same time she was also trying to figure out why she had such a propensity and desire to sell drugs. Sally 25 remarked that she had ten months to figure things out and get herself together and right with God. Upon completion of her sentence, she would like to open up a restaurant. She said that she was trying to make sure that she set definite plans for herself, so as to keep her from relapsing and returning to her old habits. Hopefully these efforts would help prevent her from reoffending.

Sally 25

Sally 25 was a 47-year-old African American female. She graduated from high school and had been enrolled for one and a half years at a vocational school. She was initially raised with her siblings by her parents. Her mother worked at the dry cleaners. Her father had a job too, but he had committed suicide when Sally 25 she was only six years old. He had been traumatized by the fact that Sally 25's older sister had died on December 10th at age 18 years from complications of heart disease. Three days after the death of Sally 25's sister, on December 13th her father killed himself. Sally 25 also had three surviving brothers and a 52-year-old sister, who had been working as a District Attorney for the past thirteen years. The sister was divorced and had two children. One of her brothers was a construction home builder. But her youngest brother worked odd jobs. Her youngest brother was the only one in her family that had ever been in trouble with the law. He had been arrested in the past for drug offences. At the time of the interview Sally 25 stated that he was on rehabilitation for drug addiction.

Sally 25 married at 17 just to get out of the house. She noted that she could not stand living at home. She wanted to have a baby very badly and she and her husband tried numerous times to get pregnant. After five miscarriages she stopped trying to have children. Although she came from a very religious and family oriented background she got divorced after only four years of marriage, when she was about 21 years old. For 14 years she worked as a supervisor at a glass plant until the glass plant closed down. Then in 1988 she married a man she had met in vocational school and stayed married to him for 14 years until she divorced him in 2003. Her mother died when she was 27 years old. Her family was reeling from the death of her mother, and two days after her mother's death a friend of the family introduced Sally 25 and her two brothers to cocaine. She liked the feeling she got when she was high on cocaine. But she stated that she used cocaine for only a month. Then she decided to quit using cocaine, and she quit cold turkey. That was not her first exposure to drugs. She had had tried marijuana a few times when she was in her twenties.

In 2002 she moved to another town after filing for divorce from her second husband. Her youngest brother had moved to the same town as well. Her youngest brother had established himself in the town as a drug dealer. He seemed to be making a considerable amount of money from drug sales. The attraction of the money he was making lured her into selling cocaine. Thus Sally 25 started selling drugs as well. She sold drugs for four years without getting caught. Her source for the drugs was the top dealer in the town but unbeknownst to her he also happened to be targeted by the police. As it turned out a wired informant had followed her dealer to her house. The informant had approached her, as she came out of her home to talk to the dealer, and asked her for four grams of cocaine. She had sold him four grams of cocaine. Forty-five days later she was picked up, taken to jail and charged with the sale of cocaine.

She was assigned a public defender, but she was not happy with the representation of the public defender. When she asked him to make a motion of discovery he had informed her that she would have to pay $300 if she wanted him to get it for her. Generally speaking, she indicated that the public defender just did not help her case at all. He convinced her to take a plea bargain even though she did not want to. The plea deal was for eight years at 30%. She eventually accepted the plea deal. As part of her plea deal, she stayed at the county jail for three months before getting out on probation. Three years into her probation she failed a drug screening test. Just prior to the drug screening test, she had discovered that she had sclerosis of the liver and tuberculosis. Sally 25 said that when she got the diagnosis, she was depressed about it. She just gave up and started doing drugs again; she just did not care anymore. Consequently she failed the drug screening test. Her probation officer violated her and she was arrested. The court determined that she should serve out her sentence in prison since she had violated the terms of her probation. She was transferred from jail to TPFW.

She had been taking medications for her liver and while in prison she had received five shots for hepatitis C. She was also taking anti depressants, blood pressure medication and medication for her high cholesterol. She was diagnosed with depression when her mother died and had had four nervous breakdowns in her lifetime. She specified that prison had helped her. In her opinion, there were some good programs offered at TPFW. Four of the programs that she recommended were; "Change is Possible" which teaches inmates how to deal with stress and finances; "Thinking for Change;" "Commitment to Change;" and "Better Decisions." Prison had rehabilitated her from cocaine and alcohol abuse. She was scheduled to go up for parole on the first week of August.

She planned that upon release, she would join a halfway house. While in prison she received a lot of support from her family, but she noted that she would not want to go back to her family upon release for fear of falling in with the wrong crowd again. To help distance herself, from the wrong crowd, after release, Sally 25 planned on moving to another town and getting a job either at Goodwill or at the Marriott Hotel. She was licensed as a subcontractor. She hoped that with her sub contractor license she would be able to get a well paying legal job.

Sally 25 also intended to attend 90 meetings of Alcoholics Anonymous and Narcotics anonymous in 90 days. That would mean attending at least 2 meetings a day. She stated that attendance at Alcoholics Anonymous was mandatory for her rehabilitation from drugs to be effective. Her free time would be spent in a Baptist church that offers a "Celebrate Recovery" program. She intended her immediate days after release to be spent on and participating in the halfway house programs and meetings. She would also endeavor to get an Alcoholics Anonymous sponsor.

Sally 25 said she learnt in prison as part of her rehabilitation process, that "If I remember and miss the feeling I have when talking to my family during the holiday's, then that was enough to prevent me from ever coming back to prison again." Thus she would use that as a mantra, in the future, after her release from prison; whenever she felt herself about to relapse she would remember the emptiness she felt in prison around the holidays.

Sally 26

Sally 26 was a 39-year-old Hispanic female. She was born in Texas. She was raised in a single parent household by her mother. Her mother divorced her father when Sally 26 was only 11 months old. After the divorce, her mother moved with the children to California. Sally 26 was the youngest of six children. She grew up with three brothers and two sisters. Her family was very dysfunctional. The majority of her siblings had been in trouble with the law. One of her sisters served 17 years at the California penitentiary for armed robbery. Another sister had been in and out of jail on assault charges. One brother was in jail for an attempt to do bodily harm. The incident had occurred when he was trying to defend his younger brother; another brother now 57 years old fought in Vietnam War; and, her other brother was in jail for a DUI.

She got pregnant at age 15 years. She dropped out of high school after getting pregnant and got married as soon as she found out that she was pregnant. She had a son, who was 23 years old, in the Navy and in Iraq. She later on had two more children, a daughter, who was 20 years old, and was on probation, and a son who was 18 years old. Her son worked at two full time jobs. Her youngest two children never finished high school. They both dropped out of high school just like Sally 26 had done as a teenager, though Sally 26 subsequently received her GED in prison.

Sally 26 divorced her first husband and the father of her children when she was 21 years old. She noted that her husband had cheated on her with her best friend. When she discovered the affair she filed for divorce. She had remarried in 2000 to a different man and though still married to the man, they had separated a while back. Her two sisters are heroin addicts and that was how she got introduced to drugs. She started selling heroin back when she was 14 years old but she had never tried it because she saw the way it affected her sisters. She also started drinking around that time but she emphasized that her drinking was just social drinking. She obtained heroin from her sisters' drug dealer for resale (although her sisters were not aware of it). She sold heroin throughout the period that she was married to her first husband.

Shortly after her divorce from her first husband at the age of 21 years, she started "full blown selling" of heroin, methamphetamine, and crack. She indicated that she would sell "punts" of methamphetamine to truck drivers. She stated that her ex-husband had gained full custody of their children after the divorce. He had also threatened to have her visitation rights to the children taken away, if she was ever to go on welfare. Thus, in order not to get on welfare, Sally 26 decided to start selling drugs full time.

During the ensuing few months after her divorce she had met another drug dealer, and they fell in love. She moved in with him and they both sold drugs together. About five years into the relationship, he became very physically, mentally and sexually abusive. She recalled one incident whereby they were in a hotel room and he wouldn't let her out. He was basically holding her hostage against her will, and he raped and sodomized her that night. He was high on methamphetamine when he did that. After that incident she moved to Tennessee to get away from him.

Shortly after her arrival in Tennessee, she got a job as a bartender. That was when she realized how easy it would be to sell drugs. She was being approached by different people at the bar where she worked. They would ask her "if she was holding anything." Bartending made it easier to sell drugs so she started selling crack cocaine in east Tennessee. Initially the bulk of the cocaine she sold at the bar was the cocaine she had brought with her from California. She specified that she was addicted to the money and power that came from selling drugs. She also noted that she was never jumped into a gang or initiated into a gang, but she did hang out with the Crypts and they accepted her. She did this for survival and for protection.

In 1997 she was at a club called "Outdoors Ebony." She had been drinking inside the club, but had decided to go outside for a breath of fresh air. So she walked out to the driveway of the club. As she was standing outside the club, a girl she had sold to previously had driven up to her on the driveway. The girl was a known crack addict and bought drugs from everyone. She dropped $300 out of the car window and told Sally 26 that she wanted $200 worth of powder and $100 worth of crack. Unbeknownst to Sally 26, she was wired and had a camera in her purse. She was a paid informant. Sally 26 stated that she sold the girl the powder and the crack; but that the moment the girl drove off she had a gut feeling that the girl was an informant. Sally 26 figured that it would be in her best interest to move, since she had a sinking feeling that the girl she had sold to was an informant. She had a feeling that she was going to be arrested because of that sale. So she left for California. She was in California for a year. She stayed with her mother and sisters. Her sisters were still selling cocaine in California. She tried cocaine powder during that year in California, but she was not too crazy about it, so she stuck to mainly drinking alcohol. She had been in California for about a year when she was contacted at her mother's house. She had received a call in October of 1998 from Detective Cox in Tennessee. He informed her that if she turned herself in she would only have to serve 11 months sentence. Apparently the girl she had sold drugs to, at the club, had a camera on her which had caught a glimpse of Sally 26's license plate. Initially Sally 26 was not inclined to turn herself in, but her mother finally convinced her to turn herself in. Therefore, she flew back to Tennessee and sold some cocaine and had a little fun before turning herself in on November 16, 1998.

Her court date was scheduled for March 6, 1999. She was assigned a public defender. She noted that she was satisfied with the public defender's representation of her, with regards to her drug charges. She was looking at the possibility of 15 years if she took it to trial and so her defender suggested that she accept a plea bargain of eight years at 30%. She did not think it was necessary to challenge anything. She never saw the audio or transcripts and never got a motion of discovery until after she was sentenced. She served a year at Hamblin County jail and was then placed under house arrest. While she was still under house arrest, she managed to get a job at General Furniture, where she built hutches and buffet tables. She met her second husband after one month of working there. She married him about nine months later. He cheated on her soon after they were married. He also started smoking crack and was verbally abusive. About two and half years after the marriage she kicked him out of her home. She said that she was turned off guys for a while, so she became a lesbian for a while.

She met a girl and they began to date. They moved in together, and were together for about two years without incident. Two weeks before her house arrest was over, her probation officer called the police station and notified the police that she was driving under an expired California license. She had not bothered to get a Tennessee license since she was not planning on staying in Tennessee. At that point in time, all of her court fees, community service hours (896 hrs) and restitution were paid off completely. Her probation officer violated her when she was stopped by the police and she spent two and a half months in jail prior to being reinstated for another year of house arrest. She successfully completed the extra one year of house arrest and was subsequently moved to state probation.

After her two and a half month stint in jail, she got a job working at a plant, James Industries. She worked there for three years until it closed down. She then got a job at Magic Logistics as a forklift operator. She worked there for five years. Her original probation officer had retired and she was given a new probation officer. One day she called her probation officer and told her she was going to be 15 minutes late because she was held up at work. It was 4:45 p.m. and the probation office was 30 minutes away. Her probation officer informed her that if she did not show up at precisely 5:00 p.m. she would violate her. Once she realized that she was going to be violated for this she stopped reporting. That was in October. She started selling cocaine again since she knew she was going to go to prison. She indicated that she wanted to save up money so she wouldn't be a financial burden to her family while incarcerated. She noted that her mother worked much too hard to have to worry about her.

Once she had saved up enough money to support herself and thus not be a burden to her family she turned herself in on December 15, 2005. She was at the county jail for about nine months. From her jail cell she was taken to her probation hearing. Sally 26 said that when she got to the probation hearing, she was charged with introduction to a penal facility. The charge was due to the fact that while at the county jail, someone had sent her two sealed envelopes with two marijuana joints in each envelope. She elaborated that the letter had been sent by some of her friends, who said that they knew she was getting out soon and they were aware of the fact that she did not use marijuana. But they wanted her to sell the marijuana such that she would have something to get back on her feet with. She claimed she did not know what were in the envelopes until an officer conducted a random search. The envelopes were still sealed. As a result of the envelopes with marijuana she got three years at 30%. She recounted that at the time she did not know how to fight the charge, she was not even sure about the possibility of fighting the charge. Thus she just accepted the charge. She was transferred to TPFW on September 18, 2007. She had been at the prison ever since then. She was eligible for parole a few days after the research interview. She elaborated that the reason she sold cocaine was to have money to send to her children and mother. She had wanted to make life easier for her mother who worked very hard. She had been diagnosed with depression prior to incarceration, and she had been suicidal in the past but she stated that she was completely cured of that and therefore refuses to take medication for depression.

She learnt in prison that she could work hard and have a good income without resorting to selling drugs. She had taken some of the rehabilitation and self help classes offered at TPFW. Some of the programs she had completed included, "Thinking for a change," "Theo Therapy" and "Victims Impact." She specified that the classes or programs have played a big part in the way she now thought things through. She clarified that she now viewed herself as being at a newborn stage in regards to rehabilitating herself. When she gets out of prison, she planned on continuing her education by getting an associate's degree in psychology. She did not want to re-offend. Hopefully her plans and the insight she had gleaned from the prison programs would help her have the fortitude not to re-offend again.

Chapter 6

Data Analysis
Study Design

The primary unit of observation for this study is the subset of inmates that were incarcerated for drug offenses in the state-run maximum security Tennessee Prison for Women (TPFW). Data was provided by the Tennessee Department of Corrections. This data provides detailed demographic information with regards to race, type of drug offence and a host of other information. All the women on the list were included as part of the research regarding the prison population and a subset of these were personally interviewed. Each participant was assigned an interview number to protect their anonymity.

The interview process involved face-to-face personal accounts of background information on each participant such as educational and socioeconomic background, and then recording their responses to specific open-ended questions. The respondents were allowed to elaborate with regards to their responses. The core questions provided the general basis for their responses. The TDOC gave written consent for the face-to-face interviews. The respondents also voluntarily gave their consent to be interviewed. The questions deal with the circumstances leading to the women's initial contact with criminal justice officials up to and through their subsequent incarceration. They are listed in Appendix 'B'. The state of Tennessee was chosen because it is a southern state and thus will provide an excellent opportunity for women drug offenders' account of their contact with the criminal justice system in the South. The experiences of African American women offenders will be compared with the experiences of Caucasian women offenders

Sample

The total prison population at the time of the interviews was 733 inmates. Out of that total, 159 of the women prisoners were incarcerated for drug offences.

Ninety of them could not be interviewed due to the fact that some of them were transferred, released, or had medical situations. The balance could not be interviewed because they changed their minds about participating. Thus the analysis was based on the information and interviews from 60 women inmates.

Data Source

The following tables provide summary and comparison data based on the responses of the 60 interviewed inmates. All the inmates were asked the same core questions.

Table 6.1 First Arrest for Drug Offence.

	African-American		Caucasian		Total	
	n	%	n	%	n	%
No	14	77.8%	29	69.0%	43	71.7%
Yes	4	22.2%	13	31.0%	17	28.3%
Total	18	100.0%	42	100.0%	60	100.0%

Table 6.1 lists the ratio of inmates polled with regards to their arrest circumstances. Analysis of the data indicates that 71.7% of the inmates have had prior drug arrests. African Americans had prior drugs arrests at a rate of 77.8% compared to Caucasians at 69.0%.

While drug arrests are specific to drug crimes, it is important to understand what the inmate's initial contact was with the criminal justice system. This involves understanding the violation of criminal law that led to the inmate having contact with the police or criminal justice system.

Table 6.2 Circumstances that Led to Initial Contact with the Criminal Justice System.

		African-American		Caucasian		Grand Total	
		n	%	n	%	n	%
Drug	Selling	12	66.7%	19	46.3%	31	51.7%
	Possession	3	16.7%	5	12.2%	8	13.3%
	Scrip fraud			6	14.6%	6	10.0%
	Manufacturing			2	4.9%	2	3.3%
Non Drug	Check fraud			4	9.8%	4	6.7%
	Assault	2	11.1%			2	3.3%
	DUI			2	4.9%	2	3.3%
	Grand larceny			1	2.4%	1	1.7%
	Theft	1	5.6%	3	7.3%	4	6.7%
	Grand Total	18	100.0%	42	100.0%	60	100.0%

In Table 6.2, the two most significant reasons for having had initial contact with the law were selling drugs at 51.7% and possession of drugs at 13.3%. Out of all circumstances leading to initial contact, 78.3% were drug related. Drug related crimes formed the basis for initial contact with the criminal justice system. Conversely, 21.7% of the inmate's interviewed had their initial arrest for non-drug type offenses. Tables 6.1 and 6.2 indicate that nearly three quarters of the individuals interviewed broke drug laws for their first offense and then continued to break drug laws in later crimes. It is noteworthy that 51.7% sold drugs and many sold them to support a habit or to make a living. A National 2004 study by the US Department of Justice states that "17% of state prisoners and 18% of federal inmates said they committed their current offense to obtain money for drugs."[1] The implication is that since drugs can only be purchased on the black market and the costs are thus very prohibitive to many users, then the only way for a drug user to be able to afford illegal drugs is to sell them back into the same market place. According to Boaz of the Cato Institute it is because of drug prohibition that there is a new set of economics that forces users to commit crimes to pay for the drugs they use.[2]

Table 6.3 Inmates that Used the Drugs They Were Convicted of Possessing/selling.

	African-American		**Caucasian**		**Total**	
	n	%	n	%	n	%
Yes	14	77.8%	41	97.6%	55	91.7%
No	4	22.2%	1	2.4%	5	8.3%
Total	18	100.0%	42	100.0%	60	100.0%

The interviewed inmates indicated overwhelmingly that they also used the drugs they were selling. Ninety-one point seven percent abused the drugs they were selling. The rate for Caucasians was 97.6% and for African Americans, 77.8%. On average, almost nine out of ten dealers were users at the time they were apprehended for selling drugs. This supports the premise that the women were often selling drugs to support their drug consumption habit.

1. US Department of Justice - Bureau of Justice and Statistics, Drug Use and Dependence, State and Federal Prisoners, 2004, NCJ 213530, October 2006 http://www.ojp.usdoj.gov/bjs/dcf/duc.htm (accessed December 25, 2008).
2. Boaz, D. On Drug Legalization, Criminalization, and Harm Reduction speech June 16, 1999 http://www.cato.org/testimony/ct-dbz061699.html (accessed December 25, 2008).

Table 6.4 Reason for First Drug Arrest.

	African-American		Caucasian		Total	
	n	%	n	%	n	%
Selling	16	88.9%	24	57.1%	40	66.7%
Possession	2	11.1%	10	23.8%	12	20.0%
Fraud			5	11.9%	5	8.3%
Manufacturing			2	4.8%	2	3.3%
Scrip Forgery			1	2.4%	1	1.7%
Total	18	100.0%	42	100.0%	60	100.0%

It is important to note that while Table 6.2 examines the criminal violation that led to first contact with law enforcement, Table 6.4 on the other hand summarizes the specific drug related crime that led to first drug arrest. The data shows that selling is the most significant reason for the first drug arrests in both African American and Caucasian respondents at a corresponding rate of 88.9% and 57.1% respectively. Caucasians were twice as likely to be arrested for possession as African Americans while African Americans were 1.5 times as likely to be caught for selling.

This raises the question as to why these women progressed from users to dealers and then to being incarcerated for drug crimes. Since 71.7% of them had multiple arrests for drugs and were aware of the consequences of using and or selling drugs, it would then seem that some more effective community or prison rehabilitation programs would be more beneficial than arrests. Based on comments from the interviews, many of the inmates felt that while programs in prison were somewhat rehabilitative, they were more concerned about being able to stay away from the drug scene upon release. So their drug use is not a problem while they are in prison, simply because drugs are not readily available to them in prison. The issue or problem arises when they go back into their communities. Then, the probability is great that they might relapse to using drugs again. This was echoed in the responses of the respondents during the interview. Generally, most of the respondents recognized the necessity and importance of keeping away from their old peers and influences and the need to forge new relationships outside of their former drug community. This they believed was necessary if they were to succeed in staying away from drug use.

If better education means that there is the more likelihood of securing a good legal viable job and subsequently removes the need to sell drugs to support oneself, then the educational level of inmates becomes important as a determinant factor for incarceration or recidivism. When women get out of prison, they have to cope with the stigma of having a felony record when seeking employment. The matter is compounded by lack of education.

Table 6.5 Education Level for All 159 Inmates Incarcerated for Drugs at TPFW.

	African-American		Caucasian		Total	
	n	%	n	%	n	%
Graduate Degree			1	1.0%	1	0.6%
College Graduate	1	1.7%	3	3.0%	4	2.5%
Some College	4	6.7%	5	5.1%	9	5.7%
GED	7	11.7%	28	28.3%	35	22.0%
Twelfth Grade	14	23.3%	19	19.2%	33	20.8%
Eleventh Grade	17	28.3%	7	7.1%	24	15.1%
Tenth Grade	4	6.7%	7	7.1%	11	6.9%
Ninth Grade	6	10.0%	11	11.1%	17	10.7%
Eighth Grade	1	1.7%	7	7.1%	8	5.0%
Seventh Grade			2	2.0%	2	1.3%
Sixth Grade			2	2.0%	2	1.3%
Ungraded	6	10.0%	7	7.1%	13	8.2%
Total	60	100.0%	99	100.0%	159	100.0%

Forty-three point four percent of all African Americans incarcerated at TPFW earned grade 12 education or above as opposed to 56.6% of Caucasians. Only one out of the 159 inmates had a graduate degree and none of the African American inmates interviewed stated that they had graduated from college. There is a GED program offered at TPFW as well as some vocational training. There is also a pilot program at TPFW whereby a few select inmates can take up to six classes over a two year period; but, generally the inmates are not well qualified for the job market when they are released.

The study indicated some compelling factors that were implicated in the women's dependence on drugs.

Table 6.6 Percent that Were Raped or Sexually Molested as Children

	African-American		Caucasian		Total	
	n	%	n	%	n	%
Yes	4	22.2%	11	26.2%	15	25.0%
No	14	77.8%	31	73.8%	45	75.0%
Total	18	100.0%	42	100.0%	60	100.0%

The data in Table 6.6 indicates that 25.0% of the inmate respondents were sexually abused as young children. Of the total respondents, about 22.2% of African Americans and 26.2% of Caucasians were sexually abused as children. According to some of the respondents the abuse started as early as when they were 6-1/2 years old. This finding reconciles with research conducted by Kendler et al in 2000. In the study Kendler et al surveyed 1,411 female adult twins. The findings indicated that young girls who were sexually abused were four times more likely to become drug or alcohol dependent.[3] So young girls, who were abused are more likely to turn to drugs or alcohol to mask the pain of their abuse. A significant percentage of the prison respondents were sexually abused as children. Thus there is a possible relationship or connection between these women's abusive childhood and their subsequent incarceration for drug offences.

Table 6.7 Percent of Inmates Interviewed that Were Treated or Diagnosed as Having a Mental Condition, Depression, Schizophrenia, Bipolar Disorder.

	African-American		**Caucasian**		**Total**	
	n	%	n	%	n	%
No	15	83.3%	24	57.1%	39	65.0%
Depression	1	5.6%	5	11.9%	6	10.0%
Bi Polar	1	5.6%	3	7.1%	4	6.7%
Bi-polar, depression			4	9.5%	4	6.7%
Bi-polar, schizophrenia			2	4.8%	2	3.3%
Depression, nervous breakdown	1	5.6%	1	2.4%	2	3.3%
Bi-Polar, anxiety disorder			1	2.4%	1	1.7%
Depression, suicidal			1	2.4%	1	1.7%
Depression, anxiety			1	2.4%	1	1.7%
Grand Total	18	100.0%	42	100.0%	60	100.0%

The data in table 6.7 indicates that of the respondents, 83.3% of African American and 57.1% of Caucasians stated that they had no prior mental disease or issue. Caucasians reported being diagnosed with depression and/or bi-polar disorders at a rate that is twice more than for African Americans.

The circumstance of the arrests for drug violations also produced an interesting insight into law enforcement strategies for apprehending drug users.

3. Kendler, S. et al Childhood Sexual Abuse and Adult Psychiatric and Substance Use Disorders in Women, General Psychiatry Vol.57 No. 10 http://archpsyc.ama-assn.org/cgi/content/full/57/10/953 (accessed December 26, 2008).

Table 6.8 Circumstance of Arrest.

	African-American		Caucasian		Total	
	n	%	n	%	n	%
Informant -sell to	12	66.7%	18	42.9%	29	48.3%
Violating parole	5	27.8%	11	26.2%	16	26.7%
Possession	1	5.6%	4	9.5%	5	8.3%
Scrip fraud			4	9.5%	4	6.7%
Undercover - sell to			3	7.1%	3	5.0%
Prescription resale			1	2.4%	2	3.3%
Search warrant			1	2.4%	1	1.7%
Total	18	100.0%	42	100.0%	60	100.0%

The data in Table 6.8 shows that almost half of the women were arrested and subsequently convicted of drug offenses because they sold to informants. Informants accounted for 66.7% of African American's arrests versus 41.5% of Caucasian arrests. Thus the data indicates that African Americans are 1.5 times more likely to be arrested because they sold to informants than Caucasians. It must also be noted that informants are current drug users or dealers whom in exchange for non-penalty and payment will turn in other drug offenders. So in essence a part of the war on drugs, inadvertently sanctions the paying of drug offenders, or waiving of prosecution of known drug offenders, such that they can act as informants in the arrest and subsequent prosecution of other drug offenders. These informants get governmental money and can practically be assured that they do not have to serve time (despite their continued drug offences) so long as they continue to act as informants against their peers.

Table 6.9 Private Attorney (PA) or Public Defender (PD) for Representation

	African-American		Caucasian		Total	
	n	%	n	%	n	%
PA	6	33.3%	11	26.2%	17	28.3%
PD	12	66.7%	31	73.8%	43	71.7%
Total	18	100.0%	42	100.0%	60	100.0%

The majority of the inmates indicated that they utilized public defenders. All the inmates that were represented by public defenders, with advice of their attorneys' opted to plea bargain. Plea bargaining means that in lieu of going through a criminal trial, the defendant will choose to plead guilty to a lesser charge, and as such effectively waive their rights to a trial. Inherent in the idea of plea bargaining, is that the defendant will plead to a lesser charge (the lesser charge is usually negotiated between the defense and prosecuting attorneys), and since the case would not have to go through time consuming and costly trial, the expectation is that the defendant will get a less severe sentence. The process of plea bargaining effectively moves cases through the court docket faster. This is usually done at the advice of their attorneys since the belief is that opting out of a trial and instead plea bargaining would garner less prison time. In some cases they pled guilty to the attendant charges or lesser charges even when in their view they were not culpable, because they were afraid of harsh sentencing if they went through trial and lose.

There is a wider impact on society than arresting and in some cases re-arresting drug users. This impact is seen in the large number of children that are left without mothers for months and years while these women were in prison. Studies[4] convincingly point to the fact that if these children grew up without a parent or stable home, they would more likely end up inclined to break the law. Thus incarcerating women not only has an immediate impact on the families and children of the women incarcerated but also on future generations.

Table 6.10 Offspring Per Inmate.

	African-American		Caucasian		Grand Total	
# children	n	%	n	%	n	%
0	5	27.8%	13	31.0%	18	30.0%
1	3	16.7%	8	19.0%	11	18.3%
2	5	27.8%	10	23.8%	15	25.0%
3	2	11.1%	8	19.0%	10	16.7%
4	3	16.7%	2	4.8%	5	8.3%
5			1	2.4%	1	1.7%
Total	18	100.0%	42	100.0%	60	100.0%

Data from Table 6.10 shows that 70.0% of the inmate respondent had children. There were a total combined number of 96 children of the respondents' that were living without a mother. In many cases, these children were left to be raised by aunts, uncles, grandparents or fathers. The potential impact on these children is described in a study by Myers that found that the change in caregivers left these children to internalize and externalize their problems and often they performed poorly at school and turned eventually criminal behavior.[5] While these mothers were in prison, a future generation of offenders was being developed as the offspring are shuttled from another parent, grandparent, relative or other guardian, while their mothers are serving time. A Bureau of Justice study indicated that 70% of the juveniles in prison on a national level were reported to

4. Myers, B. et al (2004) Children of Incarcerated Mothers Springer Netherlands, http://www.springerlink.com/content/v2u8401x07213645/ (accessed December 25, 2008).
5. Myers

be from single parent families,[6] which in most instances were fractured. It must also be noted that when a parent is incarcerated, then the offspring have a higher than usual probability of ending up also incarcerated. Incarceration of a parent has a direct relationship to future incarceration of an offspring.

Table 6.11 Number of Inmates by Race at TPFW for Drug Offences

	African-American	**Caucasian**	**Grand Total**
# of Inmates	60	99	159
% of Inmates	37.7%	62.3%	100.0%

There is a disproportionately high number of African Americans at TPFW for drug crimes. From Table 6.11, it is clear that the percentage of African Americans inmates is 37.7%. This percentage should be contrasted with the African American population in Tennessee, which is 17%.[7] Thus African American women in Tennessee are incarcerated for drug offences at a rate twice that of their percentage ratio within the Tennessee population. This ratio suggests that there may be some racial discrepancies in drug arrests. Such differences are documented in studies such as the 2008 study by King that shows that African Americans were "3.4 times more likely to be arrested for a drug offense than whites"[8] or with Blumstein who exclaims that there is high disproportionality in incarceration rates for African Americans versus whites.[9]

The type of offense also shows that African Americans are incarcerated more for Schedule II drugs than Caucasians at TPFW. African Americans are incarcerated for Schedule II drugs at a rate of 1.5 times that of Caucasians.

---

6. Beck, Allen J.Survey of Youth in Custody, 1987. Bureau of Justice Statistics Special Report. http://www.eric.ed.gov/ERICDocs/data/ericdocs2sql/content_storage_01/0000019b/80/1e/4d/b9.pdf (accessed December 26, 2008).
7. US Census Bureau 2000 http://quickfacts.census.gov/qfd/states/47000.html (accessed December 26, 2008).
8. King, R. 2008 Disparity by Geography: The War on Drugs in American Cities http://www.sentencingproject.org/Admin/Documents/publications/dp_drugarrestreport.pdf (accessed December 26, 2008).
9. Blumstein, A. 1993 Racial Disproportionality of U.S. Prison Population Revisited, University of Colorado Law Review, 64: 743

Table 6.12 Type of Offense

	African-American		Caucasian		Total	
	n	%	n	%	n	%
Schedule I						
Schedule II	57	95.0%	65	65.7%	122	76.7%
Schedule III	1	1.7%	8	8.1%	9	5.7%
Schedule IV			3	3.0%	3	1.9%
Schedule V						
Schedule VI	1	1.7%	2	2.0%	3	1.9%
Attain Obtain Drugs By Fraud			9	9.1%	9	5.7%
Promote Manufacture Meth			3	3.0%	3	1.9%
Drugs - Certain Amounts			1	1.0%	1	0.6%
Drugs: Mfg,Sale,Poss	1	1.7%	4	4.0%	5	3.1%
Promoting Manufacture Of Meth			2	2.0%	2	1.3%
Simple Poss/Casual Exchange - 3rd Offense			1	1.0%	1	0.6%
Unlawful Drug Paraphenalia			1	1.0%	1	0.6%
Total	60	100.0%	99	100.0%	159	100.0%

Table 6.12, shows that 76.7% of the total 159 drug offense inmates were arrested for Schedule II drug charges which include cocaine, crack and amphetamines. African Americans have a 95.0% incarceration rate for Schedule II offenses versus 65.7 % rate for Caucasians. It is important, that when inmates are released back into the community, that they have the necessary foundations, that will keep them from re-offending. Thus if they do not reoffend they will not be re-arrested. Therefore, the basis of any rehabilitative program would not only focus on weaning offenders from their substance abuse and criminal behavior, but also focus on ensuring a successful transition back into their communities.

There are essentially two factors that should be considered subsequent to offender reintroduction to society. These factors are: (1) the terms of parole and, (2) the social preparation of the inmate. Often the success of reintroduction to society is simply measured by whether or not the parolee or a former inmate that had served their time ends up coming back to prison. If a parolee is rearrested prior to the end of the parole period then that parolee has failed the terms of parole. When the reported data in Table 6.13 is analyzed, it shows that nearly 68.3% of the inmate respondents were at one time imprisoned for parole violations. That is a significantly high percentage of failure of parole.

Table 6.13 Percent of Interviewed Inmates that Violated Parole

	African-American		Caucasian		Total	
	n	%	n	%	n	%
Yes	12	66.7%	29	70.7%	41	68.3%
No	6	33.3%	13	31.7%	19	31.7%
Total	18	100.0%	42	100.0%	60	100.0%

Some examples given for violating parole included; being in a house when an arrest was made; not being able to find transportation to get to the parole meeting; and, not passing the drug test. Certainly the reasons for parole violation are usually non-violent. Usually parole violations are often extensions of the original crime. The cost of returning an offender to prison for this violation may not serve the public interest or provide additional safety to society.

About three quarters of respondent inmates seem to think that prison programs have rehabilitated them, but their statements are not substantive indications of how well they will cope within their community when released from prison. Although the programs are considered effective by the inmates while in the controlled environment of the prison, it is possible that the prison programs will not be effective with regards to preparing them for reintegration back into their respective communities.

Table 6.14 Percent of Inmates that Found Prison Rehabilitative

	African-American		Caucasian		Total	
	n	%	n	%	n	%
Yes	14	77.8%	33	78.6%	47	78.3%
No	3	16.7%	4	9.5%	7	11.7%
Not required			3	7.1%	3	5.0%
Somewhat	1	5.6%	2	4.8%	3	5.0%
Total	18	100.0%	42	100.0%	60	100.0%

Certainly after release it will be more difficult to stay away from drugs, since life on the outside is not regulated as in prison and there is peer pressure to use drugs as well as the lure to sell drugs to earn a living. However, all the respondents stated that they would like to give up the "drug life" and they all cited specific examples of changes in lifestyle they would hope to undertake upon release. The hope is that these lifestyle changes will help keep them from reoffending. The reality is that there is no legislated support for individuals that are trying to stay clean while working on a legal and self sustaining employment. It is important as a matter of public policy to consider the various factors that lend towards the incarceration of these women for drug offences. These factors would be considered in the concluding chapter. Polices that will address the underlying factors will go a long way towards reducing the number of women that are incarcerated for drug offences. Invariably it is important that inmates are taught life skills that will help them chart the course of staying sober and being gainfully employed when they leave prison and re-enter mainstream society.

Chapter 7

Rehabilitation Programs and Release Preparation

There are various programs provided for inmates at the women's prison. These programs are geared towards the goal of helping inmates achieve successful re-entry into mainstream life. As a pertinent part of the study, prison administrators, especially the ones that provide oversight for intervention programs were also interviewed. It was important to interview these administrators at Tennessee Prison for Women (TPFW) to garner an understanding regarding administration and effectiveness of their programs. These interviews thus, would provide a (counter) balance to inmate's perspective and account of programs provided at TPFW. The majority of these programs are voluntary, that means that the inmates can choose not to participate in them. A few of the programs are necessary for conditions of parole to be met. Invariably the overarching goal or objective of the programs at TPFW is to help inmates successfully transition back into society and as such live a life free of crime or substance abuse when they return to their communities.

According to Nuñez-Nito, there are two basic parts to inmate re-entry into society programs.[1] These two components are: "correctional programs that focus on the transition to the community (such as prerelease, work release, halfway houses, or other programs specifically aiming at reentry) and programs that have initiated some form of treatment (such as substance abuse, life skills, education, or mental health) in prison that is linked to community programs that will continue the treatment once the prisoner has been released."[2] In order to appreciate the magnitude of the number of inmates that must be reintegrated into the community annually, it is important to look at data from Bureau of Justice Statistics. According to a national level Bureau of Justice Statistics report, "each year more

---

1. Nuñez-Nito 2007 *Offender Reentry: Correctional Statistics, Reintegration into the Community, and Recidivism* CRS Report for Congress http://assets.opencrs.com/rpts/RL34287_20071217.pdf (accessed August 10, 2008).
2. Nuñez-Nito

than 650,000 offenders are released into the community and almost 5 million ex-offenders are under some form of community-based supervision."[3] Since there are over 2.3 million adults incarcerated nationally, this fact translates to about one in one hundred adults in prison.[4] These individuals at some point are going to serve out their time and then come home. They are going to be coming home to different communities. Thus, more and more communities are now coming to the realization that it is in their best interest to have intervention programs that will help ease these past offenders successfully back into the community.[5]

There are different programs offered at TPFW. Some of these programs include Inmate Education, Correctional Recovery, Exodus and Spiritual Programs. In addition, TPFW also have Inmate Classification and Corrections Compliance programs.

Inmate Education Programs

Connie Seabrooks is the current principal of Inmate Education Program at TPFW. As such, she is responsible for coordinating and administering broad ranging non-compulsory inmate educational programs. These programs not only educate but also hopefully impart new educational skills to the inmates. These skills will hopefully help them garner better jobs when they are released, thus making it less likely that they will reoffend and subsequently return to prison. Different research studies appear to indicate that educational proficiency is negatively co-related to recidivism. That means that the more educated former inmates are, the less the probability that they will reoffend. Education has been proven to help reduce recidivism. Successful educational programs for offenders are designed such that academics are coupled with instruction on how inmates should interact with their community and channel their emotions in manners acceptable to society.[6] In an important study by the Department of Education it was noted that,

> inmates who receive schooling, through vocational training or classes at the high school or college level, are far less likely to return to prison within three years of their release. The study, which followed more than 3,000 prisoners in

3. Nuñez-Nito
4. Liptak, A. 1 in 100 U.S. Adults Behind Bars, New Study Says *New York Times February 28, 2008.* http://www.nytimes.com/2008/02/28/us/28cnd-prison.html (accessed August 10, 2008).
5. Miller, S. 2005. A Shift to Easing Life after Prison. *Christian Science Monitor*, February 23, 2005 http://realcostofprisons.org/blog/archives/2005/02/ma_talk_in_ma_a.html (accessed August 10, 2008).
6. Vacca, J. Educated Prisoners Are Less Likely to Return to Prison: *Journal of Correctional Education*, December 2004 http://findarticles.com/p/articles/mi_qa4111/is_200412/ai_n9466371 (accessed August 10, 2008).

> Maryland, Minnesota and Ohio, found that three years after their release, 22 percent of the prisoners who had taken classes returned to prison, compared with 31 percent of the released prisoners who had not attended school while behind bars. We found that for every dollar you spend on education, you save two dollars by avoiding the cost of re-incarceration. [7]

The educational school system was started at TPFW during the early 1960's. Then the institution had programs to help inmates earn their General Education Diploma. Since then the programs have expanded to include Academic and Vocational Programs, and recently an academic program operated at TPFW by a David Lipscomb Professor. In addition to the principal, there are five vocational instructors, four academic teachers, two assistants, two librarians and a records specialist.

As recently as January 2007, David Lipscomb University under the initiative by Professor Richard Goode commenced a separate college credit program at TPFW. This program, though separate from Ms Seabrook's programs at TPFW, is administered at the prison under the auspices of Principal Seabrook. The David Lipscomb program allows inmates to take four college classes over a period of two years. According to Richard Goode, these classes are traditional classes from David Lipscomb's Arts and Humanities curriculum that are relocated to TPFW. These classes include Biblical Ethics, Legal Procedure, literature and writing, Criminal Procedures, History and Art. These courses stress critical and ethical thinking, effective communication skills and ultimately can lead to the Associates of Arts degree or a relevant certificate for interested inmates.

The program involves a "cohort of 15 inside or inmate" students. These students as a cohort are expected to commit to and complete the two year program. The two year program involves taking a different class in spring, summer and fall semesters for the stated period. These 15 student inmates will be matched up each semester with up to a maximum of 15 David Lipscomb students, for a total of no more than 30 students in each class.[8] According to Richard Goode, the perspectives for developing this program were as follows:

1. Offer selected components of the LU curriculum to qualified inmates at the Tennessee Prison for Women
    - a. These courses should stress critical and ethical thinking, and effective communication skills.
    - b. The course offerings should lead either to the Associates of Arts degree or a relevant certificate.
    - c. Other venues and programs may be added as approved by the TDOC and LU.

---

7. Lewin, T. Inmate Education Is Found To Lower Risk of New Arrest By, *New York Times* November 16, 2001, http://query.nytimes.com/gst/fullpage.html?res=9A02E1D8143BF935A25752C1A9679C8B63 (accessed August 10, 2008).
8. Goode, R., Background notes on the TPFW program. March 14, 2008

2. Mentor student inmates as they matriculate through the program.
3. Integrate student inmates and "free-world" students in academic inquiry (e.g., the classroom) so as to enhance educational experiences, transcend "walls" of hostility and further the work of restoration and reconciliation in our society.
4. Explore service learning opportunities for free-world Lipscomb students in the TDOC and its facilities (e.g., internships, student teaching, nursing practicum, and training of adult literacy teachers).
5. Raise a greater awareness on the Lipscomb campus of both the criminal justice system, and the needs of incarcerated.
6. Connect Lipscomb's student inmates with willing members of Lipscomb's larger, external community (i.e., Lipscomb's faith and corporate friends).
7. Connect the talents of the student inmates with the needs of the Nashville community.
8. Serve local and regional communities by contributing to the reduction of recidivism.
9. Learn from, and advise other prison-based college programs.
10. Explore offering courses for TDOC staff members. (Each state employee has the benefit of taking at least one college course per semester, paid for by the state. Lipscomb should investigate offering courses to prison staff.)
11. Collaborate in the theological assessment of the criminal justice system."[9]

At the thrust of the above stated reasons by Goode, is the underlying idea that inmates should have an opportunity to be rehabilitated while incarcerated, and should thus be able to make the transition to gainfully employed citizens once they have served their time and are back in the community. The women at TPFW can take classes in lieu of having a job in prison, though they get compensated a little bit more if they meet the criteria to take the David Lipscomb classes. As compensation for taking the course the inmates get paid $0.17 per hour.

The program was started in January of 2007 and the funding is from money raised by Professor Goode from local groups at a cost of $450 per student per semester for a total of $6750 for all 15 students. So far in this pilot program there are only enough funds to support one group of 15 students during the first two years of the pilot program. The subsequent group or cohort will only start, when this first cohort has completed the program. The criteria for entrance is to have at least two years left on the inmate sentence; to be discipline free for 12 months; take an ACT[10] like test; write an essay; and get a letter of recommendation from their prison employer. When the course was announced there were over 100 inmates that showed genuine keen interest in signing up for the courses. There were also many more that wanted to have the opportunity to sign up for the classes but could not due to scheduling conflict with their in prison

9. Goode.
10. ACT is a standardized achievement examination for college admissions.

jobs. From the more than 100 plus viable interested inmates, 15 women were selected based on the above mentioned criteria.

During the process of this research, the opportunity presented itself to be present for one of the David Lipscomb classes. It was the day the students were taking their final exam, and presenting their final research for the semester. It was very quiet in the room while they were taking their exams and all students were intently focused on completing the final exam within the time allotted. Professor Goode had brought in pizza and drinks since that was the final day of class for the summer semester. This provided a great opportunity to mingle with the 15 select inmates that had taken the course in conjunction with their 15 Lipscomb University student peers who were registered for the class. As part of the requirement of the class they had to drive out to the prison to take the classes each week with their inmate peers.

After pizza, three student inmates presented their final presentations for the class. While all students had to give oral presentations during the duration of the course, only three presentations were slated for that particular day. The topics were chosen by the students from a list provided by the professor. To get around the limited access to research materials, since the inmates do not have access to the internet, the professors had to provide research material to the students. The three student presenters were very articulate, and were able to take questions regarding their presentations.

One of the outstanding presentations of that day was titled "Critical Resistance." The student inmate started out showing a diorama of an inmate reaching through bars to try to touch a picture of her family and children. The thrust of her presentation was that prisoners are silhouettes of themselves upon incarceration. An inmate is given a number and important access to family is withheld. Once incarcerated, the inmate is assigned a number and in the process loses their identity. The presentation goes on to suggest that incarceration for some offences can be justified, but arbitrary long prison sentences are not rehabilitative. Her presentation touched on the fact that invariably most inmates will serve out (complete their sentence) their time and come out to live in the community. The length of time an ex convict served in prison is not usually indicative of the degree of rehabilitation. The presenter stated that education was the best way to be able to make better decisions when out of prison. However, with her long life sentence she felt that she would run out of opportunities for education and was glad to have the opportunity to take this college level program while incarcerated. Her presentation focused strongly and adamantly on using education as a good weapon against crime. According to her presentation, education was put on a back burner by government, and punitive measures in lieu of proactive educational measures are the rule of the political day. This marginalization led to higher crime rates. During the course of her presentation, the presenter gave examples to buttress her presentation point. For instance, she noted that while incarcerated, she had noticed a lot of inmates that were in prison for committing

TennCare[11] fraud. These individuals she stated were really just people trying to take care and look after their families the only way they knew how, given their limited circumstances. Again she reiterated the point in her presentation that education would have allowed them to make other better decisions.

In the Q&A after the presentation, one of the inmates said that she felt that the media targeted certain ethnic groups to support ideas like anti immigration. She said that prior to being incarcerated, she thought Latinos, and African American were the only ones that committed crimes and got arrested, but since being in prison and especially since taking this class and researching topics for classes, she has now come to the conclusion that such media portrayal is a myth. She has seen Caucasians, African American incarcerated at TPFW, and so she now believed that crime is across the racial board.

When the discussion turned to crime and policy, one of the professors made an insightful comment that a progressive politician is portrayed as being soft on crime, if the politician were to propose spending more money proactively on education rather than on building more prisons. At first glance you could not tell the difference between the students at a regular university classroom and the women at the prison.

At the end of the class, the opportunity presented itself to interview some of the inmate students. Following are some comments about the course:

> Question: What do you like about this course?
> Susan 1: I might not have been able to do this before but here I have learned to concentrate for long periods of time; the course helps me to concentrate better. I find that the course builds confidence in what I can do.
>
> Question: In your opinion, how does the David Lipscomb class compare with the vocational classes?
> Susan 2: The other programs are more specific and what do you do if you can't find a job as cosmetologist. You do not have anything else to lean back on. Besides, having a criminal record might make it hard to find a job. This program lets me think through what else I can do to better myself.
>
> Question: Will you continue to complete your college degree when you get out?
> Susan 2: Yes, definitely and I would like to continue to a masters.
>
> Question: What would have helped you not commit your crime?
> Susan 4: Maybe having a chance to go to school and not marrying young (19 years old). I tried to get money for school but gave up trying to get loans or grants because they were hard to get. If I was in school I would maybe not have married so young.

11.TennCare is a healthcare reform program that is supposed to replace Medicaid in Tennessee.

Apart from the David Lipscomb program, there are also three levels of academic programs that are taught at TPFW. These are as follows: (1) Adult Basic: which provides basic education from non-reader up to the equivalent of 5th grade educational level; (2) Intermediate: which provides educational instruction equivalent to grade six level through grade eight and, (3) General Education Development[12] (GED) level: This academic level program provides instruction from grade nine level up through grade 12. The classes are also structured so as to help students master proficiency needed to take and pass GED. Once an inmate has passed the GED exam she will receive her GED certificate, which certifies that the taker has attained American high school-level academic skills.

The vocational program offers six different areas of specialization. Students can take specific prescribed hours of instruction in order to earn their certification in each area. The six different areas of study for vocational studies include: (1) Culinary Arts: This program teaches students the foundations of the hospitality industry; (2) Cosmetology: Students in this program can take classes in different areas of cosmetology including hair design/maintenance, barbering, nail technology etc. Students can take up to 1,500 credit hours to qualify for the test to earn Tennessee State Board Licensing. An extra 300 hours of classes qualifies a student for earning an instructor permit; (3) Horticulture: Classes in Horticulture focus on fundamentals of greenhouse management and landscaping; (4) Residential Construction Technology: This program has three different phases, with the idea that upon successful completion of the program, the student should be adept at the fundamentals of building construction, including carpentry. (5) Computer/Office Technology: The focus of this program is on learning skills that will be necessary for working in a modern office environment. As such classes within this program focus on data input; keyboarding, literacy etc; (6) Career Management for Success: This section of the vocational program teaches students the fundamentals of applying and interviewing for jobs. Thus components of classes in this program include being taught how to fill out applications, dress for success; as well as how to create successful resumes.

It must be noted that all these classes are voluntary. Inmates at TPFW, do not have to attend the classes if they don't want to. In order to be admitted into a specific program or class, the individual had to fill out an application for that particular program. The applicant is then rated according to their qualifications. If an inmate qualifies based on the criteria for the particular program she is interested in, then she would be placed in the program based on openings available.

Principal Seabrooks thought the courses were very effective. She based this assumption on the fact that there was usually a great demand by former inmates for transcripts and references, to be sent to their prospective employers. According to Principal Seabrooks, 40 student inmates earned their GED's in 2007. These programs are available to the entire prison population and not just for those incarcerated for drugs offences.

---

12. The basic program for GED was started in 1966.

Correctional Recovery Academy

The Tennessee Department of Corrections is invested in treating drug-abusing offenders through a variety of programs. One of the programs is called Correctional Recovery Academy (CRA) subcontracted to Spectrum Health Care (SHC). SHC is a private, not for profit charitable organization that tries to improve the lives of individuals impacted by addiction and/or mental illness.[13] It is accredited by the Commission on Accreditation of Rehabilitation Facilities. Spectrum provides specialized treatment for substance abusing criminal offenders based on a cognitive-behavioral skill building approach. Spectrum's programs teach incarcerated and court-involved substance abusers practical ways to achieve a law abiding life that is free from drugs and crime.[14] The Drug Program/Correctional Recovery Director is Mr. Leonard. He is responsible for directing inmate recovery programs. He is a retired military person. While he was in the military he focused on alcohol and drug counseling. He received certification and licensing in alcohol and drug counseling and has been in that field for 27 years and is a veteran of working with substance abusers. He is a licensed counselor with four contract staff working under his supervision. Two of his staff members are licensed, while the other two are working towards earning their licensure.

The CRA program is nine months in duration and the inmates, as mandated by the TDOC, are screened for admission into the program using the Texas Christian University (TCU) Drug Screen II.[15] The screen is really a series of questions used to assess drug use severity for treatment referral. Leonard said the test is administered by asking respondents 15 questions about their drug use within the past twelve months preceding incarceration. A respondent can score from zero through nine. A score of three and above indicates that there is a critical need for treatment to help lower relapse and recidivism. On the other hand, a score of one, two, or three indicates that the respondent should be in outpatient Alcohol/Drug program, which is a less intensive program. A score of three indicates that the patient is at the middle of the road with regards to drug issues or problems. All incoming inmates are screened and the screening is administered in groups to increase the honesty of the respondents. The screening results are recorded on the mental health classification record. When the classification board meets they recommend where to classify the inmates, given the length of their sentences, and their performance on the screen. Individuals that have very short sentences or sentences over five years are not eligible to participate. If an inmate is selected to participate in the program they go on a waiting list. The TDOC will then go down the list and select inmates to participate in the pro-

---

13. Spectrum Health Systems web site http://www.spectrumhealthsystems.org/ (accessed August 10, 2008).
14. Spectrum Health Systems
15. See Appendix C

gram, from the waiting list based on their classification. For those that score 3–15 on the screen, they are then given a 120 question TCU/Brief Intake Interview,[16] to qualify for participation in Therapeutic community. There are four main sections in this interview relating to: (1) Background information; (2) Psychosocial functioning in the past 6 months; (3) Drug use background; and, (4) Drug use problems in the past year.

Presently there are 64 inmates in the program and if an inmate has more than a five-year sentence or there is no possibility of parole, it means they are not eligible to participate. Participation if preferred for those inmates that will be out of prison within two years. There are certain other criteria for being eligible to participate in the program. An inmate will be allowed into the program if they are bi-polar (depending on how severe the bi-polar disorder is) but usually will not be allowed to participate if schizophrenic. If a participant gets ill, develops full-blown AIDs, or poses security issues then they would be removed from Therapeutic Community (TC). Therapeutic community is a program where you have peer influence and structured mediation using group processes to help individuals learn and assimilate social norms, "to interact in structured and unstructured ways to influence attitudes, perceptions, and behaviors associated with drug abuse."[17] According to Leonard, the majority of the participants in the program do not leave once they start. He thought the program is effective at reducing drug dependency and recidivism. Therapeutic Community is mandatory once an individual is eligible for it and there is room for them in the program.

The CRA Program Handbook for Women outlines what CRA is and the tools that are used such that substance abusers "can be taught the necessary skills to live a successful life without re-offending and returning to prison."[18] The "approach places a strong emphasis on a) developing relapse prevention skills to avoid further crime substance abuse, b) learning anger management techniques, c) problem solving skills, d) developing a lifestyle balanced between work and recreation, and e) spirituality."[19] The group meets between the hours of 5:30 p.m. and 8:30 p.m. with daily morning and evening meetings. There are three phases of the academy. Phase I is the orientation where the inmates complete the assessment and then establish individual treatment plans and learn the requirements for participation in therapeutic community. Phase II is the main treatment in which participants continue with their individual recovery plan and learn anger management as well as counter criminal addictive thinking. In Phase III there is emphasis placed on relapse prevention and teaching on how to be-

---

16. TCU/Brief Intake Form http://www.ibr.tcu.edu/pubs/datacoll/Forms/bi.pdf, (accessed August 10, 2008).
17. National Institute on Drug Abuse Research Report Series – Therapeutic Community, http://www.drugabuse.gov/ResearchReports/Therapeutic/Therapeutic2.html (accessed August 10, 2008).
18. Spectrum Health Systems: Correctional Recovery Academy, Program handbook for Women, 2002 SHS, Inc. (accessed August 10, 2008).
19. Spectrum, 4.

come a leader in the community. Phase III or conclusion phase also involves a complete transition accountability plan and career planning.

Prior to being under contract to Spectrum, Leonard worked for the previous subcontractor at the prison, which was Correctional Counseling, Inc., of Memphis Tennessee, which used Moral Recognition Therapy (MRT). Their web site describes "

> MRT as a comprehensive, systematic attempt to treat substance abusing offenders from a purely cognitive behavioral perspective. Its objective was a systematic treatment system designed to enhance ego, social, moral, and positive behavioral growth in a progressive, step-by-step fashion. The MRT approach used 12 to 16 steps, and attempted to change how the drug abusers made decisions and judgments by raising moral reasoning." [20]

Leonard indicated that he preferred the MRT workbook since it elucidated stages of change in inmate's prior life that the patient had missed. This process he believed helps inmates reconcile the aspects or parts of their life that they missed growing up. The reconciliation might help them resolve the issues that drove them to a life of crime. Research appears to indicate that cognitive behavioral treatment programs help reduce recidivism. In a Washington State Institute for Public Policy study on recidivism, the research vigorously analyzed 25 cognitive behavioral treatment programs and "found that these programs significantly reduced recidivism by 8.2 percent."[21] The idea is that the Therapeutic Community program at TPFW will help reduce recidivism rate amongst women that are released from the prison.

Exodus Program

After talking to sixty inmates one important indelible striking impression, is that all of these individuals will return to their communities after serving their sentences, and the majority of them will have only minimal support in their quest for a life free from drug offences. When the door closes behind them as they leave prison there is the dire need to make sure that they have improved skills and knowledge that will help them prevent recidivism. It is likewise important that they have a place to live and perhaps a job as well, when they are released back into the community. This is what the exodus program is designed to do, to help inmates break out of the destructive lifestyle of substance abuse and offences that led to their incarceration.

---

20. Correctional Counseling, Inc. http://www.ccimrt.com/ (accessed August 10, 2008).
21. Evidence-Based Adult Corrections Programs: What Works And What Does Not *Washington State Institute for Public Policy* http://www.wsipp.wa.gov/rptfiles/06-01-1201.pdf (accessed August 10, 2008).

Christina Kerr is the treatment Manager for Exodus program. As such, she is under the direction of Exodus Program Manager. She is responsible for administration of "treatment" within the Exodus program. As such, she is directly responsible for the two sub-programs under Exodus, namely pre-release and substance abuse. Before they can be eligible to join the Exodus program, inmates have to go before the parole board and at the same time, have sufficient time left on their sentence to complete the program. There are various criteria for being eligible for Exodus program, but as mentioned earlier, the most important criteria is that the inmate must first of all go before the parole board. After the parole hearing before the parole board, if immediate release is recommended by the board, then the inmate is not eligible for the program. On the other hand, if the parole board mandates successful completion of the program as part of the terms of release from prison, then the inmate is eligible to participate. In the instance that a parole hearing is not available to the inmate for at least two years then they will not be considered for Exodus. If an inmate fails parole hearing but is supposed to go back before the board in a year to two years then they can be eligible. If on the other hand, the inmate is not scheduled to go before the parole board within two years then that inmate is not eligible for Exodus.

If an inmate cannot physically work, that is also a disqualifying criterion. On the other hand, if an inmate is on disability but wants to work, they can be allowed to join Exodus once the inmate has received medical clearance. Inmates that have significant health issues are not eligible to participate in the program. Inmates with mental health issues, such as schizophrenia and serious bi-polar disorder, are not usually eligible, but if their mental health can be managed such that they pose no threat to community, they can then be eligible. They must have to get medical clearance. The inmates that participate in the Exodus program are usually minimum trusty classification.

Ninety to Ninety five percent of Exodus participants are voluntary and about five percent are mandated by parole board. Participants within the Exodus program are considered to be on a "work program," but they are paid considerably more than participants in other prison work programs. Exodus participants are paid $0.55 per hour. The program utilizes the same screening test and acceptance criteria as the Correctional Recovery Academy. That means that Exodus program utilizes TCU Drug II screen. In addition, there is a risk assessment component, which takes into consideration, the individual's history, background, and record of repeat offences. Inmates that are considered to be at high risk of re-offending are not accepted into the program. These are usually inmates with scores of around three or lower. Levels 6–15 is a good score for Exodus intervention to be effective.

There are three phases to Exodus program. (1) Phase I: This phase involves the classroom portion, whereby participants are taught as well as learn different views pertaining to criminal thinking, substance abuse; issues that brought them to substance abuse. They are also presented with evidence that showcases the impact of their prior behavior and lifestyle on "victims." All kinds of victims "visit" the class at this portion of the program. It is important to note that the victims that visit are not only drug "victims." According to Ms. Kerr, they even bring in victims of other crimes so that there is a deeper impression on inmate participants of what the other side of the "criminal picture" looks like. In these meetings, victims of theft, murder, rape and drugs are brought in to expose inmate participants (perpetrators of crime) to the impact or consequences of their actions on the victims. While these are not all drug specific a lot of these are significant to substance abuse offenders because some of the inmates were under the influence of drugs at the time the crime was committed. Jane B, an Exodus participant, said that she never thought about how crack was affecting the families of the individuals she sold to, till she took Exodus and Drug Rehabilitation classes.

(2) Phase II: Community Service is the main component of this phase. This involves the process whereby Exodus participants start community service. It is scheduled for Mondays, Wednesdays and Fridays from 8 a.m. to 1:30 p.m. During this period, participants will actually go out into the community and work. They are taken to participating projects like Second Harvest, Humane Society and Future Children's Garden. Every, Tuesday and Thursday morning, they have career development. In career development, they learn about basic job skills pertaining to work ethic, resume writing and basic job skills. Afternoons on Tuesdays, Wednesdays and Fridays, are spent on sessions with "Next Door Halfway House."[22]

> The Next Door is a six month residential transitional living program located in downtown Nashville, Tennessee, that provides recovery support services for women with an addiction to alcohol and drugs. . .While at The Next Door, residents will have weekly case management assistance with job placement through in-house Workforce Development staff, recovery support services for their addiction, relapse prevention planning, mentoring services, individual counseling and access to Psychiatric Nurse Practitioner Services if needed. After completion of The Next Door program, women will have the opportunity to receive support through The Next Door's Continuous Recovery Management Program where they may meet regularly with other previous residents for educational and community activities.[23]

The sessions are focused on teaching the inmates basic life skills that people usually take for granted. According to Kerr, inmates have to be coached on basic relationship, money management, and coping skills. In addition, they learn how to take care of themselves. In some cases these individuals may move into the halfway house and pay rent after release.

---

22. Next door halfway house is a six month residential transitional living program. It is located in downtown Nashville, and provides recovery support services for women with addiction to alcohol and drugs.

23.The Next Door. http://www.thenextdoor.org/the_next_door_downtown.asp (accessed August 8, 2008).

Sally 15, a participant, said she plans upon release to go to a halfway house to help ease back into life. For her, finding a job would be of utmost importance since she had never really had a job apart from the few jobs she had in prison and selling drugs. Education would also be an important new influence in her life and she was laying the ground work by taking the GED. She said that she was going through a process and did not want to jump straight back into life and overwhelm herself and get high again. In her own words, "I know my location, and that location is bad right now; but I do know my direction, and my direction is good."

According to a past resident of Next Door, when she "arrived here at The Next Door, I was greeted by a host of wonderful people and I could feel the love all around me even though I was in fear and doubt. After being here right at a week, I started to feel more comfortable and at ease within myself . . . so, I started being more motivated about what I wanted out of this program. I knew right away that I wanted to continue to be clean and sober and I wanted to be successful so that I could give back what had been given to me."[24]

(3) Phase III: This is the third and final phase of Exodus and it involves Work Release. During this phase participants are expected to get a job and work full time five days a week. During this phase they are also expected to participate in Alcoholics Anonymous (AA) and Narcotics Anonymous (NA) meetings every Wednesday nights from 6–7:30 p.m..

Kerr said that the success of a program like Exodus could be very crucial in helping reduce rate of recidivism. She further elaborated, that releasing former inmates without jobs and skills to support themselves is surely a large contributor to high rate of recidivism. Since the program only started three years ago, she was not sure if there was empirical evidence to show that it actually and statistically reduced recidivism. But it is important to note that during the course of inmate interviews, one of the most common threads amongst the interviewees was the idea that transition back to a different lifestyle was essential to their not reoffending. For example, Jane 13 said that she "is going to stay close to her family and try and keep away from her former drug friends and from drugs and the drug culture. Hopefully these changes will help her stay out of trouble."

As part of Phase III, the inmates were working at two places that employ inmates, Tricor and Swett's Restaurant in Nashville. The relationship with the Tennessee Rehabilitative Initiative in Correction (TRICOR) is to "provide an environment where offenders learn work ethics and marketable skills which will assist with a successful reintegration into society."[25]

Kerr provided an example of when a work status of an inmate participant in phase III of Exodus might change. This particular participant took an Avon order while on her job. She was written up by her job site supervisor; this fact changed her working location. She thus had to work "in compound," inside the prison in lieu of working outside. The process of Classification also has an im-

---

24. The Next Door

25. Tricor. http://www.tricor.org/content/view/12/27/ (accessed August 9, 2008).

pact on where a participant can work at.[26] Kerr said that anecdotally, Exodus has a 50-80% success rate.

Spiritual Programs

"Spirituality is about realizing what makes us a human being by recognizing, accepting, appreciating and nurturing the inner spirit."[27] Chaplain Yolanda Walker is a paid Chaplain of the State of Tennessee. Within that capacity, she serves as the director and Chaplain of Spiritual Programs at TPFW. Chaplain Yolanda Walker is a graduate of Tennessee State University with a bachelor's degree in Sociology. She serves as a paid Chaplain and Volunteer Coordinator for the Tennessee Prison for Women. She holds membership in the following associations: the American Association of Christian Counselors, The American Probation and Parole Association, and The Tennessee Correctional Association. She is also a Registered Addiction Specialist Intern for the Breining Institute.

She coordinates and manages all the different spiritual programs that are available for inmates at TPFW. The spiritual programs are voluntary and inmates can attend only if they choose to do so.

There are various spiritual and Christian programs offered at TPFW. Some of these spiritual programs include, Anger Management, Making peace with Your Past Program and Serenity/Substance abuse programs. The Serenity/Substance Abuse program used to be managed by Volunteers, as a 12-week program, but when Chaplain Walker took over the program, she turned it into a 50-week program for substance abuse, and other addictions.

Although all the programs are voluntary, the Serenity Program however requires participants to sign up. The staffing of spiritual programs at TPFW is covered by volunteers except for the Serenity Program, which is manned by Walker with aid of outside speakers. According to Chaplain Walker, the majority of the programs have been at TPFW for at least 10 years. Many of them developed in churches as Bible studies that were brought to prison. The Serenity Program is based on the book "Power to Choose" by Mike O'Neil. The program "is an adaptation of the twelve steps of Alcoholics Anonymous (AA) with an emphasis on how to solve problems in substance abuse addicts lives." The emphasis of "twelve steps to wholeness" is to bring deliverance to people who are still in bondage in major life areas-those who continue to suffer from not just addictions but from guilt, fear, anger, self-deceptions, self-destructive compulsions, obsessions with self and codependency."[28]

There is a lot of anecdotal information that seems to imply that spiritual programs have a positive impact on recidivism, but there is no concrete empiri-

---

26. Classification is the process, utilized by Tennessee Department of Corrections, to determine custody levels for each inmate.
27. Walker, Y., Chaplain at TPFW, Oral interview July 2008.
28. O'Neil, M., 1992. Power to Choose: Twelve Steps to Wholeness, Sonlight vii

cal research that specifically shows a positive co-relation between spiritual programs in prison and reduced recidivism. In fact a 2006 study, which researched the relationship between faith based prisoner reentry programs and reduced recidivism, concluded that there was no statistically significant relationship between the two criteria.[29] Despite the lack of statistical evidence connecting the two criteria, the fact is that inmates at TPFW seem to appreciate attending the various support spiritual programs available to them.

29. Mear, D., 2006. Little Evidence Faith-Based Prison Programs Reduce Recidivism *Florida State University*. http://www.newswise.com/articles/view/524066/ (accessed August 10, 2008).

Chapter 8

Classification and Procedures

Inmate Classification

Wanda Biggers is the Classification Coordinator at TPFW. She is responsible for classifying all inmates at the prison. The process of classification involves sorting inmates by possible likelihood of misconduct as well as ensuring that the charges from court are correctly recorded for each inmate. State prison systems are usually organized by security level, the higher the security level, the more restrictive the setting. At TPFW, the classification system is based mainly on score sheet. Upon arrival at a reception center, new inmates are scored within a classification system that is used to determine the appropriate level of security. The classification custody assessment is based on a nine question form. This form has questions relating to history of assault, disciplinary actions and prior convictions. Scores of six or less are a minimum custody level, 7–16 medium security and 17 or more is close custody. The intake is based on the National Institute of Corrections' (NIC) classification model using a standard form. It is important to make sure that classifications are based on complete information and that cut-off points result in correct assignment. According to a summary from the TDOC web site, there is a wide variety of prisoners passing through the classification system here. There are 744 beds to house inmates at the prison. As of early August 2008 there were 733 inmates assigned with the remaining places open due to upcoming assignment or transfers.

> The Tennessee Prison for Women (TPFW), located in Nashville, is the primary facility for female felons in the state. TPFW has several missions. It is a reception and classification center for female offenders entering into the TDOC system. The prison also houses inmates in all custody levels, including pre-release participants, work release inmates, and those women sentenced to death. The security designation is maximum.[1]

---

1. State of Tennessee; Tennessee Prison for Women. http://www.state.tn.us/correction/institutions/tpfw.html (accessed January 12, 2009).

An inmate that is classified as Minimum Direct will have restrictions in moving around the prison structure. This level of classification indicates that the inmate requires direct continuous supervision, within a secure area. This classification is usually reserved for inmates with escape history, severe offences, or those that have medical or mental health issues or pending charges and/or have not been classified yet. On the other hand a minimum restricted inmate requires minimum supervision within secured areas, but may not meet the criteria to be classified as minimum trusty.

A minimum trusty inmate has demonstrated the ability to function without direct supervision so they can get out and work on such outside jobs with minimal security or periodic supervision e.g. highway maintenance jobs. It is also important to note that classification can change at any time, due to a need for change in custody level, for instance a minimum trusty inmate can be immediately re-classified as a minimum direct, if the inmate gets into a fight, but usually inmates are reviewed yearly to see if there is any change in classification level. Except for extenuating or immediate circumstances[2] which can lead to immediate classification changes, the normal routine for classification review is yearly. According to Tennessee Department of Corrections there are six main minimum security level classifications, and they are as follows:

> *Minimum Direct*: A custody level for inmates that allows them to be housed and to complete tasks outside the secure perimeter of an institution while under continuous supervision.
> *Minimum Restricted*: A custody level for inmates who are suitable for minimum supervision within secure confinement but who may not meet the criteria for minimum direct or trusty assignment.
> *Minimum Security Housing*: A facility with a fenced, unarmed perimeter that is specifically designated to house minimum direct or trusty inmates (i.e., boot camp, technical violators unit, and institutional annexes).
> *Minimum Trusty*: A custody level for inmates that allows them to be housed and complete tasks (including work) outside the secure perimeter of an institution while under periodic supervision.
> *Special Alternative Incarceration Unit* (SAIU) or Boot Camp: A highly regimented, short term, military style program for selected non-violent inmates. (TCA 40-20-201)
> *Technical Violator Unit*: A minimum-security, short-term incarceration program for technical probation or parole violators who have no new felonies.[3]

---

2. Such immediate circumstances that would warrant immediate classification would include getting into a fight, discipline issues, pending charges, and detainers (pending in other state).
3. Administrative Policies and Procedures, State of Tennessee, Department of Corrections. http://www.Tennessee.gov/correction/pdf/404-07.pdf (accessed December 26th 2008).

The policy at the prison is to classify the inmates with the least restrictive level that does not compromise the safety of the public or the staff at the prison.[4] So if an inmate is classified as minimum trusty they can work outside the prison. They are usually taken to their job site by an officer, and while at the job site they are under the supervision of the employer, at the end of the work day the officer will pick them up to take them back to prison. Every inmate in work release has a job.

Correctional Compliance

For most individuals the word prison connotes a facility filled with felons, but this usual oversimplification overlooks the tremendous oversight and administration required to provide a standard of care and safety for convicted inmates. It is important to have the administration and personnel in place to manage the prison effectively. As such, TPFW has a staff of 165 security personnel, 22 unit managers, and 66 administrators. At the top of the hierarchy at TPFW is Warden Steele, who provides the framework for care, custody, and control of the women sentenced to serve time in the prison. She is likewise responsible for the safety and security of the correctional facility. As warden, it is important to have set policies and procedures that should be followed in the management and administration of the prison.

The Correctional Compliance Manager is responsible for ensuring that policies and procedures are adhered to at TPFW. TPFW is accredited by The Commission on Accreditation for Corrections. In order for the prison to keep their accreditation, they must follow the standards that are necessary for such accreditation. Files and documentation should be kept up to date. There should be records of any actions, disciplinary or otherwise taken during the year at the prison. Inmate's sentences from the courts should be accorded or matched to judge's orders. Standards from the American Correction Association (ACA) are utilized at the prison. These functions fall under the auspices of the Correctional Compliance Manager. The Correctional Compliance Manager is Alice Curuthers. In addition to making sure all policies and procedures are carried out properly, she must keep the facility ready for the annual inspection by the TDOC who conducts random checks on the application and tracking of policies and procedures. As part of the process of maintaining their accreditation, TPFW is subjected to yearly inspection by the Accreditation Department for Tennessee Department of Corrections.

Every three years, there is a full accreditation review by the Commission on Accreditation for Corrections, whereby they review the facility for compliance. In the case that there are deficiencies then the issue must be resolved within 60 days to keep within compliance.

---

4. Administrative Policies and Procedures

Curuthers works closely with senior administrators at the prison as well as with the Accreditation Department for Tennessee and the Commission on Accreditation for Corrections, to ensure that the objectives of the facility are carried out according to standards. The standards used as performance references by Curuthers include a combination of those provided by TDOC as well as those standards published by ACA in the Standards Supplement. An example of the multitude of items that are covered under the procedures that could lead to audit write ups are something as seemingly small as a butcher knife that was not properly chained to the table in the kitchen area,[5] or the interactions of staff and inmates. Curuthers has the responsibility of making sure that all staff members comply with procedural standards and that there are records to constantly track that the procedures are being followed.

The Tennessee Department of Correction became the first adult correctional system in America to have all of its institutions accredited by the American Correctional Association. Some penal institutions in other states chose not to be accredited.

Staff Training

Hilda Griggs is the training Specialist for TPFW. Under the auspices of her position, she has to ensure that all personnel are trained to perform the procedures as demanded by Tennessee Department of Corrections' policy and procedures. This requires a detailed knowledge of all the procedures, polices and current training methods.

The training manual and policy for Tennessee Department of Corrections requires that any employee that works in direct contact with an inmate should have at least 40 hours of training. On the other hand, if the employee does not work in direct contact with an inmate they have to have at least sixteen hours of training. An employee can choose to take more than the 16 or 40 hours that is mandated by TDOC. This training is usually conducted at the Tennessee Corrections Academy state training facility in Tullahoma. Pre-service or New employee training is six weeks at the academy.[6] This six weeks training is for security personnel. After six weeks at Tullahoma, the staff would come back to TPFW for on the job training for three weeks before they are assigned a shift. After one year, the staff participates in an annual training update for 30 hours at the Academy. This update usually occurs upon the hiring anniversary date. Some specific jobs also require additional hours, for instance the hostage negotiating team requires a total of 88 hours for hostage release training. There is also a firearms instructor that works with firearm rated officers. To carry firearms the

---

5. Usually all kitchen utensils are supposed to be chained to the kitchen table.
6. Note; if the position is non-security position then pre-service training is two weeks at the Academy. Non-security positions would include nursing, teaching, auxiliary and counseling positions.

officers need to go to the Tennessee corrections academy in Tullahoma, Tennessee, and receive 30 hours of specialized training.

According to Griggs, training is streamlined such that every position gets the needed training required of that position. That is important in providing a safe and secure prison.

Chapter 9

Drug Court

Drug court is an alternative to prison sentence for individuals that have committed drug crimes. The main focus of drug court is to rehabilitate drug users in lieu of just sending them to prison. As such drug courts tend to concentrate on reducing recidivism and substance abuse by engaging participants in a judicially structured and monitored substance abuse treatment.[1] Drug Courts came into existence during the late 1980's due to various factors.

> In the late 1980s in response to a justice system overburdened by drug crimes, various social and political forces during that time – most importantly, the crack cocaine epidemic and the subsequent "war on drugs" – created an environment in which court dockets were overwhelmed by drug cases and prisons were filled to capacity with drug offenders.[2]

The results of the TPFW study indicated that 48% of the women inmates interviewed were initially arrested for selling drugs. 78% of the respondents abused the drugs they were subsequently convicted of selling. This information would suggest that there may be a connection between drug use/addiction and sales. Invariably the majority of users turn to selling, either on a small or large scale to support their drug habit. The possibility of police or criminal justice contact is higher with selling than with private consumption at home. On another note, almost half (47%) of the women inmates interviewed indicated that they had been arrested previously for drug offences. This fact underscores the need for rehabilitation. If such rehabilitation efforts were to prove effective after

---

1. Adult Drug Courts: Evidence Indicates Recidivism Reductions and Mixed Results for Other Outcomes. *United States Government Accountability Office*, 2005. http://www.gao.gov/new.items/d05219.pdf (accessed January 15, 2009).
2. Gottfredson, D. 2005. Long-Term Effects of Participation in the Baltimore City Drug Treatment Court: Results from an Experimental Study Department of Criminology and Criminal Justice Universoty of Maryland College Park: Marylandhttp://www.crim.umd.edu/Faculty/userfiles/25/Gottfredson.JEC3.pdf (accessed February 23, 2009).

an initial arrest for drug charges, then the number of inmates with prior drug arrests should be reduced. If rehabilitation is the possible key to preventing repeat drug offences, then there seems to be the case for instituting it while the inmates are still within the prison system. The drug war would be better served on all sides if addicted inmates are actually rehabilitated while serving time in prison for drug offences. This idea is the core basis of drug court.

There are different drug courts located around the country but the majority of them do not have residential rehabilitation programs. Within Tennessee, there are a number of drug courts, but Nashville has the only residential rehabilitation drug court program within the state. Richard Taylor is the 2009 current Program Director for the Davidson County Drug Court Program (DC4) in Nashville, Tennessee, which is a residential rehabilitation drug court. The program at DC4 "strives to assist the offender in overcoming his/her addiction, eliminating criminal behavior, developing life skills, obtaining vocational training, completing basic education and attending to other specific needs."[3] While there are some rehabilitative programs offered inside TPFW, the main difference between those programs and DC4 program is that in DC4, offenders are in a constant environment of rehabilitation and with peers who are focused on sobriety. According to Richard Taylor, "there is no therapeutic effect to being in a jail with other addicts." This sentiment was seconded by an inmate alum of the program who stated that "it is easier to get into jail and do time than to be confronted and change your life."

Taylor elucidated the process by which offenders can get into the program at DC4. The majority of offenders are referred to the court by the public defenders office or a judge. The criteria for entering the drug court program is that they need to be felons that were convicted of a drug related non violent felony such as burglary, theft of property or possession of drugs. Once admitted to DC4, there are seven available full time counselors that provide treatment to residents. Administration of treatment is divided up into four phases. In Phase I, which lasts about one month, the inductees go through the rigors of medical and psychiatric examination every morning. Based on the results of assessments during this phase a treatment plan is then developed, and the inmates now move into Phase II. During Phase II which runs for about eight to nine months, there are group meetings and individual counseling sessions which use the twelve step type recovery program. In these sessions, emphasis is placed on telling the truth and self policing; this is supposedly different from the atmosphere at the prison where you try to keep your mouth shut and not self police. Part of the rehabilitation effort is dependent on the offenders dressing, talking and interacting and emoting with other adults in a manner that is more typical of sober adults in society. "During this phase, residents are slowly integrated into the community by attending five outside support meetings of Alcoholics Anonymous and Narcotics

---

3. Davidson County Drug Court http://drugcourt.nashville.gov/portal/page/portal/drugCourt/programOperations/ (accessed October 10, 2008).

Anonymous."[4] From this phase the residents then segue on to the next Phase. Phase III lasts for about an eight to nine month period. During this period residents begin to work offsite, and this process helps participants reintegrate within the community. Throughout the process, participants are subjected to random drug tests to make sure there is no reversion to drugs, which would be possible cause for rejection from the program. During this phase, with the advice and help of a counselor, they develop a post rehab plan for living. Work plans are created to provide guidance on how the residents will reintegrate back into the work force. Once they have successfully completed Phase III without failing any drug tests they advance to Phase IV, whereby they are sent to a transitional living facility. They still have to participate in the mandatory drug testing and therapy. The drug testing is usually administered at the facility on Mondays and Thursdays. The core idea is to have a combination of rehabilitative process from drugs as well as integral offsite efforts to help reintegrate rehabilitated drug offenders back into society armed with life skill training and work assistance.

The DC4 facility is constructed without the perimeter security walls that are typical at prisons. The sleeping chambers are large shared rooms, housing six or seven occupants. Each occupant has an individual bed, a bookcase and a nightstand. No walls separate the beds; as such the occupants do not have a lot of privacy within their living quarters. This was structured purposefully so that the occupants will live a life without privacy. The lack of privacy is supposed to be an important part of the psychology of becoming sober. The residents at DC4 are allowed to wear regular civilian clothes unless they are being sanctioned for minor infractions. In that case they will be required to wear traditional black and white striped jail uniforms for the duration of their sanction or punishment.

The Tennessee Drug Court Annual Report from 2006-2007 states that, "a significant motivator for the offenders to stay in the program is a combination of deferring prosecution by not pleading guilty and post-adjudication where the sentences may be waived contingent upon completing the program."[5]

There are programs at TPFW, but the depth of the program offered at DC4 offers a possible insight to an alternative to incarceration that appears to yield some positive indicia with regards to reducing recidivism where drug offenders are concerned. As mentioned earlier, one of the common refrains noted from the female respondents at TPFW, was that they were going to try and get away from their past drug life, relationships and environments. DC4 seems structured to help former drug offenders have a shot at turning their life around and away from the "drug life."

The following data is taken from DC4 web site which summarizes the throughput since its inception in 1997.

---

4. Nashville County Drug Court http://drugcourt.nashville.gov/portal/page/portal/drugCourt/programOperations/ (accessed October 10, 2008)
5. GAO, 36.

Table 9.1 Tennessee Residential Drug Court Statistics

Description	Data
Number of participants since inception	1,138
Number of graduates since inception	411
Number of participants terminated since inception	482
Number of successful completion since inception	623
Graduation rate	46%
Retention rate	47%
Primary drug of choice	crack

During the course of the research there was the opportunity to attend a "graduation" ceremony for some of the recent graduates of the program. In attendance were the Mayor of Nashville, Karl Dean and the Nashville Chief of Police, Ronal Serpas. In his speech Serpas said that "drug courts work . . . congress has finally decided drug courts work . . . we can't build our way out of the problem with more prisons and beds" which is an endorsement that rehabilitation may be more effective than incarceration. One of the graduates said that "It has been the greatest experience coming through here. It made me realize I can be someone and a productive member of society. The counselors gave me courage and hope to go on."

While empirical measures of the benefits of drug courts versus conventional prisons would be useful, a Congressional Research Services Report on offender reentry indicates that caution should be taken when attempting to draw conclusions about the efficacy of policy measures based solely on recidivism statistics.[6] Not only is recidivism hard to define because it could include all encounters with law enforcement or only encounters that lead to new charges being placed but often the data sets are not accurate due to state and national level inaccuracies.[7] In a speech at the National Conference of the International Community Corrections Association in 2003, Travis stated that "drug courts reduce recidivism; yes, they reduce drug use; but they also result in healthy children born to sober mothers, a very important indicator of social reintegration."[8]

Drug courts offer an alternative to traditional incarceration and studies show that they are more effective than traditional incarceration in rehabilitating drug offenders. Thus as a matter of public policy it is important to explore the possibility of utilizing drug courts as an alternative to incarceration for individuals that are arrested for drug offences. The issue would be how to convince the general public and politicians that drug courts or other possible alternatives to incarceration offer a more feasible solution to incarceration. The case of Propo-

6. Nuñez-Neto, Offender Reentry
7. Nuñez-Neto, Offender Reentry
8. In Thinking About "What Works," What Works Best? The Margaret Mead Address at the National Conference of the International Community Corrections Association Presented by Jeremy Travis, Senior Fellow

sition 5 in California proffers an insight on how tough it is to change the mindset of the populace regarding incarceration. Proposition 5 was a California ballot initiative that was supposed to change the way drug programs worked in California. In addition it was supposed to provide drug offenders diversionary programs that would allow them to be treated and rehabilitated for their drug addiction in lieu of prison term. Proposition 5 also contained sections that would have allowed for broad changes within the state's parole system. The changes within the parole system would have demarcated new rules for parole violation, as well as offered treatment for paroled offenders both before and after they leave prison.[9] But it was defeated at the ballot during the 2008 November elections. There was no majority consensus for the proposition.

---

9. Smith-Heisters, S. 2008 The Nonviolent Offender Rehabilitation Act: Prison Overcrowding, Parole and Sentencing Reform (Proposition 5). ,*Reason Institute* http://igs.berkeley.edu/library/hot_topics/2008/Nov2008Election/Prop5main.html (accessed January 5, 2009).

Chapter 10

Discussion and Conclusion

This research study was undertaken with the hopes of better understanding the circumstances leading to incarceration of women drug offenders in Tennessee. Drug offender inmates at Tennessee Prison for Women were interviewed, with the hope of understanding the circumstances of respondents' police or criminal justice contact. The Tennessee Prison for Women in Nashville was chosen for this research because it is the largest prison for women within the state of Tennessee. It is located a few miles from down town Nashville. Both the main prison and the prison Annex are surrounded by 17 foot fence with about five coils of razor wire. It is a 744 bed facility, though as of early August 2008 (at the conclusion of the interviews) there were 733 inmates residing at the prison. Eleven beds were then empty due to upcoming assignments and transfers. A total of 159 inmates were incarcerated at TPFW for drug offences during the period of the interviews. They were all given the opportunity to participate in the process. Out of the 159 inmates, 99 of them were not able to participate in the interview process, either because they were transferred, in treatment, on work program, or simply because they decided at the last minute not to participate in the interview.

Limitations of the study

The findings should be interpreted based on the context of the possible limitations of the study. This study as mentioned earlier utilized all the population of drug offence inmates at TPFW, but it must also be noted that the prison was chosen because it is the largest women's prison as well as the main prison for women within the State of Tennessee. It was also a matter of convenience to study inmates at the prison, since it is located conveniently to downtown Nashville. Thus TPFW was not chosen randomly out of all the women's prisons within the Southern part of United States or the country in general. As such it is important to note that this study cannot be statistically generalized to the entire United States female drug prison inmates. It should also be borne in mind that the details of the women inmate interviews were their personal recollections and statement of facts or circumstances pertaining to events that occurred prior to and subsequent to their incarceration. As such, the research could not crosscheck the validity and truthfulness of the aforementioned recollections. The fact that 99 drug inmates at TPFW could not be interviewed for whatever reason should also be duly noted.

Nonetheless, the study provides a very insightful, detailed and current personal recounting of circumstances leading to the respondents' initial contact with police or the criminal justice system and subsequent events leading to their eventual incarceration at TPFW. The interviews provide personal perspectives on the current "War on Drugs," and this is especially important where women are concerned, because there is a dearth of drug research pertaining to female offenders. The bulk of research on drug offenders usually focuses on the male offender.

Discussion and Conclusions

It is a matter of empirical fact that crime rate is on the decrease, yet data also show that the rate of incarceration of women is on the increase for all types of crime. But the most increase is seen in the area of drug crimes. This book focuses on the circumstances leading to incarceration of women in Tennessee for drug offences. As such the study utilized personal interviews focusing on personal recollections of inmates' circumstances of arrest and subsequent incarceration. From the findings of the interview one of the most glaring issues is that the majority of these incarcerated women respondents are not well educated and they likewise come mainly from low to middle class background. Less than 10% of the women respondents either attended college or earned degrees. There was only one Caucasian respondent that stated she earned a graduate degree, and no African American earned a graduate degree. Eleven percent of African American respondents earned their GED while 28.9 percent of Caucasian respondents earned their GED. Of the total respondents, 30.8 percent earned their GED or above, with 38.2 percent of Caucasian respondents with earned GED or above. Conversely, 20.1 percent of African American respondents earned their GED or above. This is an interesting finding, thus this study clearly shows that the majority of the inmate respondents did not earn their GED. This has clear implications with regards to drug and criminal policies. Studies generally show that majority of incarcerated women are from poor socioeconomic and low educational background. This research also demarcated four general groups of respondent drug offenders. These respondent groups are as follows: (1) The respondents that became dependent on drugs because they had an underlying medical condition that necessitated prescription for painkillers from their medical doctors. They thus became addicted to the prescribed painkillers and segued into abusing other illicit drugs.(2) Another group of respondents started abusing drugs and alcohol, as a panacea to the physical and emotional pain of rape, incest, death or child abuse. Research show that about sixty percent of incarcerated women in state prisons, had been either physically or sexually abused, in some cases the abuse started at a young age and continued into adulthood.[1] (3) The third group of respondents were introduced to drugs via their peers, friends or family and they subsequently enmeshed themselves within the drug culture and lifestyle. (4) The final group of respondents was attracted to making big money or in some cases making just enough money to survive and they see selling and manufacture of drugs as a good avenue towards that goal. They also saw their friends and peers making money through drugs and as such were attracted to the allure and possibility of making a lot of money via dealing in drugs. They subsequently and usually ended up abusing the drugs they were dealing in.

Regardless of the group category that each of the respondents belong to, one of the common recurring theme with all the women interviewed, was the desire to get away from the drug culture life. There was also a fervent desire not to have to reoffend such that they will not be re incarcerated. Some of the women had more concrete ideas or plans on how to ensure that they do not get ensnared back in the drug culture, but the majority of the women interviewed only knew that they were desperate to break away from the drug culture, but they did not appear to have detailed plans on how to stay away so as to not re-offend.

These women are going to face tough odds in their stated efforts to stay away from drugs and crimes once they are released. They have to find legal employment, housing, reconnect with families and friends in their respective communities while trying to stay away from drugs. It would be tough for these women not to go back to the drug life, if they don't have legitimate job opportunities. Research shows that finding a satisfying job could keep an individual engaged in line of activity or work for a long time but the problem for them is how to find a legal satisfying job.[2] In the case of these respondents, they already have a disadvantage, because upon release from prison they will have a criminal record and are not well educated. These are significant impediments to successful, satisfying job opportunities. There are also a host of federal and state policies that are counterproductive to inmate re-entry and success upon release from prison. It will be hard for these women inmates to go back to school and earn degrees through financial aid, because the Federal Higher Education Act was amended in 1998, to preclude anyone with a drug conviction from receiving financial aid for post secondary education.[3] The amendment precludes any student that has been convicted of any possession or sale of drug offence under any applicable state or federal law, from receiving any grant, loan or work assis-

1. Ward, J. 2003. Snapshots: Holistic images of female offenders in the criminal Justice system. *Fordham Urban Law Journal*, http://findarticles.com/p/articles/mi_hb6562/is_2_30/ai_n28999749/pg_25?tag=artBody;col1 (accessed January 9, 2009).
2. Shover, N. 1983. The Latter Stages of Ordinary Property Offenders' Careers, *Social Problems*, 31: 208-18
3. Anonymous Author, Barriers to Re-Entry for Convicted Drug Offenders. *Drug Policy Alliance.* April 2003 http://www.drugpolicy.org/library/factsheets/barriers/ (accessed January 14, 2009).

tance.[4] At the same time, under the federal "One Strike" eviction policy, any tenant or any guest of the tenant who is involved in criminal drug activity can be evicted by public housing agencies.[5] Likewise tenants can be denied admission to public housing if they are using drugs, are in a drug treatment program or had been convicted of a felony drug offence.[6] With respect to other social services, it is important to note that a person is permanently barred[7] for life from receiving cash benefits or food stamps, if they have had a felony drug conviction.[8] Thus when they are released, it will be just about impossible for these women respondents to receive cash benefits or food stamps, to tide them over until they settle into regular jobs.

Some of these factors make it difficult for former drug offenders to achieve an appreciable measure of success in re-entry. In some cases they revert back to substance abuse and the familiar life of drug related crimes, as such recidivism rates are high where female drug offenders are concerned. Therefore the key to successful reentry of these women back to their communities will involve educational, job placement as well as rehabilitation and support services. According to Jennifer Ward, in 2003, different studies have indicated that a woman's economic situation has a direct bearing on her criminal behavior.[9] The implication is that women resort to criminal behavior out of economic necessity. As such, the majority of female offenders are poor, usually have children and are self supporting.[10] Generally drugs play an important role in the increasing incarceration of women. For example about eighty two percent of federal criminal cases involving women offenders involved at least one drug offence, and about forty percent of convicted women offenders at the state level were under the influence of drugs when they committed their crimes.[11] Usually women are the primary care givers of their minor children and the subsequent arrest and incarceration of these women have serious implications for the future of these children. The separation that occurs with incarceration causes strain on the mother-child relationship and can lead to emotional and behavioral problems for the children.[12] These children are thus more likely to be drawn into criminal activities and as such are more likely to be incarcerated. Thus the incarceration of women offenders can have implications for young upcoming generation of their children.

---

4. Barriers to Re-Entry.
5. Barriers to Re-Entry.
6. Barriers to Re-Entry.
7. States have the opportunity to either modify or opt out of the ban.
8. Barriers to Re-Entry.
9. Ward, J., 2003. Snapshots: Holistic images of female offenders in the criminal Justice system. *Fordham Urban Law Journal*, http://findarticles.com/p/articles/mi_hb6562/is_2_30/ai_n28999749/pg_25?tag=artBody;col1(accessed January 9, 2009).
10. Ward.
11. Ward.
12. Ward.

The underlying indication of this research is the realization that "Get Tough" drug policies are enforced in such a way that both addicts and dealers are punished with equally long sentences. It should also be recognized that drug enforcement is targeted almost exclusively at inner cities, lower income neighborhoods, with the end result that harsh drug enforcement policies in effect are aimed at largely lower socioeconomic and minority populations, regardless of the fact that drug abuse and addiction has no socioeconomic demarcations. Throughout, this discourse the fact that drug addiction is bad cannot be overemphasized, but at the same time it must also be recognized that there are also other addictions in our society that are not good. The difference is that such addictions are treated as sicknesses that should be treated. The consensus appears not to be the same for drug addiction especially illegal drug addiction.

The stark reality is that abuse of drugs is not good but then again so many other things in society can be likewise considered not so good as well. Tobacco and alcohol impact a morbidity and death toll on our society that is exponentially more than the morbidity and death toll from illegal drugs. Likewise lack of effective gun control can be considered a bad thing, especially considering the recent spate of high profile mass killings with guns in recent years.[13] Empirical research shows that the leading causes of death in USA for the year 2000 were tobacco (18.1% of total US deaths), poor diet and physical inactivity (16.6%), and alcohol consumption (3.5%).[14] Some other actual causes of death listed in order of magnitude include motor vehicle crashes (43,000), incidents involving firearms (29,000), and illicit drug use (17,000).[15] The table below showcases the data for annual causes of death in USA for the year 2000.

---

13. (1) Columbine killing occurred on April 20, 1999. In that instance, two high school students enacted a gun assault on their high school. They shot and killed 12 students, a teacher and they turned the guns on themselves. (2) March 26th 2006, A gunman entered a Rave after party in Seattle Washington, and shot and killed 6 people and wounded two, prior to turning the gun on himself. (3) April 16th 2007, 32 people were killed and many more wounded at Virginia Tech, when a distraught student opened fire at students at the educational institution. (4) October 7th 2007, a part time deputy police officer, shot and killed six people and critically injured one person at a post homecoming party, inside a duplex in Crandon Wisconsin, before killing himself with his gun. (5) March 29th 2009, a gunman that was having marital problems opened fire at a Pine lake Health and Rehab nursing home in Carthage, North Carolina, and shot and killed eight people, and wounded three others before he was shot and subdued by a police officer. (6) April 3, 2009, 14 people including the shooter were killed, and four wounded in Binghamptom, New York when a distraught immigrant who was jobless went to American Civic association immigration center and shot the people inside. That was the 5th mass killing in one month within USA. (7) April 4th 2009, three police officers were killed in Pittsburg when they responded to a domestic dispute call.

14.Mokdad, A., James S. Marks, Donna F. Stroup, Julie L. Gerberding, 2004. Annual Causes of Death in the United States, 2000, *Journal of the American Medical Association*, 291, No. 10, (March 10, 2004) 1238-1245.

15. Mokdad, .1238-1245.

Table 10.1: Annual Causes of Death in the United States[16]

Annual Causes of Death in the United States	
Tobacco	435,000
Poor Diet and Physical Inactivity	365,000
Alcohol	85,000
Microbial Agents	75,000
Toxic Agents	55,000
Motor Vehicle Crashes	26,347
Adverse Reactions to Prescription Drugs	32,000
Suicide	30,622
Incidents Involving Firearms	29,000
Homicide	20,308
Sexual Behaviors	20,000
All Illicit Drug Use, Direct and Indirect	17,000
Non-Steroidal Anti-Inflammatory Drugs Such As Aspirin	7,600
Marijuana	0

Table 10.1 suggests that illicit drug use accounts for the second lowest annual causes of death[17] in the United States for the year 2000. But tobacco, alcohol and guns are legal. They are supposed to be regulated to preclude their abuse. Likewise illicit drug abuse is a serious societal problem, but the question that begs to be asked is this, should policies not be focused on treating drug addiction as a disease rather than treating it as a particular and separate brand of ultimate evil that must be stamped out at all costs, notwithstanding the grave injustices that are meted out whilst in the process of stamping out illicit use of drugs.

It is important to note that "Get Tough" sentencing often tends not to demarcate between offenders that are users versus offenders that are dealers. Our prisons are increasingly being filled by non violent drug offenders, especially minority drug offenders. The majority of women offenders incarcerated at both federal and state prisons are African American, notwithstanding the fact that the majority of their crimes are non violent property, drug and public disorder crimes.[18] It is also noteworthy to mention that African American women are more likely to be arrested than Caucasian women for drug offences as a result of heavy drug enforcement policing in minority communities.[19] This is despite the fact that research suggests that jobs, more accessible drug treatment, alternative

16. Mokdad, .1238-1245.
17. It is important to note that for their article, Mokdad et al included drug related suicide, homicide, motor-vehicle injury, HIV infection, pneumonia,, violence, mental illness and hepatitis, as part of the criterion for calculating the death rate relating to illicit drug use.
18. Ward
19. Ward.

sentences or possibly decriminalization of non-violent drug offences would be more successful approach to the issue of drug problem.[20]

From a policy perspective it is important to address the success or failures of our current "Get Tough" policies, especially as it relates to women drug offenders. Both anecdotal and empirical researches suggest that such policies are not having an effect on reduction of drug addiction or crimes. Although the current political atmosphere reeks of "Get Tough" on street crimes, including non violent drug crimes, there seems to be an imperceptible softening of the "war on drugs" approach. This is evidenced by some of the current states initiatives regarding drug policies and minor crimes in general. For instance in California, proposition 36 was passed in 2000. Under this proposition first or second time drug possession arrestees would not be at risk for incarceration, rather they would be evaluated for treatment.[21] On the other hand the defeat of proposition 5 in California, underscores the need for better public discourse as to alternatives to the drug issue. In his opening statement before Joint Economic Committee hearing, Senator Webb underscored his concern for the impact of conviction and punishments especially on minority communities.[22] He also specifically noted the racial disparities that are inherent in sentencing for drug offences,[23] whereby African Americans are disproportionately sentenced for drug offences than their Caucasian counterparts. One main thrust of his opening statement was that current drug policies do not seem to be achieving its stated goal of reducing drug addiction and sales.[24] As such Senator Webb indicated the need for alternatives to incarceration. Such alternatives will include diversionary programs and drug court, which have been shown by research to produce outcomes that have better social benefits, public safety and reduced incarceration.[25] One of the most important conclusions drawn by Senator Webb in his opening statement is the assessment that the United States imprisons more people for drug offences than it should, while providing little or no treatment options for drug users.[26] Ultimately he concluded that as a matter of policy, the United States of America has failed to utilize a reasonable approach which would involve interlinking criminal jus-

---

20. Hagedorn, J., 1994. Homeboys, dope fiends, legits, and new jacks. *Criminology*, 32, no. 2, 197–219.
21. Webb, J., Opening statement of Senator Jim Webb, Joint Economic Committee Hearing , Illegal Drugs: Economic Impact, Societal Costs, Policy Responses, June 19, 2008 http://jec.senate.gov/index.cfm?FuseAction=Hearings.HearingsCalendar&ContentRecord_id=9d0729b4-eefe-2b3e-7931-fb353bebe2a8&Region_id=&Issue_id (accessed January 9, 2009).
22. Webb.
23. Webb.
24. Webb.
25. Webb.
26. Webb.

tice and drug treatment.[27] His conclusions resound with the majority of research relating to drug, criminal justice and policy.[28]

It is important to note that in recent months; at least two states of the union have flirted with the idea and possibility of legalizing marijuana on a broad scale. Currently 13 states allow the use of medical marijuana. The State of Oregon is one of the states that already has current laws that allow for medical use of marijuana. Its medical marijuana use law was approved by voters in 1998. Under the law a chronically or terminally sick patient can get a medical marijuana authorization card. The card would allow them to buy marijuana from specific private medical marijuana grow sites.[29] Thus with the card, individuals can acquire marijuana legally for medical pain management. Recently Representative Ron Maurer (R- Oregon) has sponsored a House Bill 3274 that would invariably allow the state to operate a marijuana production facility.[30] Therefore under the bill, the state would have control of distribution of marijuana to pharmacies.[31] The pharmacies would in turn fill marijuana prescriptions for registered card holders. This would purportedly improve public safety since only state facilities can grow marijuana under the bill, thus reducing the likelihood of illegally selling marijuana to individuals without a card.[32] The bill also incorporates the imposition of a $98 per ounce tax on marijuana, which would help cover state costs for operating and securing the production center[33] as well as generate considerable revenue for the State of Oregon. Inherent in the proposal of the bill is the alluded perspective, that there seems to be a softening in the general perception of drugs, specifically marijuana as ultimate evil that must be stamped out from society at all costs.

This seemingly imperceptible softening of harsh drug laws can be seen playing out not only at the federal level but also in other states of the nation. Currently, there is more inclination on the part of different states to push for drug sentencing reforms, in an effort to reduce prison populations and cut costs. Recently U.S. Attorney General Eric Holder stated that states should be allowed to make their own rules and laws regarding medical marijuana.[34] He also announced that there would be a stop to federal raids on pot dispensaries in Cali-

---

27. Webb.
28. Pratt, T., 2009. Addicted to Incarceration: Corrections Policy and the Politics of Misinformation in the United States. Woodland Hills: Sage, 90-95.
29. Loew, T., State may take over growing medical pot, *Statesman Journal*, March 12, 2009. http://www.statesmanjournal.com/apps/pbcs.dll/article?AID=2009903120336 (accessed April 1st 2009)
30. Loew
31. Loew.
32. Loew.
33. Loew.
34. Stateman, A., Can marijuana help rescue California's Economy? *Time* Friday March 13, 2009. http://www.time.com/time/nation/article/0,8599,1884956,00.html (accessed April 3, 2009).

fornia.[35] This approach indicates a softening by the current administration of the hard-line approach utilized by prior administrations in dealing with the issue of medicinal pot use. California is one of the other states that have also legalized marijuana. It was one of the first states in the nation, to legalize medicinal marijuana.[36] Marijuana was legalized in California in 1996.[37] Recently Assemblyman Tom Ammiano (D-California), introduced The Marijuana Control, Regulation, and Education Act (AB 390).[38] The Act, is meant to legalize marijuana, but at the same time, have it regulated in a manner similar to that of alcohol and tobacco, whereby taxed sales to individuals 21 or older is allowed.[39]

The National Organization for the Reform of Marijuana Laws, asserts that, "the bill could generate more than $1 billion in tax revenues and reduced enforcement costs. The bill would create a structure where producers or distributors would have to pay a $50 per ounce excise tax, or about $1 per joint."[40] This bill if passed would effectively generate much needed revenue for cash strapped California, in terms of revenue generated from imposed taxes as well as cost savings that would be generated from elimination of prosecutorial/incarceration costs for marijuana use and possession. Marijuana or "pot" is the largest agricultural cash crop of the State of California, surpassing milk and cream which is the second largest agricultural commodity of the state.[41] Pot generates over $14 billion yearly, while milk and cream generate about $7 billion annually.[42] Only about $200 million in medical marijuana sales taxes are subject to taxes every year.[43] Thus currently the bulk of marijuana sales in California are not taxed because regular marijuana sale is illegal. If it is legalized and taxed, the possible revenue generated is estimated to surpass $1billion yearly.[44]

Proponents of the bill claim that such revenue will go a long way towards helping fiscally strapped California. The State of California is so fiscally strapped, that they are laying-off public employees and some schools are instituting four day school week in order to shave costs of operation. That is the idea behind the bill to legalize marijuana in California. Opponents of the legalization bill believe that the focus should not only be on the projected possible revenue, but also on the potential for the harm that such legalization could bring. Such potential harm could be compared with the harmful effects wrought by use of legalized drugs (alcohol and tobacco). The suggestion being that legalization of

---

35. Stateman.
36. Stateman
37. Stateman.
38. Tam, D., Marijuana legalization supporters say bill could save billions. *The Times-Standard* March 8, 2009, http://groups.google.com/group/talk.politics.medicine/browse_thread/thread/9812b9160465171f (accessed April 1, 2009)..
39. Tam.
40. Tam.
41. Stateman. .
42. Stateman..
43. Stateman.
44. Stateman.

marijuana could lead to a corollary spike in marijuana use. But it must be noted, that if marijuana is to be used as an analogy to alcohol, then as mentioned earlier in chapter one, research pertaining to alcohol prohibition, did not indicate a spike in usage of alcohol after prohibition was abolished.

Another state that is trying to ease the application of its harsh drug laws is New York. The state of New York is well known for its strict and harsh Rockefeller drug laws.[45] Opponents of Rockefeller laws have always claimed that the laws were draconian, racist, unjust and ineffective.[46] The core problem of drug issue is addiction, which can be treated. Treatment proffers less possibility of recidivism than incarceration, and annually, it also costs at least a third of the cost of incarceration.[47] Drug addicts that are incarcerated in lieu of going through a treatment program are much more likely to go back to using drugs once they get out of prison. Governor Paterson of New York with his legislative leaders, decided in March of 2009, to repeal the last of Rockefeller drug laws.[48] The provisions of the prospective legislation would allow more judges' discretion in sentencing non violent felony offenders,[49] in lieu of discretion solely on the part of prosecutors. Under mandatory minimum sentences, a person convicted of selling two ounces or possessing four ounces of illegal narcotics would be sentenced by judges to a minimum of 15 years to life. The Rockefeller mandatory minimum sentencing guidelines made it difficult for judges to utilize their discretion in sentencing. With the result that minor non violent drug offenders could be sentenced to a length of time that is similar to the sentence length of a murderer. The new prospective legislation would also allow for drug treatment options, drug courts and diversions in lieu of prison sentence. The prospective legislation would also possibly allow application for resentencing by about 1500 individuals that are currently incarcerated for non violent drug offences. These reform or changes would help bring about better equity and fairness within the state's judicial system, especially when considering the fact that about 90% of incarcerated inmates for drug offences are minorities.[50] This is not justifiable since there is no research that indicates that minorities sell or use drugs at a disproportionate amount than Caucasians.[51] It will be interesting to analyze future statistical data regarding effects of the legislation on drug offences, incarceration rates, and rate of crime in New York. But most impor-

---

45. Then Governor Nelson Rockefeller, a Republican, pushed through harsh mandatory minimum drug sentencing legislation in 1973, that he felt were necessary to combat drug related, specifically heroin "reign of terror."

46. Virtanen, M., New York to ease its landmark tough drug laws, http://www.google.com/hostednews/ap/article/ALeqM5iOKFwHiHOzd75gNbI2C7vt7uHGbAD976JK400 (accessed April 3' 2009).

47. Virtanen.

48. Virtanen.

49. Virtanen.

50. Virtanen.

51. Virtanen.

tantly, is the acknowledgement by some of top New York's elected officers, that the punitive and harsh drug laws of the state need to be reformed.

It is important to reconcile research with public policy, and research has shown that our current "Drug Policies" are not working. United States have one of the highest incarceration rates of the industrialized nations, and yet the high incarceration rates have not mitigated the issue of our drug problem. In fact despite the billions that are allocated yearly within USA to fighting crime and drug offences, America has more problems with drugs and crime than any of the industrialized nations, who tend to have a less punitive approach to drug problems. There is the case to be made for possibly rethinking our current drug policies and as such reconciling such policies with research. That would involve exploring and utilizing alternative policies for dealing with current USA drug problems or issues. Diversionary programs, drug courts, extensive rehabilitative programs for incarcerated women, mental health treatment as well as educational, supportive and social services will go a long way towards mitigating the need for drugs and the economic need to sell; certainly more so than current punitive approach. The current punitive approach, for the last decade has managed to skyrocket the number of women incarcerated for drug offences. This increased incarceration rate for minor drug offences is especially pronounced in minority communities. This research hopefully provides indicia regarding the possibility of rethinking our current focus on prohibitory drug policies in lieu of more of a focus on regulatory and rehabilitative drug policies, while at the same time including a directed focus on educational, supportive and social services.

Future research will need to focus on the following questions:

(1) Will there be agreement that prevention, education and treatment should be the focus of public policy with regards to drug offences?
(2) Will there be support for revamping current drug policies.

In the end the solution might be a combination of three choices regarding drug policy;

(1) Reconcile current drug policies with current research on drug offences and consider focus on alternatives to incarceration for non-violent drug offences.
(2) Legalize some drugs
(3) Treat it as a health problem.

Appendix 'A'

Schedule for Rank of Drugs Potential for Abuse

The Controlled Substances Act (CSA) was enacted into law by the Congress of the United States as Title II of the Comprehensive Drug Abuse Prevention and Control Act of 1970. The CSA is the Federal U.S. drug policy under which the manufacture, importation, possession, and distribution of certain drugs is regulated.[1] There are five schedules ranked by the drugs potential for abuse:

"Schedule I: (A) The drug or other substance has a high potential for abuse; (B) The drug or other substance has no currently accepted medical use in treatment in the United States; (C) There is a lack of accepted safety for use of the drug or other substance under medical supervision. Include: heroin, marijuana, methaqualone, and LSD.

Schedule II: (A) The drug or other substance has a high potential for abuse; (B) The drug or other substance has a currently accepted medical use in treatment in the United States or a currently accepted medical use with severe restrictions; (C) Abuse of the drug or other substances may lead to severe psychological or physical dependence. Include: cocaine, methadone, phencyclidine (PCP), amphetamine preparations, and barbiturates.

Schedule III: (A) The drug or other substance has a potential for abuse less than the drugs or other substances in schedules I and II; (B) The drug or other substance has a currently accepted medical use in treatment in the United States; (C) Abuse of the drug or other substance may lead to moderate or low physical dependence or high psychological dependence. Include: all barbiturates except Phenobarbital and certain codeine preparations.

Schedule IV: (A) The drug or other substance has a low potential for abuse relative to the drugs or other substances in Schedule III. (B) The drug or other substance has a currently accepted medical use in treatment in the United States; (C) Abuse of the drug or other substance may lead to limited physical dependence or psychological dependence relative to the drugs or other substances in Schedule III. Include: Darvon, Phenobarbital, meprobamate, Valium, and Librium.

Schedule V: (A) The drug or other substance has a low potential for abuse relative to the drugs or other substances in Schedule IV; (B) The drug or other substance

---

1. Wikipedia. Controlled Substances Act. http://en.wikipedia.org /wiki/ Controlled_Substances_Act (accessed January 5, 2009).

has a currently accepted medical use in treatment in the United States; (C) Abuse of the drug or other substance may lead to limited physical dependence or psychological dependence relative to the drugs or other substances in Schedule IV. Includes opiates with non-narcotic medicinal ingredients."[2]

---

2. U.S Drug Enforcement Title 21 - Food and Drugs Chapter 13 - Drug Abuse Prevention And Control Subchapter I - Control And Enforcement Part B - Authority To Control; Standards and Schedules Sec. 812. Schedules of controlled substances http://www.usdoj.gov/dea/pubs/csa/812.htm#b (accessed January 19, 2009).

Appendix 'B'

Questions asked of the participants

The following questions were asked of the inmates interviewed.

1. What is your family and educational background?
2. Have your parents ever been arrested?
3. Have siblings ever been arrested or convicted for crimes?
4. Was this your first arrest for drug offence?
5. If no how many other times were you arrested and what were the circumstances surrounding the arrest?
6. Do you also use the drugs that you were convicted of possessing/selling?
7. Did you have a job prior to this arrest and subsequent incarceration?
8. What circumstances led to your initial contact with the criminal justice system?
9. What circumstances led to your initial contact with drug?
10. Did you have a public defender or private attorney?
11. Did you plea bargain or did you go through a trial?
12. If you plea bargained, who suggested the idea.
13. Why did you decide to plea bargain?
14. Why did you decide to go through trial?
15. Were you satisfied with your attorney during the whole process & why?
16. Have your time in prison thus far been rehabilitative?
17. Have you ever been treated or diagnosed as having a mental condition, depression, schizophrenia, bipolar disorder etc
18. What are your plans after you get out of prison?
19. Do you want to want to come back to prison?
20. What will you do to help prevent you from coming back to prison?

Appendix 'C'

TCU Drug Screen II

TCU Drug Screen II

Instruction Page

The following questions ask about your drug use (including alcohol) in the past 12 months. Please answer them by marking only one circle for each question. If you do not feel comfortable giving an answer to a particular question, you may skip it and move on to the next question.

If you are an inmate, please refer to the 12-month period immediately before you were locked up; that is, the last time you were in the "free world."

Also, alcohol is a drug. Your answers to questions about drug use need to include alcohol use, such as drinking beer.

The example below shows how to mark the circles --

	Yes	No
1. I like ice cream.	○	●

TCU DRUG SCREEN II

During the <u>last 12 months</u> (before being locked up, if applicable) –

Question	Yes	No
1. Did you use <u>larger amounts of drugs</u> or use them <u>for a longer time</u> than you planned or intended?..	O	O
2. Did you <u>try to cut down on your drug use</u> but were <u>unable</u> to do it?..............	O	O
3. Did you <u>spend a lot of time</u> getting drugs, using them, or recovering from their use?...	O	O
4. Did you <u>get so high or sick</u> from drugs that it –		
a. <u>kept you from</u> doing work, going to school, or caring for children?..................................	O	O
b. <u>caused an accident</u> or put you or others in danger?..............	O	O
5. Did you <u>spend less time at work, school, or with friends</u> so that you could use drugs?..	O	O
6. Did your drug use <u>cause</u> –		
a. <u>emotional or psychological</u> problems?.....................................	O	O
b. problems with <u>family, friends, work, or police</u>?.........................	O	O
c. <u>physical health or medical</u> problems?...	O	O
7. Did you <u>increase the amount</u> of a drug you were taking so that you could get the same effects as before?..	O	O
8. Did you ever keep taking a drug to <u>avoid withdrawal symptoms</u> or keep from <u>getting sick</u>?..	O	O
9. Did you <u>get sick or have withdrawal symptoms</u> when you quit or missed taking a drug?..	O	O

10. Which <u>drug</u> caused the <u>most serious problem</u>? [CHOOSE ONE]

- O *None*
- O *Alcohol*
- O *Marijuana/Hashish*
- O *Hallucinogens/LSD/PCP/Psychedelics/Mushrooms*
- O *Inhalants*
- O *Crack/Freebase*
- O *Heroin and Cocaine (mixed together as Speedball)*
- O *Cocaine (by itself)*
- O *Heroin (by itself)*
- O *Street Methadone (non-prescription)*
- O *Other Opiates/Opium/Morphine/Demerol*
- O *Methamphetamines*
- O *Amphetamines (other uppers)*
- O *Tranquilizers/Barbiturates/Sedatives (downers)*

11. How often did you use each type of drug during the last 12 months?

	DRUG USE IN LAST 12 MONTHS				
	NEVER	ONLY A FEW TIMES	1-3 TIMES A MONTH	1-5 TIMES A WEEK	ABOUT EVERY DAY
a. Alcohol	O	O	O	O	O
b. Marijuana/Hashish	O	O	O	O	O
c. Hallucinogens/LSD/PCP/ Psychedelics/Mushrooms	O	O	O	O	O
d. Inhalants	O	O	O	O	O
e. Crack/Freebase	O	O	O	O	O
f. Heroin and Cocaine (mixed together as Speedball)	O	O	O	O	O
g. Cocaine (by itself)	O	O	O	O	O
h. Heroin (by itself)	O	O	O	O	O
i. Street Methadone (non-prescription)	O	O	O	O	O
j. Other Opiates/Opium/Morphine/Demerol	O	O	O	O	O
k. Methamphetamines	O	O	O	O	O
l. Amphetamines (other uppers)	O	O	O	O	O
m. Tranquilizers/Barbiturates/Sedatives (downers)...	O	O	O	O	O
n. Other *(specify)*	O	O	O	O	O

12. During the last 12 months, how often did you inject drugs with a needle?

O Never O Only a few times O 1-3 times per month O 1-5 times per week O Daily

13. How serious do you think your drug problems are?

O Not at all O Slightly O Moderately O Considerably O Extremely

14. How many times before now have you ever been in a drug treatment program? [DO NOT INCLUDE AA/NA/CA MEETINGS]

O Never O 1 time O 2 times O 3 times O 4 or more times

15. How important is it for you to get drug treatment now?

O Not at all O Slightly O Moderately O Considerably O Extremely

Scoring for the TCU Drug Screen II

Page 1 of the TCU Drug Screen is scored as follows:

1. Give 1-point to each "yes" response to 1-9 (Questions 4 and 6 are worth one point each if a respondent answers "yes" to any portion).

2. The total score can range from 0 to 9; score values of 3 or greater indicate relatively severe drug-related problems, and correspond approximately to DSM drug dependence diagnosis.

3. Responses to Question 10 indicate which drug (or drugs) the respondent feels is primarily responsible for his or her drug-related problems.

The TCU Drug Screen II was developed as part of NIJ Grant 1999-MU-MU-K008, *Assessment of a Drug Screening Instrument*.

For more information on the TCU Drug Screen II, please contact:

Institute of Behavioral Research
Texas Christian University
TCU Box 298740
Fort Worth, TX 76129
(817) 257-7226
(817) 257-7290 FAX
Email: ibr@tcu.edu
Web site: www.ibr.tcu.edu

Bibliography

Baum, D. 1996. *Smoke and Mirrors: The War on drugs and the politics of failure.* Boston: Little, Brown.

Beck, A. 1987. *Special Report: Survey of Youth in Custody.* Bureau of Justice Statistics http://eric.ed.gov/ERICDocs/data/ericdocs2sql/content_storage_01/0000019b/80/1e/4d/b9.pdf (accessed December 21, 2008)

Bewley-Taylor, D., et al. 2005. *Incarceration of drug Offenders: Costs and Impacts.* The Beckley Foundation Drug Policy Programme.

Blumstein, A. 1993. *Racial Disproportionality of U.S. Prison Population Revisited*, University of Colorado Law Review, 64: 743

Boaz, D. *On Drug Legalization, Criminalization, and Harm Reduction* speech June 16, 1999 http://www.cato.org/testimony/ct-dbz061699.html (accessed December 25, 2008).

Bowman, K. 1958. *Some Problems of Addiction in Problems of Addiction and Habituation.* New York: Grune & Stratton.

American Bar Association and American Medical Association Report, 1958:19-21.

Brecher, M. 1972. *Consumer's Union report on Licit and Illicit Drugs.* http://www.druglibrary.org/Schaffer/studies/cu/cu8.html (accessed December 14, 2006).

Bureau of Justice Statistics, *Crime 1974–2004.* http://bjsdata.ojp.usdoj.gov/dataonline/Search/Crime/State/StatebyState.cfm?NoVariables=Y&CFID=207830&CFTOKEN=35222829 (accessed January 3, 2009).

Bureau of Justice Statistics. 2006. *Prisoners in 2006.* Washington, DC: U.S. Department of Justice

Bureau of TennCare. http://www.Tennessee.gov/tenncare/ (accessed August 18, 2008).

Bush-Baskette, S.R., 1999. "Women, Drugs and Prison in the United States." Boston: Northeastern University Press

Center for Drug Evaluation Research. Suboxone http://www.fda.gov/CDER/DRUG/infopage/subutex_suboxone/subutex-qa.htm (accessed August 23, 2008).

Chambliss, W. 2001 *Power, Politics and Crime.* Westview Press

Chiricos, T., Eschholz, and Gertz. 1997. *Crime, News, and fear of crime: Toward an Identification of Audience Effects. Social Problems* 44: 342–57

CIA Website https://www.cia.gov/about-cia/todays-cia/index.html (accessed September 7, 2008).

Davidson County Drug Court web site http://drugcourt.nashville.gov/portal/page/portal/drugCourt/programOperations/ (accessed October 12, 2008).

Dills, A., et al. 2005. *The Effect of Alcohol Prohibition on Alcohol Consumption: Evidence from Drunkenness Arrests. Economic Letters* vol. 86, Issue 2: 279–28

Drug Abuse and Addiction, National Institute on Drug Abuse. http://www. drugabuse.gov/scienceofaddiction/addiction.html (accessed January 10, 2009).

Drug Policy Alliance. 2003. *Barriers to Re-Entry for Convicted Drug Offenders.* http://www.drugpolicy.org/library/factsheets/barriers/ (accessed January 14, 2009).

Endometriosis.org http://www.endometriosis.org/endometriosis.html (accessed September 5, 2008).

Endometriosis Web MD http://women.webmd.com/endometriosis/endometriosis-topic-overview (accessed August 20, 2008).

Friedman, D. *Drugs Violence and Economics.* http://www.daviddfriedman.com/ Academic/drugs_and_violence.html (accessed August 24, 2008).

Friedman, M. 1991. *The War we are Losing. In Searching for Alternatives: Drug Control Policy in the United States.* Stanford, California: Hoover Institution.

Gottfredson, D. 2005. *Long-Term Effects of Participation in the Baltimore City Drug Treatment Court: Results from an Experimental Study.* Department of Criminology and Criminal Justice. College Park: University of Maryland

Government Accountability Office. *2006 Adult Drug Courts: Evidence Indicates Recidivism Reductions and Mixed Results for Other Outcomes* http://www. gao.gov/new.items/d05219.pdf (accessed January 2, 2009)

Hagedorn, J. "Homeboys, dope fiends, legits, and new jacks," Criminology, 32: 197–219

Hanson, G. 2002. *National Institute on Drug Abuse on OxyContin: Balancing Risks and Benefits before the Senate Committee for Health, Education, Labor, and Pensions* (accessed February 12, 2002).

Hu, T. 1950 *The Liquor Tax in the U*.S..: 1791–1947, New York City: Columbia University Press.

Jacobs, B. and Wright. *Stick-up, street culture, and offender motivation in Criminology.* 37:149–174.

Kendler, S. et al. *Childhood Sexual Abuse and Adult Psychiatric and Substance Use Disorders in Women, General Psychiatry.* Vol.57 No. 10 http://archpsyc.ama-assn.org/cgi/content/full/57/10/953 (accessed on December 26, 2008).

King, R. 2008 *Disparity by Geography: The War on Drugs in American Cities* http://www.sentencingproject.org/Admin/Documents/publications/dp_drugarrestrep ort.pdf (accessed December 26, 2008).

Kobler, J. 1993. *Ardent Spirits: The Rise and Fall of Prohibition.* New York: Da Capo Press

Levine, H. and Reinarman. 2004. *Alcohol Prohibition and Drug Prohibition: Lessons from Alcohol Policy for Drug Policy* http://www.cedro-uva.org/lib/Levine .alcohol.html

Lewin, T. Inmate Education Is Found To Lower Risk of New Arrest *New York Times*, November 16, 2001

Liptak, A. "1 in 100 U.S. Adults Behind Bars, New Study Says" *New York Times* http://www.nytimes.com/2008/02/28/us/28cnd-prison.html (accessed August 10, 2008).

Little Evidence Faith-Based Prison Programs Reduce Recidivism: http://www.newswise .com/articles/view/524066/ (accessed August 10, 2008).

Maguire. K. and Pastore, eds. 1977–1995 *Sourcebook of Criminal Justice Statistics.* Washington, DC, U.S. Department of Justice,, Bureau of Justice Statistics

Mayo Clinic. http//www.mayoclinic.com/health/polymiositis/DS00334 (accessed August 24, 2008).

Mear, D., 2006. Little Evidence Faith-Based Prison Programs Reduce Recidivism *Florida State University*. http://www.newswise.com/articles/view/524066/ (accessed August 10, 2008).

Miron, J. 1999. *Alcohol Prohibition*. NBER Working Paper No. 7130 http://eh.net/encyclopedia/miron.prohibition.alcohol (accessed July 31st 2006).

Miron, J. and Zweibel. 1991. *Alcohol Consumption during Prohibition.* The American Economic Review, Vol. 81, No. 2, Papers and Proceedings of the Hundred and Third Annual Meeting of the American Economic Association: 242–247

Miron,.J. 1999. *Violence and the U.S. Prohibitions of Drugs and Alcohol. American Law and Economics Review* 1–2: 78–114

Miller, S. "*A Shift to Easing Life after Prison*" Christian Science Monitor. February 23, 2005

Mirror of Justice. *Asset forfeiture*. http://www.mirrorofjustice.com/Real-Property-Law/52225.htm (accessed September 7, 2008*)*.

Mokdad, A., James S. Marks, Donna F. Stroup, Julie L. Gerberding, 2004. Annual Causes of Death in the United States, 2000, *Journal of the American Medical Association*, 291, No. 10, (March 10, 2004) 1238-1245.

Myers, B. et al 2004 *Children of Incarcerated Mothers Springer Netherlands*, http://www.springerlink.com/content/ v2u8401x07213645/ (accessed December 25, 2008).

National Commission on Marihuana and Drug Abuse: History of Alcohol Prohibition. http://www.druglibrary.org/Schaffer/LIBRARY/studies/nc/nc2a.htm (accessed August 17, 2006).

Nashville County Drug Court http://drugcourt.nashville.gov/portal/page/portal/ drugCourt/programOperations/ (accessed August 18, 2008)

National Institute on Drug Abuse: NIDA InfoFacts: Understanding Drug Abuse and Addiction. http://www.nida.nih.gov/Infofacts/understand.html. (accessed 13th January 2009).

National Institute on Drug Abuse *Research Report Series – Therapeutic Community*, http://www.drugabuse.gov/ (accessed August 18, 2008)

ResearchReports/Therapeutic/Therapeutic2.html (accessed August 10, 2008).

NIDA InfoFacts: Prescriptions and Over the Counter Medications. http://www.nida.nih.gov/infofacts/PainMed.html (accessed January 13, 2009).

Nunez-Nito, B. 2007. *Offender Reentry: Correctional Statistics, Reintegration into the Community, and Recidivism CRS Report for Congress* http://assets.opencrs.com/rpts/RL34287_20071217.pdf (accessed August 10, 2008).

Odegard, P. 1928. *Pressure Politics: The Story of The Anti-Saloon League*. Columbia University Press.

Official Website of the State of Tennessee: Tennessee Prison for Women. http://www.state.tn.us/correction/institutions/tpfw.html. (accessed August 15, 2008).

O'Neil, M. 1992. *Power to Choose: Twelve Steps to Wholeness*. Sonlight Publishing

Peele, P. "McCain has Two Standards on Drug Abuse." *Los Angeles Times*, February 14, 2000 http://www.peele.net/lib/mccain.html, (accessed August 8, 2008).

Pollard, J. 2000. *An Analysis of Coping Resources, Trauma and Significant Life Events in a Sample of Female Prisoners*. Paper Presented at the Women in Corrections by the Australian Institute of Criminology http://www.aic.gov.au/conferences/ womencorrections/pollbak.pdf (accessed January 9, 2009).

Pfizer Xanax web site http://www.xanax.com/content.asp?id=4&sid=1 (accessed September 7, 2008).

Pratt, T. 2009. *Addicted to Incarceration: Corrections Policy and the politics of Misinformation in the United States*. Thousand Oaks: Sage Publication Inc.

Public Law No. 223, 63rd Congress, approved December 17, 1914.

Schenkel L. 2005. *Histories of childhood maltreatment in schizophrenia: Relationships with premorbid functioning, symptomatology, and cognitive deficits. Schizophrenia Research* 76 (2–3): 273–286.

Shover, N 1983. "The Latter Stages of Ordinary Property Offenders' Careers," Social Problems, 31: 208–1

Simstad, S. Ohio State University Fact Sheet: Preventing Theft of Anhydrous Ammonia. http://phioonline.osu.edu/aex-fact/0594-1.html (accessed August 26, 2008).

Smith-Heisters,S. 2008 *The Nonviolent Offender Rehabilitation Act: Prison Overcrowding, Parole and Sentencing Reform (Proposition 5)*, Reason Institute http://igs.berkeley.edu/library/hot_topics/2008/Nov2008Election/Prop5main.html (accessed Jan 5, 2009).

Spectrum Health Systems web site http://www.spectrumhealthsystems.org/ (accessed August 10, 2008).

Spectrum Health Systems: Correctional Recovery Academy, Program handbook for Women, 2002 SHS, Inc. (accessed August 10, 2008).

State of Tennessee, Department of Corrections. *Administrative Policies and Procedures*, http://www.Tennessee.gov/correction/pdf/404-07.pdf (accessed December 26, 2008).

TCU/Brief Intake Form http://www.ibr.tcu.edu/pubs/datacoll/Forms/bi.pdf, (accessed August 10, 2008).

The Confederate Battle Flag. http://www.infoplease.com/spot/confederate1.html (accessed September 6, 2008).

The Effective National Drug Control Strategy. 1999. http://www.csdp.org/edcs /page14.htm. (accessed 19th December 2008).

The Next Door http://www.thenextdoor.org/the_next_door_downtown.asp the Next Door web page (accessed August 8, 2008).

Travis, J. "In Thinking About "What Works," What Works Best?" The Margaret Mead Address at the National Conference of the International Community Corrections Association

Turner's Syndrome website http://www.turnersyndrome.org/ index.php?option=com_content&task=view&id=40&Itemid=63 (accessed September 8, 2008).

Tricor http://www.tricor.org/content/view/12/27/ taken from Tricor web site (accessed August 9, 2008).

US Census Bureau *2000* http://quickfacts.census.gov/qfd/states/47000.html (accessed December 26, 2008).

U.S. Department of Health and Human Services. *AFDC: Aid to Families with Dependent Children*. http://aspe.hhs.gov/HSP/abbrev/afdc-tanf.htm (accessed August 24, 2008).

US Department of Justice - Bureau of Justice and Statistics, *Drug Use and Dependence, State and Federal Prisoners*, 2004, NCJ 213530, October 2006 http://www.ojp.usdoj.gov/bjs/dcf/duc.htm (accessed December 25, 2008).

U.S. Drug Enforcement Agency, *Cocaine Price/Purity Analysis of STRIDE Data* http://www.usdoj.gov/dea/concern/cocaine_prices_purity.html (accessed August 18, 2008)

U.S Drug Enforcement Agency *Title 21 - Food And Drugs Chapter 13 - Drug Abuse Prevention And Control Subchapter I - Control And Enforcement Part B - Authority*

To Control; Standards and Schedules Sec. 812. Schedules of controlled substances http://www.usdoj.gov/dea/pubs/csa/812.htm#b (accessed January 19, 2009).

Vacca, J. 2004. *Educated Prisoners Are Less Likely to Return to Prison*: Journal of Correctional Education, http://findarticles.com/p/articles/mi_qa4111/is_200412/ai_n9466371 (accessed August 10, 2008).

Visher, C.A. 1986. *The RAND inmate survey: A reanalysis. In Criminal Careers and Career criminal.* Washington, DC: National Academy Press.

Virtanen, M., New York to ease its landmark tough drug laws, http://www.google.com/hostednews/ap/article/ALeqM5iOKFwHiHOzd75gNbI2C7vt7uHGbAD976JK400 (accessed April 3' 2009).

Warburton, C., *The Economic Results of Prohibition.* New York: Columbia University Press.

Ward, J. "Snapshots: Holistic images of female offenders in the criminal Justice system". Fordham Urban Law Journal, Jan 2003, http://findarticles.com/p/articles/mi_hb6562/is_2_30/ai_n28999749/pg_25?tag=artBody;col1 (accessed January 9, 2009).

Webb, J. *Joint Economic Committee Hearing , Illegal Drugs: Economic Impact, Societal Costs, Policy Responses*, June 19, 2008 http://jec.senate.gov/index.cfm?FuseAction=Hearings.HearingsCalendar&ContentRecord_id=9d0729b4-eefe-2b3e-7931-fb353bebe2a8&Region_id=&Issue_id (accessed January 9, 2009).

Index

About the Authors

Chinyere Chigozie Ogbonna was born in Okwe, Nigeria. She completed her elementary education at Ekulu Primary School, Enugu in 1980. She graduated from Federal Government College, Enugu in 1985. She earned a Bachelor of Science Degree (Honors) in Parasitology and Entomology from Anambara State University, Enugu, Nigeria in 1990 and a Master of Science Degree in Health Care Administration from Western Kentucky University in 1996. Her Doctorate in Public Administration was earned at Tennessee State University in August 2000.

Dr. Ogbonna has held various positions in both private and public health care industries, including research positions at Vanderbilt and Vectors /Arbovirus Research division under the auspices of World Health Organization and in 2001 she served as Bioterrorism Epidemiologist for Tennessee Department of Health. She worked in Administration at the office of International programs at Western Kentucky University. She is also the author of TennCare and Disproportionate Share Hospitals. Ogbonna is currently employed as an Associate Professor of Public Management and Criminal Justice at Austin Peay State University.

Ross Alexander Nordin was born in Vancouver, British Columbia. He earned his Bachelor of Engineering Science from the University of Western Ontario, London, Ontario in 1982 and a Masters of Business Administration from the University of Michigan in 2006.

Over the course of his career he has been actively involved in engineering, finance and data analysis of large data sets. He has had senior management roles in companies in the US, Canada, and Hungary. Nordin includes studies and policy data analyses of "War on Drugs" policies amongst his varied research interest. He is currently working in advisory roles in finance for high growth companies.